T0401395

PLANTATIONS OF ANTIGUA:
THE SWEET SUCCESS OF SUGAR

A Biography of the Historic Plantations Which Made Antigua a Major Source of the World's Early Sugar Supply

Volume 1:
St. John's Parish

By Agnes C. Meeker, MBE
with Donald A. Dery

AuthorHouse™
1663 Liberty Drive
Bloomington, IN 47403
www.authorhouse.com
Phone: 1 (800) 839-8640

© 2017 Agnes C. Meeker, MBE ; Donald A. Dery. All rights reserved.

No part of this book may be reproduced, stored in a retrieval system, or
transmitted by any means without the written permission of the author.

Published by AuthorHouse 07/31/2018

ISBN: 978-1-5246-8731-1 (sc)
978-1-5246-8733-5 (hc)
978-1-5246-8732-8 (e)

Library of Congress Control Number: 2017906399

Print information available on the last page.

Any people depicted in stock imagery provided by Thinkstock are models,
and such images are being used for illustrative purposes only.
Certain stock imagery © Thinkstock.

This book is printed on acid-free paper.

Because of the dynamic nature of the Internet, any web addresses or links contained in this book may have changed
since publication and may no longer be valid. The views expressed in this work are solely those of the author and do
not necessarily reflect the views of the publisher, and the publisher hereby disclaims any responsibility for them.

authorHOUSE®

To the Meeker and Watson Families.

Content: Volume 1

Top - A Working Sugar Estate with Mill by E.T. Henry
Bottom - Post Card 1876 – Museum of Antigua & Barbuda

THE MANUFACTURE OF SUGAR, I.—CUTTING THE CANE
JULY 15TH, 1876 ANTIGUA

Introduction

Sugar.

It sits there, dormant, nestled in a small bowl or serving-size packet, waiting to be spooned into a cup of coffee or tea, spread across some cereal, dropped into a recipe for cake, pie, or other scrumptious treat in the making. It is so readily available, so easy to use, so irresistibly tasty.

But few people stop to realize the enormous economic, social, political, even military, upheaval this simple looking, widely popular food enhancer has caused in many parts of the world. In the 17th and 18th centuries, even into the 19th century and early decades of the 20th, sugar cane was a pre-eminent crop upon which economies succeeded or failed, societies grew, and money flowed like . . . well, sugar!

A region particularly impacted by sugar was the volcanic islands of the Caribbean: virgin soil enriched by crushed coral and limestone, and blessed by unlimited sunshine. The result was soil so rich for planting that the necklace of island colonies and small nation-states became a massive source of the world's supply of sugar. Antigua's 108 square miles, an island of undulating hills and indented coastline, fell into this category.

The 200-plus plantations on Antigua, founded by British explorers, owned mostly by absentee landlords, operated by managers and overseers, and worked by indentured servitude and African slaves, generated an economy that grew beyond anyone's imagination. Millions of tons of Antiguan sugar generated millions of pounds sterling which were enjoyed by the resident or absentee plantation owners, the shipping companies that carried Antiguan sugar to far parts of the world, the rum distillers who turned it into liquid gold for sale across the globe.

But the Antiguan people, those who built the plantations, managed them, cultivated the soil, planted and harvested the sugar cane; they who built and operated the vast stone sugar mills to grind the cane, freeing the liquid, boiled it, skimmed it, cooled it and agitated it; they who then packed the crystals into barrels, each weighing fifteen-to-sixteen-hundred pounds; they who loaded those heavy barrels onto mule- or oxen-pulled carts, then drove them along rutted dirt pathways to various distribution points around the island -- those folks benefited very little from the fruits of their hard labour. Antigua is renowned for having more of those windmills per square mile than any other island in the Caribbean. There were almost two hundred by the late 1700s, like freckles across the island's face.

Initially, mules or cattle were harnessed and walked in a large circle to operate huge rollers, crushing stalks of sugarcane to extract the sweet nectar. By 1750, windmills first appeared, harnessing the strong trade winds to operate the crushing equipment. But when the trade winds died, mules were again pressed into service. Steam power became prevalent by the mid-1800s, and sugar factories took over all sugar production by 1905.

Over the past 350 years, many of the magnificent stone windmills, so painstakingly hand-built by slaves or indentured servants, have been lost to earthquakes, neglect and the ravages of time. Yet more than one hundred of the stone towers still stand, sentinels marking the location of elaborate plantations, now nothing but faded memories silently requesting that their biographies be told. I have taken on that assignment.

I began my research twenty years ago, collecting photographs of the original plantation homes, most of which no longer stand. My effort gradually took on a life of its own, prompting me to search for letters, diaries, quotations, published articles, even people who still remembered "the good ole days" and could tell me interesting yarns and anecdotes about past times connected to the individual estates. They also assisted with my genealogical research. This often results in confusion because of the practice of naming the first child after the father, generation after generation.

I am not aware of any other publication that attempts to reconstruct the myriad plantations that covered Antigua. Names, of course, have changed with ownership over the years, and I have endeavored to relentlessly document each name I have successfully uncovered. Those people whose names I cannot associate with a particular estate, or the names of an estate which cannot be placed, are also noted at the end of this volume. With the passage of time, boundaries changed as smaller estates were incorporated into larger holdings, or large estates were sold off in small acreage parcels. The Parish of St. John's contained the largest number of estates, which are detailed in this Volume I. The plantations within the Parishes of St. George's and St. Peter's will be recorded in Volume II, and those in the Parishes of St. Philip's, St. Paul's and St. Mary's will be covered in Volume III.

At a point in time I had to draw closure and hope my initial effort to reconstruct an image of Antigua as it has existed over the past 350 years will bring more people forward with information, images, anecdotes about their heirs who lived here from the mid-1600s to the present. Additional information continues to become available on the internet as libraries digitize their records and individuals post genealogical sites.

The Museum of Antigua & Barbuda, in St. John's, will become the repository for this valuable collection of early Antiguan history.

All of the information from research sources is in italics, and we have used the spelling, phraseology and punctuation of the original documents.

I acknowledge that this publication may contain some errors. I hope they are few.

Agnes C. Meeker, MBE
September 2017

The Sugar Mill
by Patricia Von Levern

When I see a sugar mill on top a grassy knoll,
And view its weather beaten stone
These people must be told
Of a people who were brought here,
Torn from their native land
In chains and ropes
They came by boats
Across the treacherous seas.
They dreamed of jungles so unlike
These sleepy island lands,
And thought of loving mothers
While toiling near white sands.

Great stones were carved
Huge rocks were placed
In an ancient manner built,
By the hands of slaves,
Our fathers gave this legacy,
The Mill.
The crumbling stones
Like whitewashed bones
No modern plaster used
The old mills stand
The test of time
Cathedrals of Doom.

Tho slaves have died
Who built these Mills
Their stories buried deep
And when I see those Sugar Mills
A salutation I repeat.
Remember all who laboured
The coarsely caloused hands
These people who once worked here
Upon these sugar lands.

Their past is our foundation
Our very core of life
Has brought us to the present
Through sweat and bitter strife.
These stately Mills are silent tombs
Left here for all to see.
Grave headstones without written words
A hand hewn memory.
Now each of you, who now is here
When every time you see,
The crumbling stately
Sugar Mills
There, stands history

Preface

History with its flickering lamp
Stumbles along the trail of the past,
Trying to reconstruct its themes, to
Revive its echoes and Kindles with pale
Gleams the passion of former days.
Sir Winston Spencer Churchill

In this great future, you cannot forget the past.
Bob Marley

He didn't come to the West Indies to dance —
he came to make money as they all do. Some
of the big estates are going cheap, and one
unfortunate's loss is always a clever man's gain.
"Wide Sargasso Sea" by Jean Rhys

In the beginning . . .

When a line of volcanoes at the bottom of the southwest Atlantic Ocean began to erupt eons ago, they blew millions of tons of rock and lava upwards through hundreds of feet of ocean depth, so high the volcanic outpouring broke the surface of the ocean to form hard scrabble plateaus. This string of islands stood silent for centuries, ultimately covered with trees and tropical forestry, devoid of most animal or reptilian life, populated by hundreds if not thousands of birds of various species, colors, with voracious appetites for insects. About 1200 BC the Amerindians, pre-Columbian Carib Indians, arrived and built modest settlements. Over time, explorers began referring to these islands as the West Indies, the southern group called the Windwards, the northern group the Leewards. The largest landmass in the Leeward Islands they called Antigua; it was apparently named by Christopher Columbus after the church of Santa Maria de la Antigua, in Seville, Spain. (Columbus did not stay long; in fact, there is some question about whether he even landed in Antigua!) The smaller islands in the British Leeward group were named Nevis, St. Kitts (St. Christopher), Montserrat, Barbuda. Antigua was among those which harbored an undiscovered secret.

Its secret was its soil. Tropical winds, warm rain, and vast amounts of sunshine created a very rich soil composed of volcanic ash mixed with coral, limestone and decaying tropical vegetation. Antigua was ripe for cultivation, an asset the earliest settlers did not take long to discover.

The island was initially populated by the Amerindian people, whose archeological sites have been documented in and around the coastline of Antigua. It didn't take those early settlers long to chase them off Antigua, where they settled the island of Dominica, about one hundred miles south. The Carib Reserve was established in 1903 and is now known as the Kalinago Territory, the only remaining population of Pre-Columbian Indians in the Caribbean.

The European settlers came initially from the nearby island of St. Kitts in 1632, led by a twenty-two-year-old ship captain named Edward Warner, who went on to become Antigua's first Governor. He was the son of Sir Thomas Warner who, with a warrant from King Charles I, served as Governor of St. Kitts, Nevis, Barbados, and Montserrat. He instructed his son, Edward, to colonize Antigua for the British Crown.

Those early settlers faced mosquito-borne diseases, famine, hurricanes, and the problems associated with learning to grow new agricultural crops in an unfamiliar environment. They also encountered devastating attacks from Carib Indians as well as French, Dutch and Spanish explorers and privateers, all of whom were battling the settlers, the British and each other, for ownership of the West Indian islands.

In Vere Oliver's three volumes on the early settlers, he cites an incident in 1640 when *"(the) English at Antigua were attacked by the Caribs who killed fifty of them and carried off the Governor's lady, then great with child, her two children, and three other women. At this time, the inhabitants of Antigua consisted of about thirty families."* Another source stated that in *"1655 Mrs. Lee, wife of Capt. Lee (of Antigua), was carried away by the Caribs, and kept prisoner for three years, and many English were slaughtered."*

But the determined settlers survived.

Hungry for as much land as possible to cultivate, the pioneer settlers cut down many of the island's hardwood trees to plant their crops of indigo, tobacco, ginger, cotton and sugar. The downside of their enthusiasm was the decimation of the island's tropical forest, which led to a perpetual condition of drought causing the rivers and streams to dry up. (It is a condition which still exists: Antigua does not have a single river or stream, although dry riverbeds exist; tropically forested and mountainous Dominica, about one hundred miles south, has more than three hundred rivers and streams.)

Those early settlers established boundaries on the island, dividing Antigua's precious land into six Parishes, a reflection of their religious Anglican commitment: St. John's, St. Philip's, St. George's, St. Mary's, St. Peter's and Saint Paul's. They then subdivided the Parishes into fifteen Divisions, which made it easier to stake claims on specific acreage: Popes Head & Dickinson Bay, Falmouth, South Side Nonsuch, North Side Nonsuch & Willoughby Bay, Belfast, Old North Sound, New North Sound, Dickinson's Bay, St. John's, Carlisle Road, Old Road & Bermudian Valley, and Five Islands.

Within a few decades of their initial arrival, the other crops were phased out in favor of sugar cane and some sea-island cotton. Cotton proved easy to grow, thrived in the Antigua soil and weather, and survived well in the dry conditions. But sugar quickly became the mono-crop, occupying all of the flat and hillside land on the island for three centuries. It was Antigua's cash crop, and it delivered a lot of cash.

Historians believe sugar cane likely originated in the South Pacific and was domesticated in New Guinea and Indonesia. Over time, it spread to other parts of the world: India in 325 BC; China around 286 BC; Egypt by the mid eighth century; the Middle East by the tenth century; Madeira, Canary and Cape Verde islands and West Africa by the fifteenth century. Persia was producing hybrid cane by the early seventeenth century, and it soon was growing throughout the islands of the Caribbean.

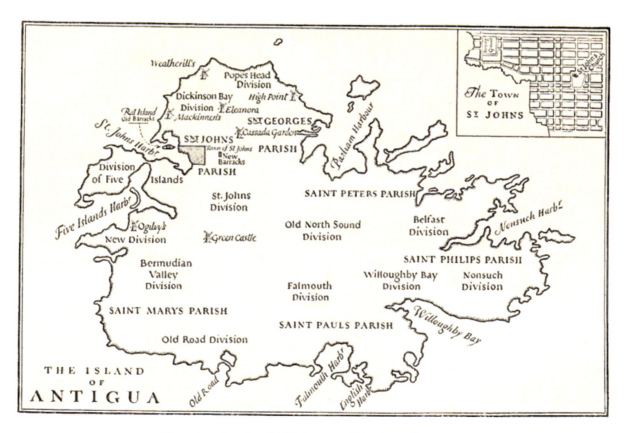

Map showing the 15 Divisions within the 6 Parishes
Museum of Antigua & Barbuda

Print by
Pierre Turpin-Chaumet - Cane

All sugar cane is derived from the several varieties of grasses in the Graminaea family. The stalk grows seven to eight feet tall, is about two inches thick, and can grow to fifteen feet when mature. It is jointed, similar to bamboo, with a soft inside full of sweet sap. It is this sap, when the stalk is crushed, that is boiled and turned into sugar crystals.

Cuttings that include one of the nodes or bands that circle the stem, are planted in soil, and from the first planting it takes between twelve and eighteen months for the stalks to mature. Once grown, several "ratoons" or crops may be cut over the next two-to-three years, but these succeeding crops produce progressively less sugar.

Sugar cane requires a lot of water, sunshine and fertilizer to reap the best returns. Unfortunately, the fields can harbour red fire ants and other pests, and the cane itself is subject to invasion by "bora" and disease. Also, the tall grassy leaves are sharp as a double-edged sword, resulting in fine paper-like cuts while being harvested, which is done by hand with a bill or cutlass: not an easy crop to harvest, especially in the hot tropical sun.

By the mid-1600s, sugar had replaced honey as a sweetener, and the European love of sugar to enhance and make elaborate fondants, cakes and other deserts had begun. Coffee houses sprang up all over London, becoming THE place to conduct business and debate political issues.

By 1700, more than half of the land on Antigua was planted with waving fields of sugar cane with the exception of the Shekerley Mountains and hilly areas in the southwest of the island. Nothing was wasted: the cane tops were used to feed animals and cover the roofs of the slave "trash" houses; the bagasse, the residue after all of the juice has been squeezed out, was used for both fuel and feed.

By 1724 no unregistered land was left on the island. The large plantations, or estates, had gobbled up acre upon acre of the fertile soil to expand their cultivation of sugar cane, which they crushed in their individually built and owned stone sugar mill towers.

The plantation estates were largely owned by absentee landowners most of whom continued to reside in Great Britain. Writing in 1825, Henry Nelson Coleridge said: *"the planters' houses were, I think, the best appointed of any that I saw in the West Indies. Most of them are very old mansions, and are constructed upon a more spacious and substantial plan that is generally deemed expedient in these days of mortgages."*

He continued: *"A small park, or lawn, is commonly enclosed round the house, and the sugar works, which, however picturesque at a distance, are a very disagreeable appendage at hand, and so well concealed by trees and bushes that in many cases their existence would not be suspected by a person with the principal buildings. I saw with great pleasure also the formation of some pretty flower gardens, for which there are such manifold facilities and delightful rewards, that it is surprising their existence should be so rare."*

Day-to-day operation of the plantations was under the direction of a manager or owner who appointed an overseer to supervise a population of slaves in the planting, nurturing, harvesting, crushing of the sugar cane, processing it, then delivering the crystals in heavy barrels to be loaded aboard ships.

It was slavery which permitted the owners and managers to employ (but not pay!) the many people required to operate a plantation. Vere Oliver notes that the sale of negroes and Indians for a life of unpaid servitude *"was authorized in*

1636, hitherto all the slaves on the plantations consisted solely of Indians and these were rapidly dying out." Some of the first slaves were American Indians captured and imprisoned by the settlers of the New World (North America), who also owned plantations in the West Indies. African slaves always comprised the major workforce, although indentured white servants from Scotland and Ireland arrived and were worked for seven years, deemed the price of their passage.

By the mid-1600s, the Irish were the main slaves sold to Antigua and Monserrat plantations. The Irish became 70% of the population on Monserrat. These white Irish were treated very harshly by their British masters; any infringement extended their indentureship, and many were sentenced to hang. From 1641 to 1652, more than 500,000 Irish were killed by the English and another 300,000 were sold as slaves in the West Indies, Virginia and New England, including more than 100,000 children between the ages of 10 and 14, who were stolen from their parents. This continued even after the Irish Rebellion of 1798, when thousands of Irish slaves were sold in America and Australia.

"The Irish Slave Trade: The Forgotten 'White' Slaves" by John Babik

In Antigua, the Irish did not adapt very well and few survived. Some of those who did eventually purchased land, as did some Scottish survivors who also opened shops on Scotch Row in St. John's. Scotch Row (now Market Street) was named after them.

Colonial Gentry, 1730-1775

"The story is told of [King] George III who, while driving with the elder [William] Pitt at Weymouth, met a splendidly accoutred carriage that far outshone the one carrying the royal person and his chief minister. Upon learning that the occupant was a West Indian, the King turned to his companion and said: 'Sugar, sugar, eh? All that sugar. How are the duties, eh, Pitt, how are the duties?'".

"The Rise of Colonial Gentry" by R. B. Sheridan.

There are many other examples of West Indians who cut a fine figure at the centre of fashion, and used their wealth to purchase seats in Parliament, to build town houses and country mansions and, in some cases, to form marriage alliances with members of the landed aristocracy. The literature is replete with accounts of repatriated West Indians; it is far from adequate in explaining how these absentees acquired their estates.

Little has been written of the relative importance of sources of wealth and income, including agriculture, trade, shipping, finance, government and the professions. Also, it is not clear whether the advantage lay with the descendants of pioneer families, enterprising latecomers, or a combination of both in the form of marriage alliances.

One contemporary maintained that the estates of absentees had been raised not by their own efforts but *"by the hardship, sweat and toil of their forefathers, among few capable competitors, in the infancy of the colonies.".* A contrary opinion was expressed by the West Indian who wrote that *"when Merchants who settle here, or Men of the Learned Professions, of the Law especially, have got a little beforehand, let them but once get Footing on a Piece of Land or on a Plantation ever so poorly settled, whether by Marriage, Purchase or otherwise, and they seldom fail (as their other Business or Practice is daily bringing them in Money) of soon becoming considerable Planters."*

Many of these individuals were able to return to Europe, to live there in affluence and splendour on their plantation profits *"whilst the mere Planters, who make the Bulk, are so far (some excepted) from being rich, that too many of them owe more than their Estates are worth."*

< >

The Revolutionary War fought in the American colonies (1775-1783) played a heavy role in the decline in trade between Colonial North America and the islands of the West Indies. With cries of "Down With Colonialism" and "No Taxation Without Representation", the Navigation Act actually precipitated the war. The West Indies relied heavily on trade with North America, but the colonials believed in "free trade" and enjoyed a considerable export and import business with French and Spanish islands as well as British.

England opposed this "foreign" trade, so Parliament passed a Molasses Tax in 1733 and a Sugar Duties Act in 1764, imposing stiff duties on New England's trade with the foreign sugar colonies. Duty on sugar climbed from 6s. 3p. per hundredweight in 1776 to 12s. 3p. in 1782. Other items sold to the islands included board and timber, shingles, staves, hoops, corn, peas, beans, flour, fish, rice, beef, pork, poultry, horses, oxen, soap, candles and iron. The American colonies imported sugar, rum and slaves from the islands.

John Quincy Adams (who in 1796 would be elected the second President of the United States) declared: *"They [the islands] can neither do without us nor us without them. The Creator has placed us upon the globe in such a situation that we have occasion for one another."* There were close ties between America and the British West Indies; as example, American owned estates on Antigua included Winthorpe's (#56) and Hart's & Royal's (#3).

By 1672, the population of Antigua was 1,370 people, 41.6% of them black. The island accounted for almost half of the Leeward Island slave population and its sugar production. By 1720, the island's slave population (23,000) had doubled to 84%, and by 1734, 86.6% of the island's 28,180 residents were black slaves. In 1831, the value of a slave was pegged at seventy pounds sterling; an acre of land sold for thirty pounds sterling. By 1833, 94.5% of the island's total population (37,031) were black slaves.

The slaves almost always took the name of the plantation on which they lived and worked, or the name of the owner or manager. They lost completely their African lineage and identity. Some were sired by managers and owners: it was well known that there were many a dalliance, both willingly and unwillingly, between master and slave. Nearly all of the proper names for areas in Antigua are derived from the old plantations, and many surnames in the current telephone book reflect the genealogy: Abbott, Archibald, Benjamin, Byam, Codrington, Edwards, Goodwin, Jarvis, Jacobs, Looby, Martin, Nibbs, Thomas, Thibou, Williams, Willock, to name a few.

The slave trade was officially abolished by Parliament in 1807, but it required another 26 years to effect the emancipation of the enslaved. In 1833, additional legislation abolished slavery in the British Caribbean, Mauritius and the Cape of Good Hope at the southern tip of South Africa. The 1833 legislation was prompted by a combination of factors, not least of which because it was felt plantation owners should be compensated for their slaves about to be freed. The British government budgeted £20 million to be divided between all slave owners.

By then Antigua's slave population exceeded 29,839 (14,068 males; 15,773 females). Emancipation did little to alter conditions for the former.

As part of the colonial system, London controlled not only the price of sugar but it also enacted various laws which impacted ownership of the estates. The Encumbranced Estate Act of 1854 and 1858, permitted any owner or encumbrancer of a West Indian Plantation to initiate proceedings. The 1833 legislation was prompted by a combination factor not least of which because it was felt that the plantation owners should be compensated for their property, i.e. slaves. The proceeds of such sales were to be divided among the estate's creditors according to the "wisdom" of the court. The purchaser would receive his property free of liabilities under a parliamentary title.

This sped up freeing slaves: the plantations continued to be their main source of employment; many continued to live in plantation-owned huts; they worked for paltry wages, and often tended small plots to provide general provisions for their families or to sell at the Sunday market. Those enterprising enough raised a few chickens, pigs or goats for sale or barter.

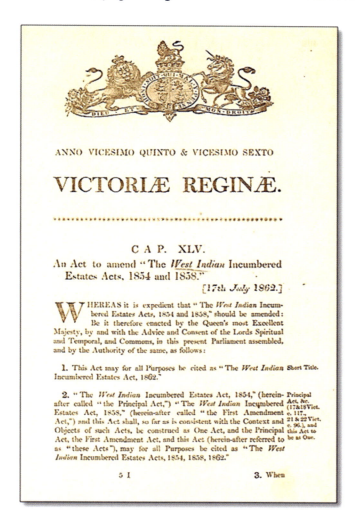

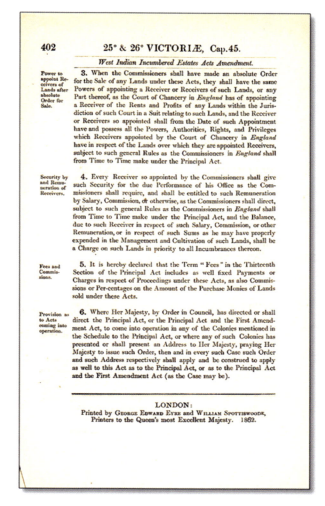

The chief desire of the newly emancipated people was to own a portion of land "in perpetuity", but this proved to be extremely difficult. Most of the land was already under cultivation and belonged to the many estates. The freed labourers could not find work if they did not live on the plantations. The planters actually devised a Contract Act under which they would provide free housing and medical attention to any labourer who agreed to sign up for a year's work without pay! However, a prolonged drought immediately after the 1833 emancipation resulted in little need for work, and the planters began to relax the residency requirement of the Contract Act.

Also, there was very little land left on which the freed slaves could plan villages. Only those in existence at the time had been large enough to be called towns: St. John's, Parham, Falmouth, English Harbour and Old Road. The rest of Antigua's villages were created after emancipation, some appearing in out-of-the-way locations, like the southwestern hills and the now extinct Hamilton's Village, which was located south of Bendals.

< >

By 1829, just prior to the abolition of slavery by the British Parliament, only 13 of the original 65 leading families of the 1730-1775 period remained estate owners on Antigua, and at least three were absentee owned.

This sped up freeing estates from legacies promised to family members back in the halcyon days, and removed debts, making the estates a more attractive purchase. In Antigua alone, 73 transactions went through the court between 1866 and 1892. (CO 318/282 26th January 1893). *"Sugar & Empire"* by Susan Lowes, and *"The Sugar Cane Industry"* by J. H. Galloway make fascinating reading about the Encumbered Estates Act, also *"Columbus to Castro"* by Eric Williams.

Some planters began to sell plots of land to their slaves and new villages came into being: Liberta is a prime example. The freed labourers gave many of the villages names meaning "freedom": Freetown and Liberta are two. Freemansville, on the other hand, was named after Freemans estate. Other villages appeared where the Moravians and Methodists had already erected chapels or schools: Jennings, Bendals, Newfield, Bethesda.

By 1840, only seven years after emancipation, there were almost thirty villages scattered around Antigua. The populations of those villages grew rapidly after a devastating earthquake in 1843, when many of the worker's homes on the estates were shattered and the planters did not want to incur the expense nor inconvenience of rebuilding them. Also, many of the workers decided they no longer wanted to live on estate-owned land: they wanted freedom from dependence upon the planters, freedom to bargain for their wages.

In the early 1850's, about thirteen years after Antigua's emancipation two thousand Portuguese from Madiera arrived in Antigua to serve a five year indentureship on the plantations. A number of Chinese also were working on the estates, but neither ethnic group could tolerate the extreme climate and working conditions of the tropics. They were not enslaved and after serving their indentureship were assimilated into the community.

There were 127 estates listed in Antigua in 1841, and by 1897 there were only 71 contributing to the amalgamation of estates (Schnakenbourg 1984-92). Various companies had been formed, such as F. Garroway Co., which purchased in 1868 Blackman's (#63), Cades Bay (#191) and Otto's (#16), and sold the estates the company owned in 1840/50, including estates to be clear of all debts and available for sale under the Encumbered Estates Act to begin fresh with new owners.

Peters, Dew and J.J. Camacho & Co. formed South Western Estate Co. for the same purpose, buying Bellevue (#36) and Briggin's (#22) in 1878 and Langford's (#6), Mount Pleasant (#7), Dunbar's (#8), Otto's (#16), Wood's (#12) and Jonas's (#85) in 1891.

Parker & Co. bought Hawes (#79), Mercer's Creek (#78), Big Duers (#89) and Little Duers (#90) and Freeman's Lower (#82). Dobee & Sons Belvedere (#38), Byam's and Bodkin's (#142). This permitted the purchase of Otto's (#16), and Blackman's (#63). Fryers Concrete Co. owned Bath Lodge, Bodkins (#142), Green Castle (#163), Bendal's (#37), Belvedere (#38), Byam's and Halliday's Mountain (#49), which was used to raise cattle. And in 1889, A. M. Lee (Lee, Crerar & Co., London) bought Montpelier (#11) from F. B. Harmon.

But the largest landowners on the island were John and Robert Maginley who, as listed in the 1872 Almanac, owned Comfort Hall (#103), Gilbert's (#80), Long Lane (#107), Lavington's (#121), Lyons (#123), Willis Freeman's (#143), Burke's (#133), LaRoche (#135) and Table Hill for a total of 4,500 acres. In 1891, they added Cedar Hill (#74) and Sanderson's (#86), bringing their estate ownership to nine. (Burke's, LaRoche and Table Hill were considered one estate.)

Sugar quickly became the lifeblood of Antigua and the source of extraordinary wealth for the absentee land owners and a good life style for the managers who supervised the estates, although they were paid a very low wage, which did not enable them to accrue wealth. The Public Record Office in London in 1907 (Ref. CO.q52/297/295) notes in their lists 16 absentee landlords as owning 58 estates between them; 8,535 acres under cultivation.

Planting of the cane began during the island's rainy season by "holeing" the soil in four-foot squares about six-to-eight inches deep. The stalks of cane were placed horizontally in the squares and covered with a mix of soil and animal manure. It was hard, back breaking work. Sprouts grow high at maturity, which required fourteen-to-sixteen months. Old stalk roots, called "rattoons", were left in the ground to sprout for several growing seasons, and while this saved the hard labour of planting, those older crops yielded progressively less juice.

A typical cane field covered ten or twenty acres. It was laid out in grids with the cane rows running east-to-west to allow the wind to pass through the tall stalks. The interval between cane fields was twelve to eighteen-feet wide, serving as both a fire barrier and a track for the cane carts during harvest, which began in January and continued through July.

Planting the cane stalks, Weatherills. Print by William Clarke, Beinecke Collection,
Hamilton College*

"An Essay Upon Plantership 1750-1785" by Colonel Martin of Antigua provides a detailed and interesting description of the planting process. His chapter on the "blast", a pest that attacks the sugar cane, notes that the cane then attracts millions of ants, often necessitating that the field be burned with the loss of any crop. To combat the "blast", planters combined a barrel of salt or fresh water, added several handfuls of Stinking-reed roots, a leaf of small Aloe cut into slices (or a quart of vulgar Great Aloe, called Dagger), and quart of Temper Lime. Mixed together, it was allowed to stand for 24 hours, then dipped with rags and wiped on the cane, a concoction which would most likely kill anything!

Upon the recommendation of Mr. P. E. Turner, who came to Antigua in 1949, cane was planted in different parts of Antigua at different times of the year, depending upon the soil and rainfall. In the wet area of Fitche's Creek, it was planted in September, while in the dry area November was recommended as the best month to plant. Turner also claimed that on Weatherill's, it was best not to plough close, but only furrow about 4-5 inches to cut up old shoots as a weeding process; space the chisels about 12 inches apart, break banks or mould to get the camber smoothed out with no depressions. (To "chisel" means to dig as deep as possible without disturbing the marl.) For fertilizer he recommended 2 Cwts. S/Amonia and 1 Cwt. S/Phosphate per acre while ratoon crops required 3 S/Amonia and 1 S/Phosphate.

Cutting the cane at Delaps Plantation - Print by William Clarke, Beinecke Collection, Hamilton College*

Cane was considered ripe for harvesting when the "arrows" appeared (the seed stem similar to grasses) in dry weather. A cutlass, or cane "bill", was used to trim off leaves, which were carted off for fodder or roofing materials for the slaves' houses. The stalks were cut into four-foot lengths, bundled and piled high on carts pulled by oxen or mules (later by locomotive) and delivered to the stone sugar mills topped with a large windmill. Because cane juice would be lost or sour very quickly, the daily amount of cane harvested had to be coordinated with the extraction capacity of the mill, sixty-to-seventy cart loads of cane, about two acres worth. The juice was delivered to the Boiling House, poured into a clarifying vat and mixed a dozen or more times in large cast iron basins called "coppers" or "taiches", to be mixed with lime (calcium oxide} to commence purification. It was then boiled into muscovado sugar. The fire to accomplish the boiling was stoked with bagasse (a byproduct of the crushed cane stalks) from outside the building; the heat was distributed through horizontal flues underneath the coppers.

Boiling the Cane Juice in Coppers - Print by William Clarke, Beinecke Collection, Hamilton College*

The juice faced further travels. The boiling liquid was ladled from the largest into the smallest copper, the heat increased, the scum on the surface skimmed off in a gutter which led to the fermentation tank. When the liquid had reached the proper caramel-like stage, it was "struck" from the smallest copper/taiche and flowed through a trough to wooden drying flats along the eastern (upwind) wall. Once cooled for several hours while being agitated with a spatula, the resulting sugar crystals were packed into "hogsheads" (barrels) or clay pots, some of which were made at what is known today as the Potworks Dam. The hogsheads were placed on rafters in the Curing House, where they drained for about one month producing molasses, which dripped from the sugar crystals. A hogshead of refined sugar weighed fifteen, sixteen hundred pounds when it was shipped to England, producing molasses, which dripped from the sugar crystals.

Shipping the casks of sugar and rum from Willoughby Bay.
Print by William Clarke,Beinecke Collection, Hamilton College*

The print above shows sailing ships at anchor in Willoughby Bay where Bridgetown was located. Bridgetown was one of Antigua's first towns so named by settlers from Barbados. The town was completely destroyed by a Tsunami in the 1700's and whilst the Church, St. Phillip's, was relocated to the hill above, there are only the remnants of stone foundations and grave stones on the shore below. Barrels of rum and sugar are seen being rolled on to a row boat to be taken out to the ships at anchor. In the distance is a sugar plantation under full steam. In about 1845 the first plantation on Antigua converted its sugar mill to a steam-powered engine to increase the percenage of juice derived from the cane. This power source was first used successfully in Cuba in 1797, but it took years to filter to the smaller West Indies islands.

Fletcher & Stewart Ltd., of Masson Works in Derby, had been concerned about the inefficiency of wind or animal driven sugar machinery for many years. In 1838 George Fletcher (born in Derbyshire) started his engineering business in Southwark, London, after being trained in the Darlington Works of George Stephenson. He visited Cuba for the firm, saw the primitive sugar machinery then in use, and decided to establish his own firm to make steam driven machinery for processing sugar cane. He moved his works to Derby in 1869.

Meanwhile, in 1840, Peter Stewart was a millwright in the Anderston district of Glasgow, specializing in the construction of sugar machinery for export to the West Indies. His firm merged with the Booker Group in 1958 and George Fletcher & Co. joined in 1956. Molasses had been the industrial waste of the sugar cane refining business. However, when folks realized that with a pinch of this, a dab of that and a handful of something else, the outcome was a delicious beverage they called Rumbullion, Rhum, Kill Devil, and of course, Rum, it quickly became the national drink of the Caribbean and ultimately replaced sugar as the area's largest export.

Rum was produced from the fermented mixture of water and molasses residue from the boiling process. Large cisterns ran along the outside of the Still House, where vapours from the stills were condensed through copper coils immersed in cooling water collected from the building's roof. Holes at the bottom of each cistern contained pipes to collect the raw rum, which flowed into casks to be aged or re-distilled to increase the percentage of alcohol before the beverage was exported.

The residents of Barbados were apparently the first to distill rum from molasses, the by-product of their sugar distillation, around 1638. Their knowledge apparently came with the Scots, who first settled the island and who had been distilling whisky for decades.

The making of rum using molasses spread throughout the Caribbean with the exception of the French islands; those settlers preferred white rum, which was distilled from the cane sugar juice, not molasses. Each island produced its own blend of rum, stored in oak casks to contribute to the flavor. The wooden casks allowed the rum to breathe, permitting a certain amount of dehydration during the aging process.

In 1702, Christopher Codrington wrote: *"the planters think the best way to make their strangers welcome is to muther [murder!] them with drinks, the tenth part of that strong liquor which will scarce warm the blood of our 'West Indians', who have bodies like Egyptian mummys (sic) . . . ."*

Ian Williams, in his book *Rum,* wrote: *"Antigua was ... small but efficient in its sugar production and was reckoned to be the best rum after Jamaica and Grenada's double distillation. Antiguans were careful in their techniques, as well, producing more molasses and even more rum with the addition of skimmings from the wash. They produced 120 gallons of rum for every 100 gallons of molasses."*

The American colonials developed a strong taste for rum, resulting in an explosive trade with the various taste preferences of the North American colonies. New Yorkers apparently favored St. Croix rum, Philadelphians preferred rum from St. Kitts or Barbados, Virginians liked Antiguan rum, while collonists resident in Maryland swilled rum from Barbados.

Rum eventually became as important to the Caribbean economy as sugar. It was even used as barter for slaves: in 1764, the price of a slave was £12 sterling, or 110 gallons of rum! Molasses, too, became an important commodity. Admiral Horatio Nelson's body was embalmed in a cask of rum after he was killed at the Battle of Trafalgar, and the British Navy prescribed a "tot" of rum for every sailor aboard its ships, a practice which was not abolished until 1970. It was thought to kill bacteria.

As example, the slave ship *Sally* carried foodstuffs, naval stores, and more than 200 hogsheads of rum on its slaving voyage to Africa. Rum, distilled from sugar produced by West Indian slaves, was the standard trade good carried on Rhode Island slave ships; the captains were known on the African coast as "rum men". The *Sally's* cargo as she departed for Africa included 17,274 gallons of New England rum!

In the early 1850s, when the Portuguese arrived in Antigua from Madeira and were eventually freed, they often set up rum shops in St. John's and in other villages around the island, residing on the floor above their stores. The only example recently existing was run by John (Bushy) Gonsalves in Bolands. Bushy blended his own rum, called Bolanda, and sold it from his rum shop next to a grocery store, the local post office, and a gas station across the road. Regrettably, Bushy passed away in 2013 and his rum shop closed.

Families such as Farara continue to operate a liquor business. A group of nine Portuguese (Emmanuel Gomes, Manuel Dias, John Vieira, Emmanuel C. Farara, G. F. Joaquion, Joseph De-Freitas, Quin Farara, John R. Anjo and Francis R. Anjo) came together in the 1900s to purchase eight of the old estates: Lynch's, (#123), Harmon's (#120), Skerret's Folly (#114), Archilbald's (#12), Brown's (#113), Hope (#119), Walrond's (#116), and Manning's (#124).

They formed the distillery on Rat Island, which still produces Cavalier and English Harbour Rum today. The primary estate was Montpelier with its muscavado-producing factory, from which they could secure molasses for their rum production. The Montpelier Sugar Factory closed in the 1950s, and the Antigua Sugar Factory closed in the 1970s, so molasses has had to be imported from Guyana. The distillery is located on Rat Island close to the Citadel and the Port.

Several old bottles of Antiguan rum were found a few years ago in the basement of Bishop Paul Moore's home in New York City. His parents had visited Antigua and it is assumed they brought the rum to the U.S. and Bishop Moore inherited it. When he passed away, Lidie Laughlin, rector of a New York parish and brother-in-law of Desmond Nicholson, the noted Antigua historian, was appointed Bishop Moore's executor.

Laughlin was aware of Nicholson's interest in anything Antiguan and thought it appropriate that one of those bottles be repatriated to the island. It was returned to Antigua for testing by Dr. Reg Murphy, Antigua's leading archaeologist, for research and possible lead content.

The Tot Club, headquartered in English Harbour, maintains the practice of the British Navy, enjoying a "tot" of rum every day. Its members meet at The Tot Club, headquartered in English Harbour. Its members meet at sunset daily in a different restaurant or other location on the island. They stand in a circle, toss down a "tot" of English Harbour Rum for Queen and Country while one member reads a passage from Lord Nelson's maritime records about British Naval History pertaining to that particular date. (The Tot Club also is instrumental in maintaining many of the hiking trails in the English Harbour National Park.)

Antigua also helped introduce sugar to Australia. In their book *Rum; Yesterday & Today,* Anton Massei and Hugh Bartey-King state that *"in 1821, a West Indian negro convict from Antigua, John Williams, helped Francis Allman, Commander of the Australian penal settlement at Port Macquarie, grow cane."* A small amount of raw sugar was made from it two years later, but no rum. However, Tom Alison Scott, son of an Antiguan sugar planter, took over Port Macquarie as an employee (not an inmate) when Williams was hanged for theft. (The) Project (was) abandoned in 1831.

< >

The first set of sugar mill towers -- the stone edifices which held the windmills -- were built around 1671, according to George Goodwin (Duer's Estate), father of Affie Goodwin, *"who used to talk a lot,"* as quoted by Pappy Smith in the popular book "*To Shoot Hard Labour.*" Pappy goes on to quote Affie: *"He used to tell me how his family came to Antigua in the time the first set of mill towers was built in the year 1671 or so. In the old days almost everybody used to say that the best tradesman were usually from the villages of Willikies and Freetown and the Goodwins always used to tell me that these people did most of the work on the sugar mill towers. They was built over two hundred years ago by the Piggots of Northern Ireland.”*

Pappy continued: *“But no nega was to know the secret of the mixture of the white lime that they used to build the towers. If ever the bakkra believe that a negra was having the least idea of how the mixture was made up, he would be a dead man when the job was done. The secret of how them mix the limestone remain everlasting secret to this day I know that they used to use a thing from Montserrat that they call ‘trickle’ and they also put in lime.”* (“Bakkra” was dialect for a white person.)

Edgar Kasper Lane of Weatherills, writing in the 1940s, said: *“When looking at the Mill Tower, one realizes how hard the slaves worked in building it. Also, it must be remembered that in those days it was all done by manpower. The mortar used to hold the stonework in place was mixed and left for three months to mature before being used.”*

Nearly every estate bordering the sea also operated a lime kiln where conch and other shells were heated at high temperature, then crushed into a powder. To make the mortar for building a sugar mill, a fine aggregate of marle dust and ghut sand was added to the powder, followed by an assortment of recipes involving treacle, cattle dung, ox blood, cactus or horse hair.

The process took a long time to mature, three months in some cases, and it set much harder than modern day concrete. Its properties also allowed it to expand to fill the many cracks between the stones. The Knowles family was the last to operate a kiln in Antigua; there is supposedly one operating today in Nevis, using coconut husks for fuel.

< >

All estate works ceased in 1905, when three large self-contained sugar factories were built in Montpelier, Bendals and Gunthorpes (Antigua Sugar Factory). Gunthorpes was the largest and most centrally located. A narrow gauge railroad replaced oxen- or mule-pulled carts to move the cane from plantations island-wide. The Bendals factory was dismantled in 1940, and the Montpelier factory closed in 1955, leaving only the Gunthorpes factory as the sole sugar manufacturer on Antigua until it closed in 1972.

An Antigua Syndicate was formed in the 1940s and most of the Plantation owners eventually sold their lands and homes to the Syndicate for a fraction of their value, a direct consequence of the rising costs of sugar production. Most of the old estate homes have long since disappeared. In an effort to preserve them in the 1970s, a few individuals accepted an offer of a ninety-nine-year lease from the Antiguan Government, a vain hope that this would encourage them to renovate, live in, and preserve the Antigua estate houses. Most of the estate houses in existence today have been purchased and renovated.

Worldwide competition from the expanding sugar beet market caused a steep decline in the market price for sugar. Coupled with union demands for higher wages and a lack of rainfall, "King Sugar" ceased to be a marketable commodity for Antigua in 1972, ending 340 years -- 1632 to 1972 -- as the major export commodity and largest employer in the island's history in 1982 the sugar business made an attempt to revive but collapsed after only two years.

In 1995/97, a survey of Antigua's windmills was conducted by Caribbean Volunteer Expeditions, an organization which recruits volunteers from the United States to assist Caribbean agencies with the documentation of historic structures. With the help of the Museum of Antigua & Barbuda, the CVE enlisted local Antiguans to assist with the field work. Their findings are on file at the Museum along with additional research by Desmond Nicholson. He compiled a map of the many mills, which he categorized within each of the island's six Parishes along with ownership taken from various old maps.

The CVE Mill Survey served as the basis of this author's research of all of the mills before they deteriorated further and were lost forever. That research, in turn, prompted a broadened effort to include the many plantations and their owners, whose mills had been destroyed, thus enabling the compilation of a far more complete historical record.

Many of the original 175 windmills have been swallowed up by the ravages of nature and neglect by mankind but more than one hundred of the painfully re-constructed stone towers still stand across Antigua as reminders of a bygone era. Those structures provide an indication of the original estate locations, along with various maps produced throughout the years.

Sugar, once covering vast acreage of Antigua, was such a dominant part of the island's gross national product, its life style, and its heritage, is now almost entirely confined to the sugar bowls in resort hotels, inns, B&Bs, restaurants and the tables of Antiguan residents.

WINDMILL TERMS

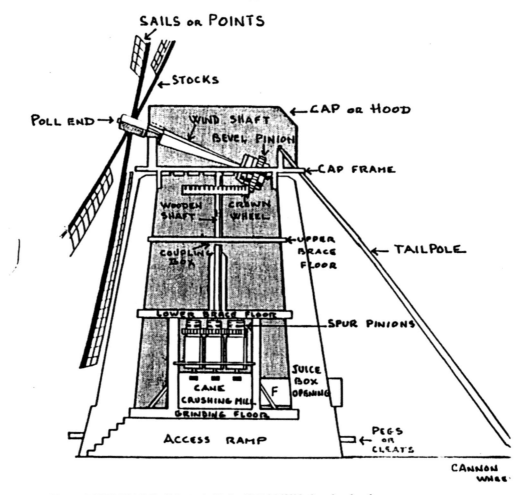

The OPENINGS IN A MILL TOWER Included:-
ENTRY (Freshly Cut Cane entry)
BAGASSE EXIT (Crushed Cane to be re-utilised as fuel)
JUICE BOX OPENING (Cane Juice to Boiling House)
EXCHANGE SLIT (for changing wooden vertical drive shaft)
PORT HOLE (for bell)
FIREPLACE (for Night Work)

FOR CRUSHING SUGAR CANE
VERTICAL ROLLERS were used until c.1794
HORIZONTAL ROLLERS gave better crushing and quicker
as shorter and a larger diameter

The SAILS drove the crushing rollers and revolved:-
4 turns a minute in an average breeze
6/7 in a stiff breeze

THE ORDER STARTING A STOPPING A MILL:-
"Turn her out!"
"Turn her in!"

The Museum of London Docklands, in the U.K., operates a special Museum on Sugar and Slavery, which is housed in the old West India Docks, London, benefitted enormously from the trans-Atlantic slave trade, with nearly three thousand British slave ships sailing from Africa to the Caribbean and North America before the trade was abolished. The landscape of East London had been transformed when the West India Docks were constructed to handle slave plantation produce.

Great Britain's burgeoning Empire was dependent upon colonial trade, and London was its financial engine. Slavery contributed greatly to the financial success of hundreds of British companies, banks and private estates, and also paid for some of the valuable artwork which currently hangs in the galleries of some of London's great museums.

The building at the Museum of London Docklands, which houses the Museum on Sugar and Slavery, was once stacked high with hogsheads of sugar that had been cut, ground and boiled by enslaved men, women and children on West Indian plantations. The building was literally a cog in the machinery of slavery, its owners were the merchants and absentee plantation landlords who pocketed millions in profits from others suffering. Most of the shipping went through the West India Docks and the Thames river was often clogged with vessels waiting their turn to be unloaded.

The Museum is a valuable and interesting resource for anyone interested in a better understanding of the historic landscape of East London from the sugar warehouses of West India Quay to the trading floors of Canary Wharf.

Ships lined up at the West India docks. – Museum of Docklands London

< >

Preservation of Existing Sugar Mills

Most of the existing sugar mills are on Government or Crown land, however in some cases, private land. It is hoped that one day the Government of Antigua and Barbuda will undertake a preservation programme and declare these reminders of our historical past national treasures. At this point in time there is no specific legislation in place. Some privately owned mills have been renovated by the owners, giving them new life, and ensuring that they will be around for coming generations. These owners are to be commended. People interested in renovating an existing sugar mill should visit the Museum of Antigua and Barbuda to research the proper design of the mills using records from the CVE Mill Survey. The mill should be left free standing, not incorporated within or attached to another building. No mill should be removed from its original location, to be assembled at another site, because it will immediately lose its historic value.

Good examples are Yepton's (#29), Galley Bay Hotel (#30), Hawksbill Hotel (#32) and Browne's/Harmony Hall (#33). Not so good are Comfort Hall (#103), Crosbie's (#2) and Hodge's (#4) for they have been built around and/or attached to.

< >

The Ravages of Nature

Many hurricanes struck the Caribbean islands without warning in the centuries prior to the invention of the telephone and telegram. Residents could check the drop in barometric pressure, but it was extremely difficult to judge the severity of an incoming storm. The result was often catastrophic damage to the planted acreage, the plantation homes, the slave huts, and the sugar mills themselves.

A major hurricane, which hit Antigua on August 27, 1772, *"buried some persons in the ruins of their houses,"* according to then Governor Payne. *"We had an exceedingly hard gale of wind, which continued for the space of 7 or 8 hours, and then subsided without doing any material damage. In the night of Sunday, the 30th of August the wind blew fres(h) . . . and continued increasing till five in the morning when it blew a hurricane from the NE . . . a melancholy darkness prevaile'd for more than an hour aft sun rise.*

"Eight o'clock the fury of the tempest in some measure abated, but it was only to collect new redoubl'd violence, and to display itself, with tenfold for the space of 4 hours . . . Some persons were buried in the ruins of their houses. Many

houses were razed. The doors, windows and partitions of the Court House were blown in, the interior completely wrecked and most valuable papers destroyed. The barracks are in a deplorable condition. At English Harbour, deemed stormproof, there was a squadron under Admiral Parry, whose flagship with others drove ashore and the hospital there was leveled to the ground, crushing in its fall the unfortunate patients and attendants. My new study, with most of its papers was blown away." The damage was so extensive the British Government provided £100,000 to Antigua *"specifically earmarked for repairing buildings and for relief to private individuals who might borrow from the government of the island."*

An earthquake devastated the island in February 1843. Thirty-five sugar mills were destroyed, eighty-two were split from top to bottom, many others required extensive repair. There were 172 mills on Antigua at that time, many of them operating when the earthquake hit, *"sending a rich stream of luscious juice through several pipes into the boiling houses."*

The loans carried a five percent annual interest; principal to be re-paid in equal installments over ten years. Those were extremely tough conditions considering the level of devastation and the time required to rebuild. As result, many mills were not reconstructed or repaired, and in other cases owners converted their operations to steam, rendering wind mills obsolete.   *"Five of the Leewards"* by Robert Hall.

The mills reduced to rubble included: Bellevue (Messrs. Shand's), Renfrew's, Belmont, Bath Lodge (Walters), Green Castle (Sir Henry Martin). Lower Freeman's, Sir George Thomas's works & mansion, Little Duers, Big Duers, Ffrys, Elliot's, Potters, La Roche's, Otto Baijer's, Mount Pleasant, Rock Hill, Delap's, George Byam's, Patterson's, Montero's, Paynter's, Gunthorpe's, Claremont (Hon. W. E. Williams), Gamble's (Adm. Tollemach's), Friar's Hill, The Wood, McKinnon's, Wm. Williams Esq.

* There are 10 prints by William Clark, 9 of which are in the "Beinecke Collection," Hamilton College.
They are described in T. Barringer, G. Forrester and B. Martinez-Ruiz, "New Haven Yale Center for British Art in Association with Yale University Free Press 2007" pp.318-321, based on Clark's unpaginated text.

*Government House being destroyed in the 1772 Hurricane
Beinecke Collection, Hamilton College.

Hurricanes of Antigua: 1632 – 1999. Museum of Antigua & Barbuda

1642 -- A hurricane hits Guadeloupe; high winds in Antigua.

1664 -- Another hurricane hits Guadeloupe; damage not as severe.

1665 -- An entire fleet of ships (Willoughby's) is destroyed off Guadeloupe.

1667 -- A "young" hurricane of small diameter devastates St. Kiitts.

1668 -- A hurricane destroys all that is left of Freeman's Estate following a French invasion.

1671 -- The yacht *Dover Castle* is washed ashore in a storm at English Harbour.

1681— One of the severest hurricanes on record strikes Antigua.

1694 -- Another hurricane pummels Antigua, extensive damage.

1706 -- An August 18 hurricane runs 18 ships aground in the entrance to St. John's harbour.

1707 -- Another August hurricane slams Antigua, destroying homes, sugar works, and agricultural fields.

1740 -- A severe hurricane hits Antigua; many ships driven ashore.

1751 -- A hurricane severely damaged the island's sugar crops.

1752 -- A major drought; storm damage to the harbour entrance and forts.

1754 -- Substantial mortality within the white population; one hurricane runs 15 ships ashore in Antigua, while a second over the entire Leeward Island chain damages plantations.

1756 -- A major storm strikes English Harbour, followed by a hurricane which damages Martinique and Antigua plantations.

1776 -- The fifth most severe hurricane strikes between Antigua and Montserrat.

1780 -- Another severe hurricane rocks Antigua.

1787 —Near miss, hurricane still caused shingles to be lost, sloops drifted.

1792 -- A major hurricane passed just north of the island.

1793 -- Another hurricane passed southeast and struck St. Kitts.

1795 -- A violent hurricane accompanied by an earthquake strikes.

1804 -- A major hurricane strikes Antigua and St. Kitts; considered one of the most severe to hit the islands along with those of 1681, 1754, 1792.

1815 -- Strong hurricane strikes Dominica, Antigua, St. Barts, in August.

1818 -- Another hurricane pounds Dominica, Martinique and Antigua on September 22.

1819 -- A hurricane damages shipping in St. John's; destroys parts of Cross Street.

1821 -- September. Floating stage at English Harbour was destroyed in a gale.

1827 -- August 17; hurricane battered Antigua, barometer fell one-half inch.

1835 -- Fifteen minute calm signaled center of the storm; 15 killed. Only four houses escaped damage on St. John's Street. The prison was severely damaged, plus St. John's properties. The Dockyard Common house and galleries were damaged. Wind increased to cause St. John's "to vibrate." Storm ended at midnight.

1846 -- Since 1664 (183 years) there had been 22 hurricanes in Antigua. On September 12th, the lifeboat *Lydia* saved three men off St. John's.

1848 -- 28 lives lost in hurricane. Great loss of property estimated at £100,000. damage to Moravian property in Gracebay, Cedar Hall, Lebanon. "Country looked as if fire, not wind, has passed."

1871 -- Hurricane wiped out entire villages, 35 lives lost. Damage to £1,500 worth of Moravian property. The Scottish Kirk was destroyed, but "the gallows nearby stood."

1887 -- July 20: slight brush of a hurricane passed Barbados.

1899 -- September 8: storm destroyed half of the houses in Freeman's village.

1913 -- Property can now be insured against hurricane damage.

1922 -- Hurricane over Barbuda; the roof of Government House blew off.

1924 -- Two storms hit! Country Pond was flooded; Nevis Street was cut in two. Storms ended a three-year drought; brought the annual rainfall to 41.57 inches.

1928 -- Another hurricane struck Antigua.

1932 -- Roof of the Barbuda school was lost along with the Puerto Rican ship *San Cipriani.*

1950 -- Two hurricanes hit Antigua within 10 days; nicknamed "Cat" and "Dog" chasing after each other. The first, on August 21st, had winds of 100 MPH; the second, on August 31st, had winds of 165 MPH. They destroyed 11,348 homes, many of them wattle/daub construction; another 2,343 were damaged, including several estate houses which were never repaired or rebuilt. 6,792 people (15% of the population) were homeless; the village of Hamilton was blown off the map.

1973 -- Late August: Hurricane "Christine"

1976 -- August 12: a hurricane damaged the base of the Sandy Island lighthouse, but it kept functioning.

1989 -- September 18: Hurricane "Hugo, with winds between 80 and 110 MPH, blew for 18 hours, brought 7.33 inches of rainfall, twice the monthly total. 509 people lost homes; 2 dead and 181 injured; 38 of 256 fishing boats were severely damaged.

1990 -- Antigua Red Cross handled $255,574 to assist "Hugo's" victims.
    -- August 27: "Hurricane "Gustave" veered north.
    -- October 5: Tropical Storm "Klaus" was upgraded to hurricane status north of Barbuda; packed winds 50 - 70 MPH; no power on the island for 25 days.

1995 -- September 4/5: Hurricane "Luis" hit, category 4 storm, winds to 140 MPH for 36 hours; 85% of homes damaged, 15% destroyed, 3 killed, 52 injured, 4,200 homeless. Red Cross handed out 15,200 food parcels, 3,000 meals, and 5,205 blankets.
    -- Hurricane "Marilyn: passed Antigua; serious flooding.

1996 -- July 8: Hurricane "Bertha", winds of 60 MPH, neared Barbuda; power out but little damage.

1998 -- Hurricane "Georges" passed over Antigua, a category 3 storm with winds of 125 - 130 MPH. Major damage to houses.

1999 -- July 20: Midday, Hurricane "Jose" hit Antigua with 100 MPH winds ABS and telephone continued to operate during the storm with an emergency call-in programme. Crab Hill was a disaster area.

-- November 19: Midday, Tropical Storm "Lenny", with 40-50 MPH winds, struck Antigua and dropped 15-to-20 inches of rain over four days. Considerable flooding and road damage; houses actually floated in Villa and Piggotts. A water spout was sighted southeast of Falmouth.

2000 -- August: Hurricane "Debby".

2003 -- August 26: Hurricane "Fabian", category 3/4, passed 200 miles off of Antigua, but demolished Barbuda. September 7: Hurricane "Isabelle", a category 4/5 storm, raged 160 miles off Antigua, eventually hit North Carolina and Virginia as a category 2/3 storm.

2014 -- October 13, "Gonzalo" was not expected to develop into a hurricane, left the island unprepared for winds of 75 mph and gusting higher, causing damage to boats in the harbors.

Antigua's Rainfall

Although it is an island, Antigua and water just don't seem to get along. It is a very dry island, in fact drought is one of the major factors which led to the demise of its profitable sugar industry. The drought of 1833 was so severe the sugar estates in the southwest corner of the island were abandoned because the owners were impoverished due to their poor crop yield, caused by the lack of water.

Large catchments for fresh water can be found on many of Antigua's hillsides. Betty's Hope, the restored sugar plantation, has one, as does the village of Willikies, New Winthorpes and Nelson's Dockyard. The Mill Reef community, when it was developing in the late 1940s, built five or seven catchments. Dams and wells contribute to the desalinised fresh water supply, and several ponds still exist on the island but they are not properly maintained.

Every plantation had one or two ponds, usually situated between the estate house and the sugar works. The ponds were used by the slaves and livestock, and for sugar production. In later years, many ponds were equipped with a metal windmill, which pumped fresh water up to the main house.

Most ponds were dug by hand; then a type of clay was smeared over the excavated sides and bottom to prevent leakage, essentially "waterproofing" the pond shell. Most ponds created today are lined with plastic sheeting.

In times of drought, these ponds provided the only fresh water available, water which could be fairly brackish as well as muddy. Once the windmill towers ceased to be used, they were often sealed up and converted into water tanks. Today, much of the island's water supply is provided by desalination. However, the capacity to store water is minimal, which continues to result in water shortages, especially during drought conditions The least amount of rainfall for an entire year in Antigua totaled only 24.16 inches in 1949, and 24.13 inches in 1997. The most rainfall ever recorded on the island was for the year 1983: 69.14 inches.

The following summarizes three periods of rainfall between 1847 and 2001. They are typical of the island's annual fresh water totals.

Rainfall: 1847 - 2001

RAINFALL: 1847-1852, taken at The Ridge - Davy's *West Indies*, pg. 384

Month	1847	1848	1849	1850	1851	1852
Jan.	2.77		2.92	1.57	3.75	.81
Feb.	1.50		1.30	1.95	6.38	2.85
March	1.72		1.00	2.60	2.85	.40
April	.57	2.92	.85	.43	2.75	
May	.86	1.17	.53	.25	5.43	4.36
June						
July	2.33	2.91	3.68	7.53	1.81	2.85
Aug.	6.38	4.00	4.26	7.52	7.31	6.24
Sept.	1.91	5.47	1.37	3.78	1.23	5.09
Oct.	3.98	7.49	2.96	1.31	3.99	.88
Nov.	6.35	4.69		.31	1.82	4.34
Dec.	2.42	1.79	3.30	3.24	5.67	4.28
TOTALS	36.51	24.16	33.19	51.23	32.10	43.96

RAINFALL: 1880-1886, recorded by the Librarian at St. John's

Month	1880	1881	1882	1883	1884	1885	1886
Jan.	11.09	2.77	2.52	3.75	2.83	2.59	2.69
Feb.	2.83	2.71	1.91	4.18	2.69	1.59	2.50
March	2.13	.66	.57	2.27	3.39	1.47	1.67
April	6.94	4.13	1.37	4.64	2.39	2.25	4.45
May	9.46	8.01	1.44	5.76	4.72	1.57	2.25
June	4.46	10.55	2.60	5.08	3.75	2/04	3.83
July	10.28	5.23	4.46	3.69	7.32	3.31	4.57
Aug.	3.96	8.60	5.45	6.19	2.44	9.85	5.68
Sept.	3.74	4.79	5.52	3.13	7.37	2.63	9.18
Oct.	3.72	12.65	2.45	10.72	5.93	9.87	4.33
Nov.	4.84	5.25	3.22	10.12	6.05	9.28	4.20
Dec.	3.36	1.30	6.55	8.69	4.71	4.70	2.78
TOTALS	66.81	66.85	42.66	69.04	53.59	50.80	48.14

RAINFALL: 1997-2001, Cedar Valley, recorded by Robert J. Meeker

Month	1997	1998	1999	2000	2001
Jan.	3.38	3.63	1.50	.0	.75
Feb.	2.38	1.75	.25	1.25	.50
March	.50	1.50	.75	7.87	.50
April	1.63	1.50	2.88	1.50	1.50
May	1.75	.88	1.00	1.50	.13
June	1.78	2.75	3.63	1.00	1.00
July	2.13	2.13	3.00	1.00	3.25
Aug.	2.17	4.86	1.25	2.50	2.50
Sept.	1.75	7.29	2.75	6.68	2.68
Oct.	3.00	6.38	8.25	1.50	1.50

Nov.	1.00	3.75	18.00	2.50	2.25
Dec.	1.88	4.50	2.33	2.88	4.50
TOTALS	24.13	45.44	50.17	35.04	29.16

< >

Antigua's Sugar Cane Production: 1828 - 1850

Year	Sugar*	Rum**	Molasses**
1828	14,976	4,169	6,540
1829	14,016	4,523	5,042
1830	15,646	3,590	8,215
1831	12,612	2,180	8,149
1832	11,092	1,795	8,231
1833	10,911	1,697	8,019
1834	20,921	2,380	13,788
1835	14,803	1,938	8,467
1836	11,741	942	6,734
1837	5,434	436	3,047
1838	18,534	1,134	12,189
1839	???	1,032	9,787
1840	16,008	1,027	10,178
1841	12,114	594	7,657
1842	11,700	896	7,135
1843	13,285	44	9,102
1844	16,702	120	10,257
1845	12,659	114	8,481
1846	7,051	297	4,659
1847	15,817	319	9,505
1848	11,313	164	5,783
1849	13,229	184	8,026
1850	8,666	100	5,126

* Sugar measured in Hogsheads (barrels)
** Rum and Molasses measured in Puncheons (an English measurement) Note that the production of rum steadily declined over the years, but the molasses used to make rum was fairly constant. Also, the years with very little rainfall -- 1835, 1846 and 1850 -- resulted in far smaller harvests than usual.

Value in Imports: £168,623   Value in Exports: £131,882
Revenues: £ 21,664   Expenditures: £ 21,771
(Tax) paid for the Poor: £ 4,188

< >

Antigua's Cattle Mills

The initial sugar plantations on Antigua crushed their cane with the use of "cattle mills." A short string of cattle, mules or horses were harnessed to a long wooden beam and walked in a circle around the sugar mill, rotating the heavy rollers to crush the cane, which was fed into the rollers by hand. In 1748 Antigua featured sixty-four cattle mills, compared with one-hundred seventy-five wind-powered mills.

In correspondence written by attorney Joshua Crump on February 22, 1755, to the managers of Parham Hill and the surrounding estates owned by the Tudway family, he advised building a cattle mill to handle the crushing task when the wind was not sufficient to properly operate the windmill. Several estates maintained a cattle mill as backup.

Writing on June 11, 1755, R. Barrister said: *"I have made 100 hhds [hogsheads] of Sugar, and should have made fifty more by this, but the whole month of February and part of March was nothing but light fluttering winds four and twenty days of the time no wind at all; you may depend upon it, I will be as expeditious as possible and will lose no time in taking in the Crop to the best advantage.*

"The season of the year," Barrister wrote in 1775, *"gives me an opportunity of letting you know that you have the prospect of a very good crop, but am greatly afraid the whole will not be taken off, for want of a Cattle Mill on each estate, the expense is but a trifle to the loss you must sustain. This I have recommended before as no Estate of the bulk of yours ought to be without one, as Calms, the rains falling is sooner than expected will be the loss of one hundred hogsheads sugar this year to you."*

Simon Farley, writing almost a year later (May 10, 1756) noted that *"many of the oxen are enfeebled by Old Age and worn out by hard labor,* and *the cows are small and many of them old and ordinary nor is there any cattle to be found except at a monstrous price. I can't think why Mr. [Attorney Joshua] Crump did not encourage your sending over the mules you have. I shall be very glad of ten or twelve if you have so many or can conveniently get them, they will do very well*

Photograph of an experimental Cattle Mill. The cane stalks are hand fed between the rollers while the animal in harness circles around driving the rollers. The juice flows into the barrels.

Foote Family Album

for the cattle mills & for other work in the plantation when the cattle mills are not at work, those we have are very useful; it is seldom any are brought here for sale and all Beasts for labour grows scarcer and dearer every day as does everything else."

He noted that *"the Cattle Mills we are now going to erect will require ten head of good working cattle, more for each mill than we now have."*

The dimensions of a cattle mill *"to be fixed to every Windmill Estate"*, and the cost to construct one are described in the Tudway Papers:

3 - Iron cases in length from out to out 24 inches, the Diameter from 21"
2 - Side Cudgeons 4 feet 4 inches in Length and 4 inches and half square,
in the middle Tapering to 4 inches at each end, the round parts 8 inches.
3 - Center Cudgeon in proportion to the side Cudgeons, with Ye Brasses Steelplaits,
Coppouses Wedges, etc."
Will cost about 45 pounds Sterling
in this currency ....74.05.00 [pounds, shillings, pence]
The Carpenter for Building...................35.00.00
The Rowlers & Spindle.....................30.00.00
* The Bridgetree...............................15.00.00
Four Sweeps.......................……8.00.00
Four Posts..20.00.00

Four Brass Blocks & Wedges.............10.00.00
Braytrees...............................8.00.00 Two
One Cistern……………………………….4.00.00 42 Cogs
@ 2/- ea...............................4.04.00
Currency........................208.09.00
Sterling @ 65 Pr. Ct £12.06.00

* this to be got in yr. Country. For want of the above, 100 hhds. Sugar & 50 hhds. Rum will be lost in this Crop.

Parham New Works was managed by my great-grandfather, John McSevney, for the Tudway family. The Tudway Family owned Parham Hill, Parham Lodge and Parham New Works. Letters from 1689 to 1849 between him and his attorney, his clerk, and his manager, shed light on many of the day-to-day workings of an estate. A complete copy of this correspondence, known as The Tudway Papers (Parham Hill #76a), was purchased by the Roberts family in 2012 and donated to the Antigua & Barbuda Museum archives. The original Codrington Papers (Betty's Hope #77a), detailing all of the estates owned by the Codrington family, were donated to the Archives by Bruce Rappaport. He also built the Archives of Antigua & Barbuda in which to house the collection. Agnes C. Meeker.

The Six Parishes of Antigua

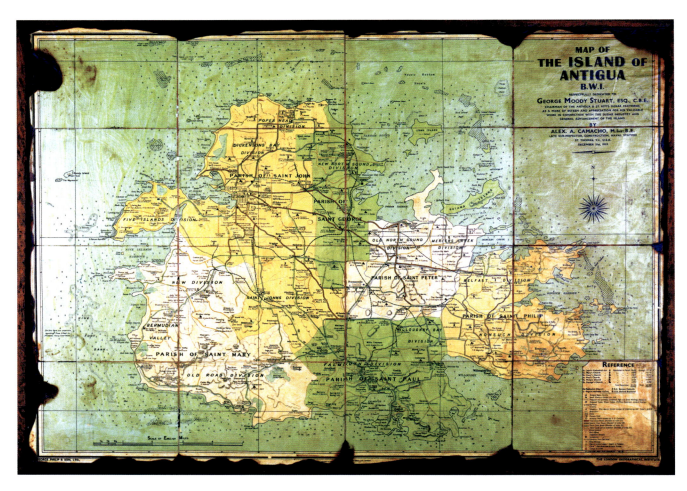

1933 Map by Alex Camacho showing the six Parishes, names of estates with owners, and the sugar railroad.
Agnes C. Meeker.

St. John's
St. George's
St. Peter's
St. Mary's
St. Philip's
St. Paul's

The Sugar Plantations and Mills of St. John's Parish

The numbered circles indicate the location of the Parish's sugar plantations and mills. In 1777/1778, this Parish embraced 17,953 acres.

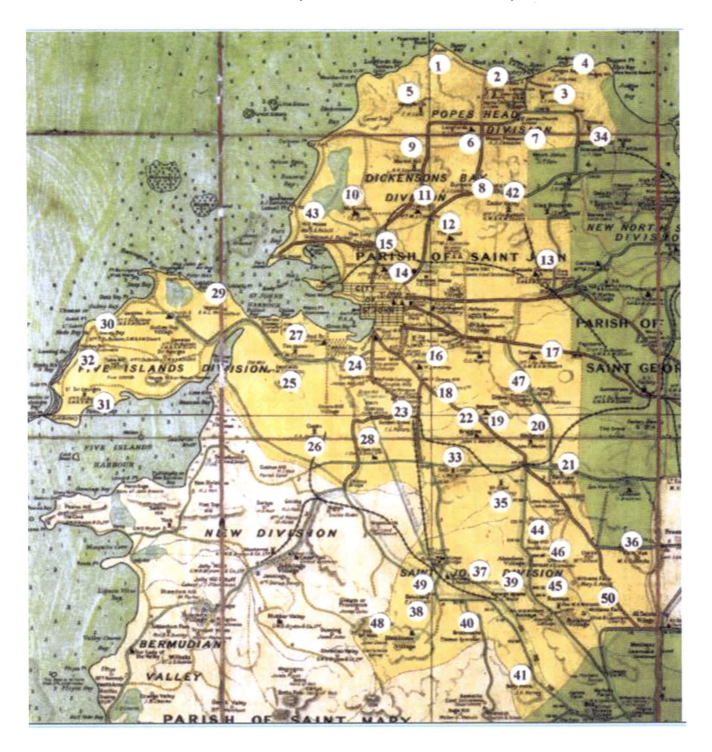

#1 - Boone's Plantation

The Ownership Chronology:

Ownership prior to 1678: Walter Burke.

1670:   William Boone, planter. On Antigua 1665,
        still living in 1710.

1672:   William Boone, still living in 1685; leased
        10 acres from Ralph Haskins, also a planter.

1676:   William Boone: A Quaker, imprisoned by
        Major Thomas Mallet

1678:   On May 20, Walter Burke, a planter, sold
        20 acres to William Boone, a planter and Quaker.
        In the 1678 census of Antigua, William Boone had four white men, two
        white women, and three white children "in family, with one negro."

1700:   William Boone married Mary Ronan.

1715:   Samuel Boone. Will dated 1716.

1717:   The Tortola census, taken in November, shows William Boone as born
        in Antigua, with "one woman and fifteen negroes."

1733:   Joseph Boone married Rachell Soanes. He died 1750.

1740:   Colonel William Dunbar. d. 1749.

1760:   John Delap-Halliday. Owned 85 acres. b. 1749; d. 1779/80.

1788:   Admiral John Hallliday Tollemache.   1777/78 Luffman map.

1790:   John Delap-Halliday. b. 1749; d. 1780. 85 acres.

1852:   John Tollemache. b. 1805; d. 1890.

1872:   Charles Crosbie.

1878:   G. John Crosbie.

1891:   The heirs of Colonel Crosbie.

c1900: John J. Camacho. (d. 1929).

c1940: Lee H. Westcott Sr.   1933 Camacho Map

1960:   Blue Waters Hotel, built by Osmond Kelsick, the only Antiguan
        squadron leader in the Royal Air Force during World War II.

2000:   The heirs of Lee Westcott. d. 2012.

2003:   The mill site is sold to Blue Waters Hotel.

< >

Boone's mill overlooking the Caribbean & Atlantic.   Inset Crosby's (#2) mill, both owned by the Westcott Family.   Post card – Museum of Antigua & Barbuda

The magnificent sugar mill on this plantation stood water-side on the northwestern tip of Antigua, where the Caribbean and the Atlantic shake hands. Early settlers had carved a rock formation, known as "Boone's Chair", enabling local Carib Indians to sit and look at the intersection of the two seas.

A prominent rumor among the settlers was *"that before you could sit in the chair, you had to make the sign of the cross and pay some money or you would suddenly be forced out of that chair and into the ocean by a spirit, so whenever I follow Affie Goodwin (Duer's estate) to sit in the chairs, we would make the sign of the cross and pay a penny or two."* The "Chair" disappeared centuries later with the construction of the Blue Waters Hotel in 2003.

"To Shoot Hard Labour" by Keithlyn and Fernando C. Smith

The mill's location was spectacular, enabling residents of the estate (and now guests at the hotel) to view ships coming and going; a suggestion that those early residents most likely enjoyed a rich bounty from the sea.

Left – Boone's mill taken in 1999. Right – 2016 incorporated into Blue Waters gardens.
Agnes C. Meeker

The location also would have enabled the mill to benefit from the trade winds, which turned its enormous sails to rotate the large sugar cane crushing rollers below. As of 1817, under the continued ownership of John Delap-Halliday, the estate still consisted of 85 acres, with labour provided by 101 slaves.

The mill remains in reasonably good shape today despite its age, and still shows some of the exterior rendering over the lime stone blocks, a finish plaster of sorts applied during construction to protect the soft lime stone.

The area around the mill now features a number of private residences as well as an extension of the Blue Waters Hotel, so the mill no longer dominates the landscape.

< >

"On the 12th (of September), Capt. Francis Burton issued a Warrant to the aforesaid Chapman to apprehend the Body of the said William Boone, and carry him to the Fort till he should be discharged by the Governor; the Fort being about five Miles from W. Boone's house.

"So the said Boon submitted, took his Leave of his Wife and Children, and was sent to Prison, where he remained five Weeks and five Days, and underwent great Hardship, for he was grievously bitten by Vermin, and through much Wet and cold was so denummed, that he was almost like a dead Man. The Governor being applied to, protested that he would not release him til he had paid Charles Goss.

"On the 14th the Governor with the Council and Assembly came to the Fort, where Boone's Wife and Children were then with him. But, though many spake on his Behalf, and the Governor's Brother, in Compassion to Boone's Family, would have had him released, nothing could be done; for Mallet had so incensed the Governor with false Accusations against Boone, that he would not release him saying, He could do Nothing of himself Nevertheless, after forty Days the said Field-Marshall Goss came to Boone's House, and took away a Cow big with Calf, which he would not willingly have sold for 3000lb of Tobacco, and having led away the Cow. Boone was set at liberty." "History of the Island of Antigua" by Vere Oliver, Volume I.

< >

In 1774, John Halliday owned seven plantations, including two of the most important, Boone's and Weatherill's (#5), in St. John's Parish. The Halliday family is of old covenanting stock and has figured in the history of Scotland, County Galloway, since the sixteenth century. John was born earlier in the 18th century, the nephew of William Dunbar, son-in-law of Francis Delap. He was Antigua's Customs Collector of 4 1/2% export duty from 1759 to 1777. He served in the island's Assembly from 1755 to 1757 and again in 1761, and apparently had large mansions on at least five of his plantations.

A meal, served at one of Halliday's homes was *"extremely pleasant, and so cool one might forget that they were under the Tropick. We had a family dinner which in England might figure away in a newspaper had it been given by a Lord Mayor, or the first Duke in the Kingdom.*

"I have seen Turtle almost every day, and tho' I never could eat it at home, am vastly fond of it here, where it is indeed a very different thing. You get nothing but old ones there, the chickens being unable to stand the voyage; even these are starved, or at best fed on coarse and improper food. Here they are young, tender, fresh from the water, where they feed as delicately, and as great Epicures as those who feed on them.

"They laugh at us for the racket we make to have it divided into different dishes. They make but two, the soup and the shell. The first is commonly made of old Turtle, which is cut up and sold at Market, as we do butcher meat. It was

remarkably well dressed to day. The shell indeed is a noble dish as it contains all the fine parts of the Turtle baked within its own body; here is the green fat, not the slobbery thing my stomach used to stand at, but firm and more delicate than it is possible to describe. Could an Alderman of true taste conceive the difference between it here and in the city, he would make the Voyage on purpose, and I fancy he would make a voyage into the other world before he left the table.

"The method of placing the meat is in three rows the length of the table; six dishes in a row, I observe is the common number. On the head of the centre row stands the turtle soup, and at the bottom of the same line the shell. The rest of the middle row is generally made of fishes of various kinds, all exquisite.

"At Mr. Halliday's we had thirty-two different fruits . . . yet in the midst of this variety the Pineapple and the Orange still keep their ground and are preferred."

"Journal of A Lady of Quality" by Janet Shaw

< >

Aubrey J. Camacho, a Portuguese from Madeira, landed in Antigua about 1878, and immediately began buying established estates. He initially owned two (Bellevue #36 and Briggin's #22) totaling 967 acres, but within three years he also owned Langford's (#6), Mt. Pleasant (#7), Dunbar's (#8), Otto's (#16), Wood's (#12) and Jonas's (#85), adding an additional 2,000 acres to his holdings, all within the confines of St. John's Parish.

His son, John J. Camacho, assumed ownership of the Boone's Estate about 1900. He was a Catholic and suffered the embarrassment of being married in the Anglican Cathedral because there was no Catholic Church on Antigua at that time.

Mr. Camacho was described as *"the most powerful and wealthiest Antiguan in his time. He had ten sons (his own cricket team!) and one daughter, who married Lee Westcott Sr. (Camacho), was responsible for starting the Ovals Cricket, Football and Tennis Clubs because the English whites refused to allow the Portuguese to join either the Antigua Cricket Club (Recreation Grounds) or their tennis club located on the premises now occupied by The Lion's Club."*

"Not A Drum Was Heard" by Selvyn Walters

Boone's Great house had been constructed of beautiful white cut stones by slaves. As its owner in the early 1900s Camacho had the building painstakingly dismantled, the white stones cleaned, and carefully moved them to Church Street to a location he had donated to the Catholic Church. The edifice became St. Joseph's Church, which was badly damaged during the earthquake of 1974. A new Cathedral was commissioned by the Catholic Church around 1998.

The architect for the new building was Richard McCullogh, the site chosen for the modern Cathedral was east of Michael's Mount below Mt. St. John Medical Center. The old church was allowed to deteriorate, but may be part beneficiary in the renovation of the entire block, which also encompasses Government House (2015).

John J. Camacho and his wife, Mary Gomez, also owned Millar's estate (#59), which was seconded to the United States during World War II to be used as the Officer's Club, as well as a house in town which was willed to the Catholic Church and became Bishop's Lodge. Bishop's Lodge comes replete with quite a large garden and has been recently put up for sale. The Camacho's had no children, donating most of their £52,624 estate to the Catholic Church.

The Catholic Church in St. John's was built in 1910 from stone taken
from Boone's estate house, cleaned and carefully moved.
Jose Anjo, postcard.

The British abolished slavery in 1833, and the British Parliament gave a legacy award (Antigua 1) to Boone's of £1,437. 4s. 1p. for granting freedom to 108 enslaved. The awardee was John Tollemache; the beneficiaries deceased were Daniel Hill and Vice Admiral John Richard Delap Tollemache. Unsuccessful were Daniel Hill, George Wickham Washington Ledeatt and William Lee.

#2 - Crosbie's Plantation
(Mount Prospect)

The Ownership Chronology:

1777/78 Samuel Martin owned land in this vicinity
  1777/78 Luffman map.

1780:   General John Crosbie. d. 1797.

1788:   This estate was known as Mount Prospect.

1790:   Ownership changed to John Crosbie Will: 1814.

1797:   Major General William John Crosbie. He served in the British Army during the French Revolution and Napoleonic wars. d.1797

1820:   The estate consisted of 210 acres, 67 slaves.

1829:   General John Crosbie

1832:   General Crosbie also owned the Hughes estate in Popeshead, which was bounded on the north by the Boone's Plantation (#1) and Crosbie's, on the east by the Langford's Plantation (#6) Crosbie's on the south by the High Road, and on the west by Boone's and Langford's. The Hughes Plantation no longer exists; most likely assimilated into one of the other named estates.

1851:   John Crosbie. 210 acres.

1872:   Charles Crosbie is listed in the Horseford Almanac as owning both the Crosbie's and Boone's estates with combined land of 300 acres.

1878:   G. John Crosbie.

1891:   Ownership shifts to the heirs of Colonel Crosbie.

1921:   W. C. Abbott. 305 acres.

1933:   Joseph Erskine.

1935/36:   Lee H. Westcott, Sr.

1950:   Lee Westcott. d. 2012.   1933 Camacho map

2000:   Ownership by the heirs of Lee Westcott.

< >

Several of the old estate buildings, and the sugar mill itself plus the cotton (or gin) house, have been turned into apartment buildings, with walls two to three-feet thick. When the land had been cleared and planted with cotton, there were no other buildings adjacent to the estate; the view from the property extended to the sea, where the Caribbean meets the Atlantic. That is difficult to envision today because the former Crosbie's estate is now one of Antigua's major housing developments.

The Crosbie Mill Apartment – Agnes C. Meeker

It is said that on a full moon night residents can hear the sounds of moaning and the rattling of chains near the shore, where slaves were once led into the sea.

John Crosbie, the Major General's son, owned a plantation known at the time as "Hughes" in Popeshead. It was bounded on the north by Boone's (#1) and Crosbie's, on the east by Langford's (#6) and Crosbie's, south by the High Road, and west by Boone's and Langford's. The Hughes estate no longer exists, assumed to have been assimilated by a neighbouring plantation.

Joseph Erskine, a Scottish sheep owner who purchased Crosbie's in 1933, actually lived on Market Street (Scotch Row), not on the estate property itself. He began cotton farming on the land, quickly lost his shirt, and sold all 305 acres to Lee H. Westcott for £600.

Westcott hailed from Waterville, New York, and landed in Antigua in 1922 while on his way to Brazil.

He was "persuaded" to remain on the island to assist in the installation of the Hornsby diesel generator, which had been given to St. John's electric power company. He purchased the Crosbie's estate from Joseph Erskine in the mid-1930s, and the estate became part of the Northern Cotton Belt when cotton was so urgently needed during World War II.

His effort to convert an overgrown 300-plus acre sugar plantation into an arable cotton farm was no easy task. Westcott was the first farmer to introduce machinery into agriculture, which he did with the purchase of an International Harvester wheeled tractor. Still, it took over a year of back breaking work by fifty employees from the village of Cedar Grove and the island of Montserrat to dig out the huge acacia (cossy or cassie) trees and to prepare the soil for planting cotton.

In the late 1940's Westcott and three other cotton farmers on Antigua spent two years negotiating with the Antigua Trades & Labor Union, but could not reach an agreement. This fruitless effort caused all four to go bankrupt, and the estate no longer participated in the development of cotton in the Northern Cotton Belt.

In addition to Westcott, the other three St. John's Parish cotton farmers to go belly-up were Martin Schaffler of Weatherill's (see #5), Aubrey Camacho of Marble Hill (see #9), and Anthony Shoul of Thibou/Jarvis & Judges (see #34). Some Montserrat workers were brought to Antigua to pick cotton, but that initiative also was thwarted by the unions.   Bankruptcy of his cotton venture prompted Lee Westcott to turn the Crosbie's estate into a real estate development, undoubtedly the largest single development of its kind undertaken by Antiguans: 310 acres of prime ocean view land.

Picking Cotton in Antigua – File Photograph Centtral Office of Information,
London, England. 1962. Historical Collection Oversize DA11 GRE)

Crosbie's Development Ltd. was formed in 1958, but the company struggled for four years, blocked repeatedly by the government administration of Antigua's first Prime Minister, V. C. Bird. Finally, after underbrush and cassie trees had again overgrown the infrastructure the company had paid to install (road, water and electricity), the company began its development plan and began selling seaside lots for 30-to-60 cents per square foot. *"Not A Drum Was Heard"* by Selvyn Walters

As of 2012, almost every surveyed lot sported a building. Initially, a covenant stipulated details of construction regulations, but it was largely ignored over the years, resulting in a somewhat scrambled layout of housing and businesses. However, the area remains highly desirable because of its proximity to St. John's and the airport.

< >

The University of Florida has a collection of the late 1700 and early 1800 papers and letters of Major John Crosby.   ufdc.ufl.edu/results/brief/2/?t=crosbie.

The William Crosbie Estate Papers, dated 1792-1816, include correspondence concerning Crosbie's estate and the land of his agent/manager, John Otto Bayer (Baijer), in Antigua. The letters provide an interesting look at the activities and attitudes of the plantation operators and slave owners in the English Caribbean colony of Antigua in the early nineteenth century.

The correspondence deals mostly with financial and operational concerns: expenses, property values, debts, loans, securities, deeds, slaves, stock, crops, rum and sugar. Other correspondents and individuals referenced in the letters include Lord Moira, Admiral McDougall, Gilbert Jones, Esq., Colonel Handfield, John Crosbie (heir), Charles Crosbie, James Wood Bursar (St. John's, Cambridge), Lady Amelia Carpenter, Colonel Knox, General Marsh, the Duke and Duchess of Newcastle, and Baron Deimar. The papers are filed chronologically.

Top -Crosbie's
Buff c.1943

Centre - the view
down to the Carribean
& Atlantic from the
main house c.1950

Bottom -Crosbie's
Buff c. 1950
with cotton drying
in the foreground.
Westcott Family

#3 – Hart's & Royal's Plantation

The Ownership Chronology

1600s: Late. Ownership by Isaac Royal (Rial, Ryall, Royall) d. July 27, 1739

1739: Isaac Royal, Jr, his son. b. 1699.

1770: The property was sold; no buyer has been identified.

1788: Barry C. Hart. See 1777/78 Luffman map.

1829: John Furlonge. 206 acres, 123 slaves.

1851: C. William and F. Shand. 206 acres. William: b. 1784; d. 1848.

1872: Thomas Jarvis. 209 acres.

1878: C. J. Manning.

1891: Victor Guffay.

1921: Amelia Gonsalves. 219 acres.

1933: Leonard Henzell   1933 Camacho map

1950s: Antigua Syndicate Estates.

1985: Lotte and Malcolm Edwards, mill site and 3 acres.

< >

The stone windmill of this estate remains intact and in excellent condition. It is the focal point in the garden of Malcolm and Lotte Edwards. The former Club Colonna Beach Hotel stood on Royal's Bay, which suggests that the estate originally stretched all the way down to the sea. It has a fascinating history.

Isaac Royal was the son of a poor carpenter, who was an early immigrant to Boston, Massachusetts. Isaac settled in Antigua in 1700 at the age of twenty-eight, a widower with a small nest egg from his deceased wife, Elizabeth Eliot. Isaac lived on the island for forty years, a pompous, fancy, thin-skinned dandy with a grand estate, he became known as "The Colonel of Antigua".

His brother, Jacob, sold rum and sugar on a ship he co-owned in Boston with his uncle, Joseph. His was a life of seaborne trade, including a raid on nearby Nevis. Toward the end of his nautical career, Jacob wrote: *Amongst my troubles and misfortunes let me inform you as my friend of my good fortune"* claiming he had amassed *"above six thousand pounds!"* during his life on Antigua.

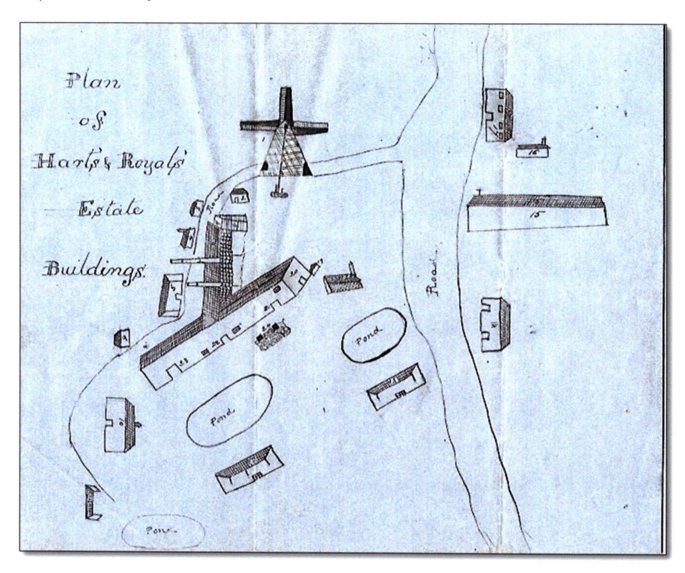

The map above is hand drawn in c1800 (and the description of the various numbered buildings is difficult to read. #1 is the mill and to the right #17 is the Overseer's house and #15 the Overseer's kitchen. Both these buildings were combined and renovated to its present state by Malcolm Edwards (1980's). The three small buildings across from the main building are #3 Managers Servants room, #4 Managers kitchen, #5 Manager's house. #9, #10, #11 and #12 are the Harness room, Horse stable, Cart shed and Cattle Pen respectively. In the main building #18 is the Still, #19 Cistern, #20 Still house, #21 Rum cellar & still house, #22 Store Room and #23 Curing house. Note the many ponds and water storage tanks, always a priority in drought ridden Antigua. There is no mention of a Buff main house at this time, but it must be supposed that Isaac Royall during the 1700's lived in the Buff.

William M. Clements Library, University of Michigan

By the early 1730s, the high-income days on Antigua were over, and Isaac Royal purchased a new estate in Medford, Massachusetts, just outside Boston. It was known as Red Hills Farm. He shipped 27 of his slaves north to the new venture, although his new wife balked moving from Antigua to Medford for several years.

His Antigua estate became absentee landlord property and it suffered the consequences. There was a continual flow of slaves between Virginia, Massachusetts and Antigua, but even an exchange of Indians captured during war skirmishes in the New World and shipped to Antigua proved "too difficult in captivity" to properly work Isaac's land, and in 1770 it was sold.

St. John's Parish estates, which abutted Hart's & Royal's, were Hodge's (#4) to the south, Weatherill's (#5) and the village of Cedar Grove to the west, Mount Pleasant (#7) to the north, and Thibou Jarvis (#34) to the east.

Malcolm Edwards, on whose property the preserved sugar mill now sits, rebuilt the small manager's house over a period of four years with the help, as needed, of a crew of 2-to-4 laborers. They used Western Red Cedar and southern pine wood, all of it imported. He, his wife and their two daughters moved into the home in 1989. The large brick kitchen oven, which was located in a separate building, has been restored and incorporated into the main body of the Edwards home.

With the development of the Royal's residential area in recent years, the remains of a large Arawak settlement have been uncovered, revealing many significant artifacts.

Ann Brown, born in 1703 as the stepdaughter of Isaac Royal, married Robert Oliver whose son, Thomas, gained notoriety as Lt. Governor of Massachusetts during the time of war. She describes Royal's Plantation: *"The 'big house' was a two story mansion set on a slight rise, complimented by the manager's quarters, a stone dwelling fifty paces off, a cane press, a still, a cistern, the busy mill, a stables for the Royall's horses, and a huddle of simple mud and thatch huts that housed family slaves."*

In 1710, there was an *"indenture between Robert Weir and John Rose of Antigua, merchant, of the other, the latter agrees to let his plantation in New Northsound to the former, late in the occupation of William Glanville of Antigua, merchant, for lease of twelve years at 300 pounds a year."* *"History of the Island of Antigua"* by Vere Oliver, Volume III.

< >

The historic Isaac Royal House purchased by Isaac on December 26, 1732, is located at 15 George Street in Medford, Massachusetts, a suburb of Boston. In 1712, Isaac granted a description of the Royal Mansion (called Hobgoblin Hall) in Antigua to Samuel Adam Drake, which is printed in Vere Oliver's *"History of Antigua and The Antiguans, Vol. III"*. Samuel Adam Drake, writing in *"Our Colonial*

Homes", said the mansion was supposedly modeled after that of a nobleman in Antigua. It is a fantastic description, but rather lengthy.

Top – The mill incorporated into the garden
Below - The Overseer's house rebuilt by Malcolm Edwards in 1989.
Agnes C. Meeker

Historic Royall House, Medford, MA.   www.waymarking.com/…/WME7T4_Royall House, _Medford

The Medford building is notable for its excellent preservation, its possession of the only surviving slave quarters in Massachusetts, and its American Revolution associations with General John Stark, Molly Stark, and General George Washington. Among its historic objects on display is a tea box thought to be from the same batch dumped into Boston Harbor on the night of December 16, 1773 (the Boston Tea Party), and a very small painting of Isaac Royal, Jr. on copper by John Singleton Copley.

The site's recorded history actually began around 1637, when Massachusetts Governor John Winthrop built his own home there. About 1692, his wooden home was replaced by a more imposing brick structure standing two-and-one-half stories high, but only one room in depth, with exceedingly thick walls.

It is this building which Isaac Royal, Sr. a slave trader, rum distiller, and wealthy merchant purchased in December 1732, together with 504 acres of land along the West Bank of the Mystic River in what was then the village of Charlestown (annexed to Medford in 1754). Isaac extensively remodeled the home between 1733 and 1737, adding a third story, encasing its eastern facade in clapboard, and ornamenting the exterior with architectural details and continuous strips of spandrel panels.

Isaac also constructed outbuildings in 1732, including the only known slave quarters to survive in New England today. Upon completion of all of his renovations, he transferred the 27 enslaved Africans from his Antigua plantation to Medford, doubling the enslaved population of that community. The Royal House has been designated a National Historic Landmark by the United States Government. It is operated as a non-profit museum, open to the public between June 1st and the last weekend in October.   Harvard University, in Cambridge, Massachusetts, owes a significant debt of gratitude to the Royal family, which donated land to the University in1786, land upon which Harvard constructed its famous Law School in 1817, the year the School was established.

Harvard still uses the Benefactor's signature -- three sheaves of wheat -- as its trademark seal. Janet Halley, the most recent recipient of the Royal Chair at Harvard, listed every previous holder of the Chair (all male) in her acceptance speech, and ended her remarks by reciting the name of every Royal slave whose name was known.   *"Red Hills Farm"* by C. S. Manegold.

< >

The Hart family genealogy includes an unsigned letter from a person seeking information *"about Barry Conyers Hart, a black freedman who came to Trinidad from Antigua in 1800. He was the father of two women who according to John Salliant: "Around 1790, two young sisters born into a slaveholding free black family began instructing Antiguan slaves in literacy and Christianity. The sisters, Anne (1768 - 1834) and Elizabeth (1771 -1833) Hart, first instructed their father's slaves at Popeshead -- he may have hired them out rather than using them on his own crops -- then labored among enslaved women and children in Antiguan plantations and in towns and ports like St. John's and English Harbour."* Soon the sisters wrote about faith, slavery, and freedom. Anne and Elizabeth Hart were moderate opponents of slavery, not abolitionists but meliorationalists. When compared to their American, British, and West African contemporaries the Hart sisters illuminate the birth of a black antislavery Christianity in the late eighteenth century precisely because they never became abolitionists. The Hart sisters shared with their black contemporaries a vivid sense of racial identity and evangelical Christianity. Yet as meliorationalists the Hart sisters did not oppose slavery as an institution, but rather the vice it spread into the lives of blacks.

The sisters, daughters of a black slave holder, both married prominent Methodist lay leaders, educators of slaves and free African Caribbean's, during the late 18th and early 19th centuries. Anne married a Gilbert, while her sister Elizabeth married a Thwaites. Daniel Burr Garling, the author's great-great-grandfather allowed them to use a warehouse in the Point area as a secondary school.

"The Sisters Hart" by Ferguson.

Vere Oliver's *"History of the Island of Antigua, Vol. II,"* notes that *"in the private burial ground at Harts (Royal's)"*, there is written on a square stone:

Sacred to the Memory
of Charles Ansll Hart
who departed this Life
on the first day of July in the year of
our Lord one thousand eight
hundred and sixteen
Aged 37 years.

Mr. Oliver also notes that there are two stone vaults in the ground with no memorial encryption. There are also eight graves with headstones.

William Shand, an owner of C. W. & F. Shand, accomplished his Antigua slave ownership through the family's merchant firm. He appears to have been in partnership with Alexander Simpson, with whom he owned the plantations Montrose and Ogle in British Guiana. In 1852 notice was given that the Shand firm, as merchants in Liverpool, had been dissolved. A shipping dispatch showed the superiority of Liverpool as a port of call compared to other British ports. Capt. W. R. Greaves, of Antigua, sailed the Shand-owned vessel *Phoenix* into Liverpool, offloaded 464 hhds sugar plus molasses plus a number of smaller packages; then loaded 100 tons of bricks plus 150 tons of goods and set sail for Antigua having spent only sixty hours on the dock! It was believed to exceed anything of the kind ever accomplished in Liverpool before.

Gore's Advertiser.

!n *"Caribbean Adventures, Journal of Thomas K. Hyde"* (edited by David H. Farquar), Mr. Hyde states:

"Today I rode to Paradise Estate (Royal's) owned by D. Furlong (ed. as of 1829) . *the mill was in the wind, and the (slaves) were boiling sugar, but (the proprietor) ordered the people to stop the mill and take the fire from under the coppers while I said prayers. I told him that I was aware it was a great inconvenience and that it might result in a loss, but the religious wants of the people were more important."*

Church records show that Agnes Marguerite Russell, born 1885 at Royals, was the daughter of Downes Nurse Russell. It is not certain what Mr. Russell did at Royals, but he was Vestryman at St. Paul's Church and received a letter from the Church when he left Antigua for Barbados in 1892/93.

< >

In 1833, Parliament paid a Legacy award (Antigua 22) to Hart's & Royal's in the amount of £1,563. 4s. 8p. for the freedom of 107 enslaved. William Shand was the only awardee.

< >

Ocean Point Resort and Spa, once The Sun Sail Club Colonna Hotel now stands on Royal's Bay, where this estate had originally stretched all the way down to the sea. The slight rise in the land from the sea meant the buff house could look out across the land to Prickly Pear island and beyond.

Nearby estates include Hodge's (#4) to the south, Weatherill's (#5) and the village of Cedar Grove to the west, Thibou/Jarvis (#34) to the east, and Mount Pleasant (#7) to the south.

Records for Hart's & Royal's are held at the National Archives in Kew, U.K.
The Royal House in Medford, Massachussetts

#4 - Hodge's (Bay) Plantation

The Ownership Chronology

1740:   Henry Hodge. d. 1750. 1777/78 Luffman map.

1820:   Langford Lovell Hodge. b. 1807; d. 1862.

1824:   Isabella Hodge. Henry's daughter. By 1829, 200 acres, 180 slaves. She died intestate and single in 1837 and is buried on the Hodges estate property.

1851:   Langford Lovell Hodge. The Almanac of the same year says he also owned the Hart's & Royal's Plantation (#3), but the Ownership Chronology for that estate lists the owners as C., William & F. Shand.

1870:   Vere Oliver, in his *History of the Island of Antigua, Vol. III* states that in 1870 the Reverend William Henry O'Bryan Hodge sold Hodges Bay Plantation to an Oliver Nugent. However, Nugent is not listed as the owner until 1891 (see below).

1872:   The Horseford Almanac lists the Hodges Bay estate at 192 acres leased to W. Goodwin, Jr.

1878:   Reverend E. Hodge.

1891:   Oliver Nugent. b. 1851; d. 1894.

1921:   H. E. Haynes. 185 acres.

1930s: Late. Dalmer Dew (the Great House).

1950s: Clarence Johnson (the mill site and land).

1970s: Sun Sail Club Colonna Hotel (the mill site).

< >

The sugar mill on this plantation's land is in remarkably good condition, having been meticulously cared for when it was incorporated into the former Club Colonna Beach Hotel. This estate also was originally waterfront property at the northern most tip of Antigua, with a commanding view of both the Caribbean and Atlantic Oceans. Subsequent development on the estate has surrounded the mill, but it can still be seen from the road.

Known as the oldest house on the island, Hodges Bay plantation house.
Maybert Dew nee Jarvis.

The Hodge's Bay Estate House is the oldest surviving home on Antigua. While a 1750 map of the island cites Henry Hodge as the owner, it is known that parts of the large house date back to the seventeenth century. A Commander Hodge was probably the builder of the house.

It was rebuilt and substantially renovated in 1939 by Maybert (nee Jarvis) and Dalmer Dew. The Dews retained the widened door-ways which used to accommodate crinoline hooped skirts, the popular fashion of the day. The room known as "the battery" contains a seventeen-century open hearth fireplace large enough to dominate the entire west wall. It could roast an entire cow and is the oldest part of the house. *"Heritage Treasures"* by Desmond Nicholson

The Dews were the last owners of the Bluff house on the Hodges Plantation. Dalmer owned Joseph Dew & Sons in St. John's, one of the major stores in the island's capital, until the 1970s. The lumber store on Old Parham Road still bears the name "Dews". Dalmer Dew also was one of Antigua's first outstanding cricketers and is mentioned in the *"Wisden"*, book, the bible of international cricket.

His ancestor, Joseph Turner Dew, had arrived in Antigua in the 1860's, and his son, Ernest David Dew (b.1868) managed Belmont (#19) estate.

Peters, Dew and J. J. Camacho formed the South Western Estates Company.

The old estate house, sitting on three-and-one-half acres, was purchased in 2013 with the intent of converting it into a boutique hotel, but the plan never materialized and the ravages of weather and time is taking its toll on this historic site.

"Joseph Dew & Sons started Antigua's first dairy milk farm at the Belmont/ Murray Estate, where they pasteurized the milk and sold it in old fashioned milk bottles. They had a milk truck that made the delivery round the island."

Margaret White, Memories

< >

The name "Hodge" was, historically, derived from "Roger", a name introduced to England by the Normans after their Conquest of England in 1066. The root of Roger is *hrod* meaning "enown" and *gari* meaning "spear". Apparently, some of the native Brits of old could not pronounce the Norman "R" and it became "H" or "D" instead; hence Hodge or Dodge as a surname.

The Hodge name is found extensively throughout the Caribbean Islands, and has been for decades. The first Hodge is believed to be an Irishman who landed on Anguilla about 1700. The 1727 records of Antigua and Anguilla list a number of residents named Hodge. Another Langford Lovell Hodge, and his son of the same name, owned estates in British Guiana, as well as Antigua, dating from the late 1700s. The Hodge family website currently lists various Hodge residents in St. Martin, St. Croix in the U.S. Virgin Islands, as well as Antigua and Anguilla.

A September 10, 1750 inventory and appraisement of the property and household effects of the original Henry Hodge, who died that year, lists his slaves, cattle, horses, household furnishings, carts and other plantation utensils. Henry was residing at Popeshead at the time: occupation, planter.

The first page of the document names and values *"52 male slaves and 12 female. Total £3,029. 1s. 0p."* The second page names and values *"28 female slaves, 40 boys,*

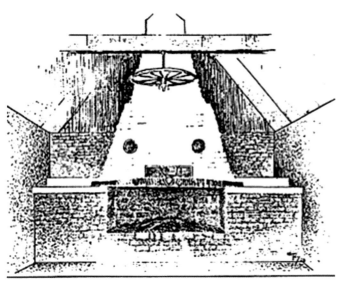

OPEN HEARTH KITCHEN RANGE OF THE 17TH CENTURY

41 girls, 6 bulls all named, 11 oxen all named, 7 cows all named, 2 horses named, carrying forward £7,375. 11s. 0p." The third page includes *"a complete inventory of the house – Hall items, First Chamber below, First Chamber above had nothing, 3rd chamber above, in the closet, in the Steward Room."* The fourth page – *"Room over Steward's room in Kitchen, in the Old Hall, in the Wine Room, in the Boiling Room, in the Still House, in the Mill. Total carried forward £7,900. 14s. ¼p."*

"Shown to them by Stephan Blizard, James Nibbs, Esqs., and Mr. John Bird. And appraised 25th September 1750 by Hamilton Kirby, Will MacKinnon, Thomas Graveney, Sam Nibbs."

At a point in time, Langford Lovell Hodge was accused of "cruel and inhuman disposition," having treated one of his female slaves with "great and unjustifiable severity and cruelty." He was Aide-de-Camp to the Governor, Sir James Leith.

The pregnant slave took her case to the Governor, who paid her some cash and gave her a note for her owner. Langford's response was to give the woman an additional number of lashes, fired off a note to the Governor, who ordered his secretary to inform Langford that the Governor no longer required his services.

Langford dressed one of his negro boys in his own uniform, mounted him on a mule, and dispatched him with an insolent note to the Governor! The grand jury refused to find Langford guilty of "great scandal and infamy."

< >

It is also known that Hodges Bay was awarded £2,756. 7s. 6p. for 201 enslaved (Antigua 25). Langford Lovell Hodge was the single awardee. And again in 1870, Hodges Bay was awarded £711. 8s. 0p. (Antigua 1070); the number of slaves were not mentioned. Awardee was Langford Lovell Hodge. Those financial awards were Legacies of British slave ownership, granted by the English Government to compensate for the loss of slaves when they were freed.

The Hodge's Bay estate came out of cultivation in the 1890s, during the ownership of Oliver Nugent, and was then used for rearing cattle. The old slave burial ground of the estate is on the south side of the main road, which currently traverses the old estate.

The area, now known as Hodge's Bay, had included The Antigua Beach Hotel built in 1938 – 1940, just prior to Europe's entry into World War II. It was owned by George W. Bennett Bryson & Co. This powerful company helped shape the history of Antigua, including the development of Hodges Bay as a residential community for the island's wealthy white population.

Two large stone gateposts stood sentry on the road where drivers entered and left the property, and to prove that the area was private, the road was closed one day a year to *all* traffic. Neither of the gateposts exist today, and the practice of blocking the road to all traffic has long been discontinued.

Records on Hodge's and Langford Lovell Hodge are in the National Archive at Kew, U.K.

< >

The home of Sandy Turner, a director of Bryson's, was converted into the White Sands Hotel in the mid-1950s by Stan Hawley. This later became the Hodge's Bay Club, which was subsequently expanded to include the Pelican Club, a popular nightclub on the Hodges Bay water front. In 2006, the property again changed hands with a major expansion, which was to include a tunnel beneath the road for access to the beach-front housing units. This project died when the primary financier, a bank in Iceland, defaulted. A new investor took over the property in 2015 and resumed work on a hotel/condo facility.

In addition to Hodge's Bay, George W. Bennett Bryson & Co., owned many of the estates on Antigua, as well as a large grocery and hardware store at the foot of St. John's, and a bottling plant. The firm was agent for many of the products Antiguans import, and it still acts as a shipping and insurance agent today. In 1891, the six estates owned by the Bennett family included Brecknocks (heirs of John W. Bennett, #40), Golden Grove (#23), Jolly Hill (#167), leased from Reverend Thomas Peters), Blubber (#168) & Rose Valley, Montero's (#164, heirs of G. W. Bennett), and Friars Hill (#11) or Freemans (heirs of H.O. Bennett).

The Claremont estate (#177) had been sold to George Macandrew, High Point (#55) to Clyde McDonald, and Nibbs (#52) to James Rocke.

In 1921, Robert Bryson owned six estates on Antigua -- Bodkin's (#142) & Willis Freeman's (#143), Diamond (#87), Dimsdale (#155), Isaac Hill (##58), Morris Looby's (#141), and Parry's (#88). Noel Scott Johnston, a Director of Brysons, owned Claremont (#177), which he most likely purchased from the heirs of George Macandrew.

In 1933, the Bryson Company had increased its holdings to include Blubber Valley (#168), Ffrye's (#118), Freeman's Upper (#81), Jolly Hill (#167), leased in 1891 from Reverend Thomas Peters (see above), La Roche's (#135), Lavington's (#121), Long Lane (#107), Morris Looby's (#141) owned in 1921 by Robert Bryson (see above), Montero's (#164), Sanderson's (#86), Thomas (#138), York's (#183), and the Bendals Sugar Factory (#37).

In August 1943, the estates formerly owned by the George W. Bennett Bryson & Co. -- Burke's (133), Cochrans (#83), Freeman's (#81/82), Hoye's, Jolly Hill (#167), Lavington's (#121), Long Lane (#107), Mercer's Creek (#78), Sanderson's (#86), Thomas (#138), and Willis Freeman's (#143) -- were acquired by Gunthorpe's Estates, Ltd., of which Moody Stuart was attorney. This evolved into Antigua Syndicate Estates Ltd., owned by a British firm, Henckell du Buisson & Co., in which Bryson retained shares

(ED: This history has been excerpted from *"An Antigua Trading Company",* a History of Bryson's, written by Mary Gleadall and published in 2012.)

Top – The Beach Hotel owned by Bennett Bryson & Co.
Bottom – Sandy Turner's home which became White Sands Hotel –
Museum of Antigua & Barbuda

#5 - Weatherill's Plantation

The Ownership Chronology

1660: This estate, originally more than 350 acres, was granted to Colonel James Weatherill by the Crown. d. c.1702.

1706: The property was converted to a sugar and sea island cotton plantation.

1730: Colonel James Weatherill, most likely the elder Colonel's son. d. 1745.

1740: Sometime prior to this year, ownership transferred to Mrs. Margaret Weatherill. It may be assumed her husband was ill for several years before he died in 1745, and Margaret took over the estate.

1766: Michael Lambert Weatherill.

1770s: Charles P. Weatherill, Provost Marshall.

1776: John Delap Halliday. b. 1749; d. 1794.

1788: Francis D. Halliday. 1777/78 Luffman map.

1829: Rear Admiral John Richard Delap Halliday Tollemach. d. 1837. 304 acres; 129 slaves.

1852: John Tollemach, owned the estate until 1869.

1871: Viscount Combermere, owned the estate until 1882.

1882: Edgar Henry Lane.

1945: Edgar Casper Lane. b. 1919.

1945: Mrs. Maginley, who apparently owned the estate for one year.

1946: Martin and Lee Schaffler. (See Crosbie's, #2.) Martin was one of the four estate owners who participated in failed negotiations with the Antigua Trades & Labour Union in the 1940s. He ran the estate until the 1970s, when estate farming in Antigua ceased.

2002: The heirs of Martin and Lee Schafler owned the estate house and 35 surrounding acres. The remaining 300 acres were sold for development.

2011: The estate house and acreage were for sale.

2013: The estate house was purchased by Victor Michael.

< >

The "new" Weatherill's estate house, which replaced the original. It is one of the few
estate houses left standing on Antigua, and has always been privately owned.
"Caribbean Style" by Suzanne Slesin

The original sugar mill at Weatherill's remains intact, along with several of the outbuildings. The estate house is not the original; the existing structure is the second home to be built, that we know of, during the Lane family era (1882 - 1945). It is one of the few estate houses left standing on Antigua, and has always been privately owned.

It is built entirely of wood and contains some unusual features, such as louvered inner walls to permit the inflow of fresh breezes. The outbuildings in the back courtyard are built of stone, and they and the mill itself date from the period 1706. Several coppers, iron tanks and other remnants of that era are strewn around the yard.

In Volumes I and II of his "*History of the Island of Antigua*" Vere Oliver notes that on July 25, 1787, 80 acres of the nearby Dickenson Bay Plantation (#10) were bounded on the east and north by the property of James Weatherill. As early as 1760, the same 80 acres belonged "*to the heirs of* (the younger Colonel) *James Weatherill*" and on the south the Plantation was bounded by the heirs of Henry Knight deceased now in the possession of Samuel Nibbs (and indentured) "*to Richard and Richard Oliver*". Its western property line was bounded by land which "*heretofore (was) the plantation of Nathaniel Knight.*"

Top photo is of the interior drawing room – note ceiling.

.

Bottom picture is of the back yard and out-buildings

"Caribbean Style" by Suzanne Slesin

The Works at Weatherill's Plantation. Print by William Clarke, Beinecke Collection, Hamilton College*

At some point, the entire Dickenson Bay Plantation apparently was assimilated into Weatherill's, or the Mackinnon's Plantation (#10) or both. The heirs of Nathaniel Knight are listed as owners who operated a cattle mill. Samuel Nibbs also may have owned the Ffryes Plantation (#118); his property and the Mackinnon estate are both shown to the south of Henry and Nathaniel Knight's estate, opposite Mackinnon's pond.

Other nearby estates to the Weatherills Plantation were Langfords Plantation (#6) to the south and Crosbies Plantation (#2) to the east. The entire area has historically been known as part of the Popeshead Division, and is still occasionally referred to as "Popeshead."

< >

The elder Colonel James Weatherill served as Captain of the privateer *Ye Charles of Jamaica,* and in 1697/98 he captured a valuable Spanish ship. He was spared incarceration because the Court refused to put him on trial for piracy. He served as a member of the Assembly for Popeshead Division in 1700/01; his son served as Aide de Camp to Governor Hart in 1723. He also owned the 575-acre Duncombe's Folly estate in St. John's Parish.

In 1746, during the Weatherill's Plantation ownership by Margaret Weatherill, widow of the elder Colonel, *"Michael Lambert Weatherill granted to Richard Oliver all* (land of the) *Popeshead Plantation charged with the widower of Margaret Weatherill and the debts and legacies of James Weatherill."* (As noted above, Richard Oliver was indentured to the property in 1760.)

John Halliday, who owned the plantation in 1776, was born on Antigua, a nephew of William Dunbar and son-in-law of Francis Delap, both prominent residents of the island. Halliday was of Scottish heritage, his ancestors having figured in the history of Scotland (Kircudbright, County Galloway) since the sixteenth century.

Halliday owned no fewer than seven plantations across Antigua, the two most important being Boone's (#1) and Weatherill's, both in St. John's Parish. He entered the Antigua Assembly in 1755, resigned the position two years later, and was returned to the Assembly in 1761. He also was the island's Customs Collector from 1759 to 1777, receiving the four-and-one-half percent export duty. It was an office of considerable importance since the port of St. John's was far superior to its only rival on the island, Parham.

John Delap Halliday was married in 1771 to Jane, the youngest daughter of Sir Lionel Tollemach, a family name identified as owners of Weatherill from 1829 (Rear Admiral John Halliday Tollemach) to 1869 (John Tollemach). He owned Gambles (#14) with 100 acres, Glanville's (#97) with 296 acres, Lavicount, Weatherill's, Delaps (#137) with 240 acres, Boone's (#1) with 85 acres, Blizard's (#53) & Rockhill with 320 acres, and another un-named estate in St. Mary's Parish with 303 acres. Halliday donated £500 toward the construction of the new Anglican Church.   *"Journal of A Lady of Quality"* by Janet Shaw

By 1829, the estate's 304 acres included four beaches: Store Bay (or Soldiers Gut), Little Bay, Rocky Bay and Dickenson's Bay. Soldier Bay was called Store Bay because, at the end of the seventeenth century, a large storage house was built there to store sugar from the plantation before it was loaded onto flat-bottom barges for delivery to the big sailing ships anchored offshore.

< >

In 1833, the Weatherill's estate received a Legacy award (Antigua 39) from the British Parliament of by £1,823. 6s. 3d. for 119 slaves about to be freed. The deceased beneficiary was Daniel Hill, so the awardee became John Tollemach, but since he also was deceased, the award was presented to Vice Admiral John Richard Delaps Tollemach (nee Halliday). The unsuccessful claimants were William Lee, George Wickham Washington Ledeatt, and Daniel Hill, who was deceased.

Many planters believed that with the abolition of slavery there would be some relaxation of labour, but Dr. Daniels, manager of Weatherill's, found all hands in the fields early the following Monday. However, at his own estate (probably Belmont #19) his people were standing with their hands on their hoes doing nothing. When he asked them why they were not working, they replied: *"it's not because we don't want to work Massa, but we want to see you first to see what the bargain would be."* After that discussion, they happily returned to work.

< >

Thomas Lane came to Antigua in 1790 as Colonial Secretary. He purchased Scott's Hill, then Marble Hill, and in 1882 Weatherill's for which he paid £1,000. When Thomas Edgar Lane assumed ownership of the estate in 1882, he rebuilt the main house at a cost of £1,000 using the original foundation of lignumvitae, and furnished the home with beautiful mahogany furniture shipped from England. The dining table sat thirty guests comfortably.

"Mr. Lane has rebuilt the dwelling-house and affected other improvements. There is an old family burial ground here and several brick vaults, but the top slabs with the MI (memorial encryption) *lost or destroyed before Mr. Lane's time. This burial ground and the one at Mount Jarvis are the only two of all the plantation family burial-places that are still kept clean and cared for. Nearly all the others have been desecrated, and are used for mule-pens or dust-heaps. Langford's (#6) was full of old iron and other rubbish."* "History of the Island of Antigua" by Vere Oliver, Volume III.

The walled Weatherill's estate burial ground dates back to Viscount Combermere (1870) and is located northeast of the main house. The gravestones have been moved to the Anglican Churchyard in Cedar Grove. The stables were east of the house, the cattle pen on the south side down the hill, and the native houses on the southwest side, also down the hill. The overseer in latter days was a Carib and he had a house near the mill on the south side of the property, which still stands.

< >

January 26, 1866, is the date of a letter sent to Viscount Combermere at Combermere Abbey by a Mr. Hartman, who had been sent to assess the value of an estate recently purchased by the Viscount. They included Gambles (#14), Weatherill's, Delaps (#137), Lucas (#136) and Glanville's (#97). A undated note in the Viscount's papers also stated that Weatherill's had been sold for £3,000 exclusive of expenses with £2,000 to be paid in return for the £2,000 paid to me by Mr. Birch.

Mr. Hartman's report stated: *"This estate (Weatherill's) is situated in what is called the Popeshead District. It appears to have had less rain than Gambles and the crop upon it is late and unpromising. The Manager thinks it will make 150 hhds of sugar, but I think he has over-estimated. Here again there is a great want of cattle, and about the same sum will be required to be laid out in purchasing Stock as at Gamble's (10 oxen at 13p. per head £130, and 4 mules at £30 - £120).*

The buildings, too, are in bad order, requiring to a greater extent than the former Estate. A new set of mill rollers, etc., have just arrived the cost of which was £368. I think it was injudiciously ordered for with a small additional cost a Steam Engine might have been put up. It is fortunate that You acted on my advice and did not send an order for Dunlap's until I was able to report to you what was required. I shall not at present put up this mill at Weatherill's, first because it is too late in the reaping season to take down the mill that is now working. And secondly because I think I may be able to make a better arrangement hereafter.

The lands of the estate are good, but owing to the small number of cattle kept on it and consequently the deficiency of manure they are poor and require bringing up. The Estate is about four miles from the Town and shipping place, and three miles from Gambles.

Salaries - Mr. Tollemache's arrangement vs. Lord Combermere's in an attempt to curtail costs: Attorney Edward Becket £79 to £60, Manager, W. H. Harper £120, Overseer £55 to £55, totals £245 to £235.

Loss & Revenue report:
1860 Weatherill's was the only instance where a loss was occurred.
1861 The estate left a very small surplus.
1863 Weatherill's was the only instance where a revenue was produced.
1864 Of the heavy loss which occurred in this exceptional year,
Gamble's and Weatherill's bore the best share.
Average annual expenses for 5 years including Salaries, laborers wages and all other items £1,148. Average crop for 5 years 100-118 Hhds.

On taking an average of the Revenue or Loss of the Estates collectively for the last 5 years to correspond with the previous Tables, the result could be that they have not met their expenses owing to the disastrous loss on crop in 1864 - but on expunging this exceptional year and substituting 1859, the average annual revenue for 5 years would be £980."

<   >

Letter to Viscount Combermere from John Tollemach, dated Saturday, March 4th:

"My dear Combermere,

Many thanks for sending me Mr. Hartman's report of the status of the Antigua Estates. That report has surprised me greatly, altho' he was liking not to represent matters in too favorable a light. Mr. Becket when in London said that the sum owing in the island was trifling.

If the stock are not in good condition, the blame really falls with Mr. Becket. He was constantly urged to plant guinea corn, instead of buying oats, etc., but he was also urged to keep the animals in good condition.

When I bought the Steam Plough I naturally reduced the number of working animals, but this was not done without due consideration. I think you have the statement that showed the reduction.

If the buildings are in base state of repair, it was unknown to me. I cannot think that Hartman's statement on the point is hardly a fair one. If the Estates are likely to produce 760 hhds, they cannot be in a bad state of cultivation, altho' no doubt, like any Estates in England, there can by an expenditure of money, be made still more productive. A Steam Mill might answer for Delap's and Lucas', but I hope you will not send one out for Weatherill's without due consideration. Unless an Estate will produce an average of 250 Hhds. of sugar, I do not believe a Steam Mill will pay.

Yrs. Sincerely, J. Tollemach

I enclose a copy of the advertisement which has been inserted every year in the Antigua Papers. Return to me."   Lancashire Archives, Preston Scotland.

Admiral Tollemach brought his nephew, William Bertie Wolseley (d. 1881) to run his estates of Weatherill's, Gamble's, Delap's, etc. but the Admiral continued to live at Weatherill's. The managers of these Estates objected to being placed under a 20-year-old boy, but eventually his fairness and integrity won them over. William moved to Bellair/Belmont (#19) in 1828 and may have owned it and received compensation for eleven slaves of £159. 3s. 3p. in 1835.

The Weatherill's plantation sugar mill was worked until 1912, and was nicknamed *"Peggy Halliday, the Greyhound of Popeshead."* It earned that name because with a strong wind spinning her blades, the windmill turned much faster than that of the Langford's Plantation (#6) across the way, which was being driven by steam.

The bronze bell, which regulated all who worked on the plantation, was cast in the Whitechapel Foundry, east of London, in the late 1700s. *"The bell was rung every morning at six o'clock and twice during the day, first for the end of the morning shift, then again at two o'clock for the start of the afternoon shift. The family coach was drawn by trained mules because they were stronger (than horses) and very sure-footed. "Father told me the mules were so well groomed you could rub a white handkerchief on the withers without staining it. A slight exaggeration maybe, though I have no doubt he said it. It must have been a sight to see. We had a mule cart for general purposes, fetching and carrying. The problem was that when the midday bell rang, the mule would do no more work for the day. It just proves that mules are not as stupid as people think they are.'*

Edgar Kasper Lane, *"Memoirs".*

The plantation's bell was stolen in 2005 from its hanging place on a beam in an opening of the mill. It has never been recovered.

"In 1939, we had riots in Antigua. It was part of my job to ride to the loading station beyond Marble Hill, almost into town. This I did as though things were normal. On my way there, on the public road, I saw a crowd armed with sticks and other weapons coming towards me. I had either to turn and gallop away or to face them. I decided on the latter. When I reached them somebody said 'That is Master Kasper's pony' and as I went by we exchanged greetings. About half a mile along the same road, the same crowd came across the Manager of Langford's estate, who was a black man. They knocked him off his horse and he was badly beaten."

Edgar Kasper Lane, *"Memoirs".*

< >

Martin and Lee Schaffler arrived in Antigua in the early 1940s, having escaped to England from Germany during the persecution of Jews at the start of

World War II. They were interred on Montserrat with other Jewish *i*mmigrants for the duration of the war. The family purchased Weatherill's in 1946 and operated it as a sugar and then a cotton plantation until the 1970s when estate farming ceased in Antigua.

When the Schafflers first arrived at Weatherill's in 1946, Mrs. Schaffler often rode into town in a horse and cart selling milk to customers along the way. Margaret White recalled that her mother was one of Mrs. Schaffler's customers, and she remembers Mrs. Schaffler driving the cart into her yard. *"It was unusual to see a woman using this mode of transportation, which was usually left to the man,"* she said.

Ms. Ella Pinkas, the sister of Mrs. Schaffler, joined the family in the 1950s to assist in running the estate. She held a law degree from a university in Germany and was a judge, but was told that because she was a Jew she would be prohibited from working. She had left Germany before the war and settled in England to pursue her career. She passed away in 2009; Mrs. Schaffler had died in 1997.

The Schafflers had two children, Janice (b. 1943) and Kiki (b. 1945), both of whom attended the Antigua Girl's High School. The two women left Antigua but visited often, and they put the Weatherill's estate house on the market in 2010 for U.S. $5,500,000. It was purchased, in 2013, by Victor Michael.

< >

Weatherill's is the site of three popular ghost stories

While babysitting for the Schaffler's children, Pat Dean retired for the night and heard deep breathing in the bed next to her. She leaped up, raced across the room, and flipped on the light, but saw no one. She checked on the children, then returned to bed. Again, deep breathing began so she spent the remainder of the night in the bedroom with the children.

Years later, when ghost stories were being told, someone mentioned that a man had been smothered in his sleep at Weatherill's by his wife's boyfriend, and the man can sometimes be seen and heard. Pat realized that's most likely whom she had heard!

Many people, including Pat Dean, have heard running water every morning at seven o'clock. When the area was checked, there was no sign of running water. The sound came from the vicinity of the bathroom and it is assumed somebody in years past probably took a shower every day at 7:00 AM.

On several occasions, in the evening, all of the outer shutters suddenly close of their own accord and must be re-opened to admit the evening breezes.

< >

In 1941, the Antigua Sugar Factory Ltd. had cane returns from Weatherill's estimated at 319 tons; 34 peasants on the Estate.

The mill from which the bell was stolen in 2005. In excellent shape it was used as a work shop. Agnes C. Meeker

#6 - Langford's Plantation

The Ownership Chronology

1660: Jonas Langford, the first Quaker to settle in Antigua.

1756: Jonas Langford. b. 1701.

1790: Jonas Langford Brooke. 1777/78 Luffman map.

1829: Thomas L. Brooke. 494 acres, 288 slaves.

1851: Thomas Langford Brooke. He owned 404 Langford acres and 280 Langford Woods (#12) acres, both in St. John's Parish; 325 Jonas' (#85) acres in St. Peter's Parish; and 231 Laroche (#135) acres in St. Paul's Parish. Total: 1,240 acres.

1872: Thomas W. Langford Brooke. The Horseford Almanac shows Langford's and Mount Pleasant (#7) with combined acreage of 621 and designated as a steam works.

1891: Aubrey J. Camacho.

1921: Aubrey J. Camacho. 791 acres in total.

1923: Aubrey J. Comacho. He is one of four plantation owners who participated in two years of fruitless negotiations in the early 1940s with the Antigua Trades & Labor Union. The other three were Lee Westcott of Crosbie's (#2), Martin Schaffler of Weatherill's (#5) and Anthony Shoul of Thibou/ Jarvis (#34) & Judges (#53).

1940s: The Antiguan Government, now the Antigua & Barbuda Police Training Academy.

< >

This estate sat surrounded by four other large plantations -- Hart's & Royal's (#3), Weatherill's (#5), Dunbar's (#8) and Marble Hill (#9). It was an early convert to steam power for the grinding rollers and related machinery within its sugar mill, along with Mount Pleasant (#7) and Dunbar's. The date 1754 is inscribed on the keystone of Langford's mill, dating the year in which it was built. The structure was later turned into a cistern for storing water

Langford's Plantation house with the mill in the foreground. Now the Antigua
& Barbuda Police Training Academy - Agnes C. Meeker

The original estate house was built of stone, and is presently used by the Antigua government as a police training center. In 2011, a new building was erected on the north side of the estate house and is a police station for the area. A number of the estate's original outbuildings and walls still exist, and are whitewashed annually with lime by the latest group of police recruits.

Jonas Langford *"arrived (in Antigua) on the 14th of the 5th month (ED: presumably 1660). "He was a Quaker, the first of that persuasion to land in Antigua. In 1664, he was imprisoned for holding a religious meeting in his house. In 1684, he was compelled to pay £9,585 sterling for church rates, and in 1690 £4,085 sterling was taken from him by the Church Warden, (and) again in 1695 a further sum of £13,044 sterling was take from him."* "History of the Island of Antigua" by Vere Oliver, Volume II.

Mr. Oliver also states that in a will dated *"14 Feb. 1709 Jonas Langford the Elder of Popeshead plantation, Popeshead Division, Antigua, merchant possessed a schedule of negros, etc., on Popeshead and Soldiers Gutt plantations: 158 slaves, 44 cattle, 18 horses, 74 sheep, 13 goats. On Cassada Garden (#13a): 79 negroes, 8 horses, 65 cattle, 56 sheep, 12 hogs. 18 Nov. 1712."*

Before he died in 1712, Jonas Langford the Elder executed a second will, stating *"I granted to Edward Byam and Francis Rogers my Popeshead plantation where I now dwell, my plantation called Soldiers Gutt ..... in trust for the use of myself and my wife Anne for our lives ..... I granted to my trustees my plantation called Cassava or Cassada Garden of 570 acres in St. John's Parish for 99 years after my death, then 1/2 to Abraham Redwood and Mehittable his wife."*

It is interesting to see how Jonas Langford the Elder accumulated so much land in a span of only 47 years, 1638 - 1685. It also demonstrates how small land holdings can be combined into a large planation. Jonas became a very powerful resident of Antigua, buying small plots from ten or more different landowners. Here's the chronology:

1638 - Langford buys 17 acres in Popeshead from John Hawkes for 8,000 pounds of tobacco.

1669 - Langford buys 15 acres at Popeshead from Thomas Ellington.

1669 - Langford buys 100 acres called Soldiers Gutt (near Blue Waters Hotel) in Popeshead from Richard Belcher.

1669 - Langford and Richard Belcher buy 87 acres from Hannah Jeffries.

1669 - Langford buys 45 acres in Popeshead from Hannah Jeffries.

1670 - Langford buys land and stock from Justinian Holliman for £60,000.

1670 - Langford buys 10 acres at Popeshead from Richard Belcher.

1678 - Langford buys 10 acres at Popeshead from James Benton.

1678 - Langford buys 10 acres at Popeshead from William Cullender.

1678 - Langford buys 10 acres at Popeshead from William Jones

1679 - Langford buys 1,000 acres called Cassava (Cassada) Gardens from John Sampson for £10,000.

1679 - Langford buys 10 acres from William Morgan.

1680 - Langford has another 126 acres in Popeshead Division.

1685 - Langford buys 10 acres from Owen McCarthy.

Antonio Joseph Camacho arrived in Antigua in 1878, a Portuguese native of Madeira. He arrived considerably later than most of the Portuguese immigrants, however he quickly began to acquire land. He owned two plantations in 1878 -- Bellevue (#36) and Briggin's (#7), totaling 967 acres and by 1891 he also owned Langfords, Mount Pleasant (#7), Dunbar's (#8), Otto's (#16) and Woods (#12), totaling 2,000 acres. Most of those plantations were clustered close to St. John's.

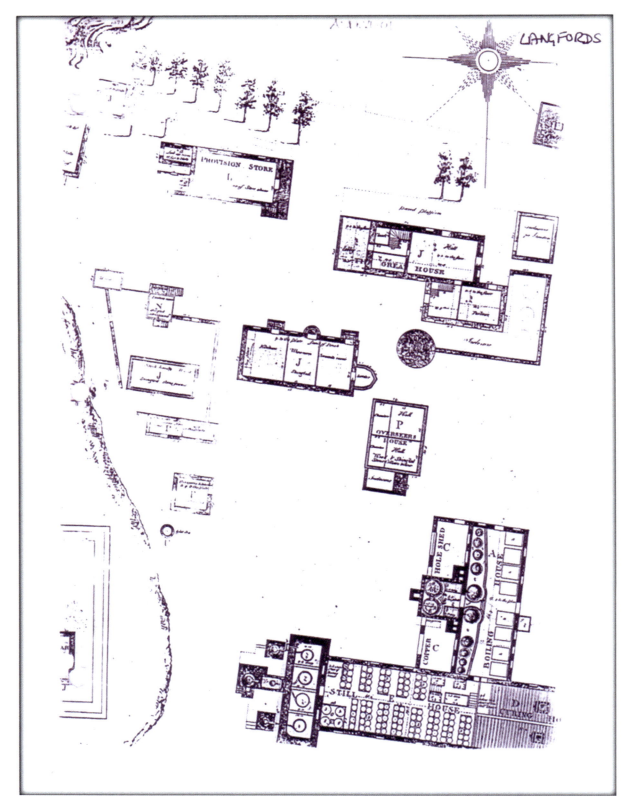

Plan of Langford's Plantation showing position of mill and Buff house in relation to the works.
Copies of Plans of the Langford Estates can be obtained from The Library of Congress, USA

< >

He had three sons: John, Emanuel and Martin. John was the one most involved with his father's estates. In 1898 he is listed as representing fourteen estates, and by 1902 he had bought another seven, making him one of the largest landowners in Antigua at that time.

Later on, his son of the same name became so fed up with having a ruined estate on his hands after two years of fruitless negotiations with the island's government and the Antigua Trades & Labor Union in the late 1940s (ED: see Crosbie's #2), that he sold everything to the government for £10,000. At the time, the Langford's estate had over 700 acres, and all of its mules, horses, cattle and sugar cane in the fields were thrown in *"brota"* (ED: slang for something for free).

A decade before that, in the 1930s, Camacho's plantation manager, Arthur Hewlett, often treated youngsters from St. John's who walked to the estate for a favorite treat known as asham, a mix of twice crushed parched corn and brown sugar, a process that originated in slave days. The Hewlett's had three children around the same age as the Willocks, so the youngsters enjoyed a visit and a treat. In her *Memories Jean (Willock) Thomas* says *"before the days of motor vehicles we walked everywhere including down to Fort James for a sea bath."*

In another instance, Helen Abbott remembers *"When we lived at Langford's I remember Daddy (ED: Fred Abbott) who was the manager, having a field of hay which he had cut and bailed, working late into the night. The hay was used as fodder for the animals. He also had a field of tomatoes along what is now Old Popeshead Road. There was a high stone bath downstairs in the house that was wonderful for playing in when filled. The stables and cattle pen were at the back and at the side of the house was a large cistern. On the north side of the house were mounting blocks where the manager's horse would be brought for him in the morning to mount prior to making his rounds of the estate. The overseer lived in a house near the cistern. The mill had been converted to store water and the animals drank from a rim around the base of the mill that contained water."*

Helen Abbott, Memories.

"At Langford's an old family burial ground enclosed by a wall containing a vault formerly used by the Hodge family (Hodges Bay, #4). Both Langford Lovell, who died in 1793, and Langford Lovell Hodge, who died in 1817, are buried at Langford's."

"History of the Island of Antigua" by Vere Oliver, Volume II.

The Langford Plantation Mill with all openings sealed in order to store water.   The letters painted on the side P.T.A stand for Police Training Academy.   At the base of the mill, the trench that provided water for the animals visible in the first photo, seems to have been broken down. Agnes C. Meeker

Nearly all of the estates had their own burial ground or cemetery, some combining with nearby estates. Vere Oliver, in his three volumes, catalogues many of these burial sites, very few of which exist today having been demolished by the backhoe and the sands of time.

Near the main road adjacent to the estate, there also is a tomb which was surrounded by an iron railing, recently repaired and fenced by the Antigua & Barbuda Police Training Academy. The inscription on the slab reads:

Sacred to the Memory
of Langford Lovell who died
29th Dec. 1793 Aged 63
Elizabeth Lovell who died
27th Dec. 1808
Ebenezer Lovell who died
29th Nov. 1798
William Lovell who died
19th Dec. 1815

< >

The British Parliament gave Langford's estate a legacy payment (Antigua 28) of £3,701. 14s. 4p. in 1834 for granting freedom to 305 enslaved. The sole claimant was Peter Langford Brooke.

Records of Langford Lovell are held at the National Archives in Kew, U.K.

#7 - Mount Pleasant Plantation

The Ownership Chronology

1668:   John Jenkins applied for patent on 150 acres.

1668:   John Humphrys, a carpenter, bought 20 acres.

1700:   Captain Nathaniel Humphrys. d. 1714.

1750:   Nathaniel Humphrys.

1777:   Alexander Willock.   1777/78 Luffman map.

1829:   Francis Willock. b. 1759, Antigua; d. 1829, England.

1830:   Frank Gore Willock.

1852:   Mrs. George Savage Martin (nee Ann Willock), married 1823.

1872:   Thomas Langford Brooke.

1891:   Antonio Joseph Camacho. d. 1894

1894:   John J. Camacho. d. 1929

1933:   Aubrey J. Camacho. 1933 Camacho map.

< >

No ruins of the sugar mill or the estate house nor outbuildings exist today, but the flat-topped hill known as Mount Pleasant remains, bristling with several communications towers. Part of an old wall runs alongside tee box #5 on the Cedar Valley Golf Course, land which was originally part of the Mount Pleasant estate. Abutting estates included Hart's & Royal's (#3), Dunbar's (#8), and Cedar Valley (#43).

A patent for 150 acres at Popeshead and North Sound was applied for in 1668, and a year later John Jenkins sold 20 acres at Popeshead to John Humphrys for £11,000.   *"History of the Island of Antigua"* by Vere Oliver, Volume I.

In 1680, Mary Humphrys, of Antigua, purchased a hill in Popeshead, plus land in St. Mary, from William Thomas for £24,000. The land abutted hers on the west. Then, in 1750, Nathaniel Humphrys is shown as the registered owner of the Mount Pleasant estate.

"On a very large (stone) ledger in the centre of a cane piece (at) Mount Pleasant, on the old family estate . . . The ledger is about a foot beneath the surface and is usually covered up with earth. A second ledger is also supposed to be nearby but never found.

Here lyeth the Body of
Cap. Nathanael Humphrey (sic)
who departed this life the 18th of
January 1714 in the 45th year
of his Age.

"History of the Island of Antigua" by Vere Oliver, Volume I.

< >

Alexander Willock was an Antigua merchant and slave trader, and is the registered owner of this estate as of 1777/78. In 1765, when the sailing vessel *Sally* first entered the Caribbean, her first port of call was Barbados. *"The Browns* (of Nicholas Brown & Co.) *had posted several letters to the island offering* (Captain) *Hopkins advice on where he might most profitably sell the enslaved Africans in his hold, but none of the letters seems to have reached him. Hopkins proceeded to Antigua where he sold what remained November 25, 1765, which accompanied the account of Alexander Willock, an Antigua slave trader who handled the sale of twenty-four captives.*

"Willock apologized for the low prices, which he attributed to the slaves 'very Indifferent' quality, and assured the Browns that, if they ever wished to 'try this market again with good Slaves I should be able to give you Satisfaction."

"library.brown.edu."

There is also a record of Willock having sold 55 slaves to a buyer named Samuel. They had been brought to Antigua on the sailing brig *Othello*, captained by Thomas Rogers.

In addition to Mount Pleasant, Willock also owned several estates in Montserrat and Tobago. He fathered 11 children, five of whom died in infancy. His son Francis Willock was born in St. John's in 1759 and died in Southampton, England, in 1829 the same year he owned Mt. Pleasant. He was declared bankrupt in 1793.

The Mount Pleasant estate was combined with Dunbar's (#8) in 1829, when Langford's (#6) converted to steam to power its sugar mill. By 1872, the combined estates held 621 acres, 192 slaves, and was designated a Steam Works. Alexander Willock, Francis Willock, and Frank Gore Willock are listed as owners of four estates: Mount Pleasant, The Folly (#33) Blizards (#53) and Samuel Byam's.

WINDMILL, MT. PLEASANT.

The Mount Pleasant Mill in full operation – Anthony Gonsalves Collection

With the abolition of slavery in 1833, the Mount Pleasant estate was awarded £1,842. 17s. 7p. (Antigua 24) by the British Parliament, for 124 slaves that were freed. The sole awardee was Robert Alexander Cuthbert, who is not shown as the estate owner, but the beneficiary was Octavia Willock and beneficiaries deceased included Alexander Willock, Francis Willock and Frank Gore Willock.

Unsuccessful claimants included Elizabeth Rebecca Cuthbert, Elizabeth Cuthbert (nee Willock), Sir Henry Willock, Rebecca Broadley, George Delmar, Ambrose Humphreys, George Savage Martin, Robert Pulsford, William Pulsford, John Gillian Stilwell, Thomas Stillwell, James Weston, Charlotte Arthuriana Williams (nee Cuthbert), the Reverend Frederick de Veil Williams, and Lawrence Blount Williams.

George Savage (b. 1789; d. 1849) married Anne Willock in 1823 at St. John, Antigua. He lived with his wife at Mount Pleasant.

Mrs. George S. Martin (Ann Willock) owned the estate, and Sir W. Martin owned both Green Castle (#163) with 605 acres and Rigbys (#162) with 263 acres, both located within St. Mary's Parish. High Point (#55) with 212 acres and

Nibbs (#52) with 131 acres were owned by heirs of Samuel Martin. They were both located in St. George's Parish.   *"History of the Island of Antigua"* by Vere Oliver, Volume II.

A. J. Camacho, the Portugese citizen from Madeira who arrived in Antigua in 1878, owned Mount Pleasant as well as Langford's (#6) and Dunbar's (#8) by 1891 as well as Otto's (#16), Woods (#12) and Jonas's (#85) for another 2,000 acres.

< >

The radar tower for V. C. Bird International Airport stands on top of Mt. Pleasant, which was the site of Antigua's first experimental wind generator in 1985. The generator was shaped like an egg beater, the name by which it became known. It was allowed to fall into disrepair when the government could not secure the spare parts to fix it. Shoul's land abuts Mt. Pleasant on the north, and part of Cedar Valley Golf Course is also nearby. To the northwest is a housing development known as Mount Pleasant.

There is supposed to be a cave in the hills (possibly Santa Maria) used by a fugitive from justice as a hideout, assisted by the villagers of Cedar Grove. There have been several attempts in recent years to find it, but no success.

Top - view of Mount Pleasant behind Cedar
Valley Golf Club. Agnes C. Meeker

#8 - Dunbar's Plantation

The Ownership Chronology

1690s: Colonel Thomas Walker. b. 1670; d. 1736.
1794: Robert Skeritt Nugent Dunbar. b. 1769; d. 1846.
1750: Heirs of Colonel Thomas Walker.
1780: John Dunbar. Baptised 1721.   1777/78 Luffman map.
1784: Robert Skeritt Nugent Dunbar.
1790: Charles Warner Dunbar. b. 1743; d. 1794.
1821: W. Dunbar owned the 165-acre estate until 1851.
1872: C. H. Okey and another. 106 acres.
1876: Heirs of Thomas W. Langford Brooke.
1933: Aubrey J. Camacho. 1933 Comacho map.
1970s: Government Agricultural Station.

< >

The sugar mill on this plantation is in excellent shape and has been landscaped with bougainvillea plants all along the bank on which the mill stands. The Dunbar's estate was situated on a hill overlooking Friars Hill Road, and became the Government Agricultural Station during the tenure of Robert Hall, the Minister of Agriculture during the People's Labour Movement. He was known for doing a lot for the island's agricultural efforts, including the Christian Valley and Green Castle Agricultural Stations. He owned Smith's estate (#161), which he actually farmed.

The Government Agricultural Station was an experimental station with a staff of agronomists who tested soil samples brought to them by land owners for testing to determine nutrient content. Plants were tested for fungus and pests, and people leaving Antigua with flowers, fruits or vegetables could obtain a certificate for customs.

This old print shows the hilltop location of Dunbar's estate house and works. The sugar mill is all that remains standing, and is in reasonably good shape given its age.   Mike Copperthite.

A small factory bottled some of Antigua's finest jams and jellies, including the very popular pineapple jam. This operation fell into disrepair and is no longer productive. However, several fields of sea island cotton are still grown and harvested annually for seed content. Antigua produces an exceedingly long thread and high grade sea island cotton, the seeds of which are harvested and provided to other Caribbean islands.

The Dunbar's estate overlooked the McKinnon's estate (#10) to the west, Langford's (#6) to the north, Cedar Valley (#42) to the east, and Friars Hill (#11) to the south. The estate was higher up the hill than the sugar mill, commanding magnificent views of the north part of the island.

The estate was combined with Langford's (#6) and Mount Pleasant (#7) in 1829, during the ownership of Charles Warner Dunbar, when Langford's converted its sugar mill from wind power to steam.

View along the Friars Hill road towards the Dunbar's mill c.1930
Museum of Antigua & Barbuda

< >

Colonel Thomas Walker (1670 - 1736) obtained a royal grant in 1691 for land forming part of the King & Queen Colony of Virginia, in North America, where he founded the village of Walkerton. He erected a manufacturing and gristmill there, as well as a cotton gin and copper shop like many settlers in the New World, he was part of the colonization of the West Indies acquiring land grants for service to their country (England). Colonel Walker's land grant became the Dunbar's estate, operated by his heirs commencing in 1750.

Martha Dandridge Custis married George Washington at the age of 27 in 1759. Dunbar's, once owned by Martha's paternal grandfather, was later sold in order to settle a debt by George Washington.

Top – Dunbar's sugar mill landscaped
with bougainvillea plants.

Bottom – View from the west side
showing the front of the mill.

Agnes C. Meeker

"Charles Warner Dunbar (1743 - 1794) passed his estate onto Robert Skerrett Nugent Dunbar (1769 - 1846)." The Dunbar family also owned an estate called Blubber and it is assumed it is this estate Mr. Dunbar passed to Robert because Mr. Dunbar's son of the same name -- Charles Warner Dunbar -- owned

the Dunbar's Plantation from 1829 to 1851 (see Ownership Chronology, above).

"History of the Island of Antigua" by Vere Oliver, Volume I.

The elder Charles W. Dunbar is quoted extensively in *Journal by A Lady of Quality* describing his plantation, which he called "The Eleanora" prior to its destruction by a hurricane in c.1774:

"Tho' the Eleanora is still most beautiful, yet it bears evident marks of the hurricane. A very fine house was thrown to the ground, the Palmettoes stand shattered monuments of that fatal calamity. This place which belongs to my friend Doctor Dunbar, is not above two or three miles from town, and as it is an easy ascent all the way, stands high enough to give a full prospect of the bay, the shipping, the town and many rich plantations, as also the old Barracks, the fort and the island I before mentioned. Indeed, it is almost impossible to conceive so much beauty and riches under the eye in one moment. The fields all the way down to the town are divided into cane pieces by hedges of different kinds . . . .

"My bed-chamber, to render it more airy, has a door which opens into a parterre of flowers, that glow with colours, which only the western sun is able to raise into such richness, while every breeze is fragrant with perfumes that mock the poor imitations to be produced by art. This parterre is surrounded by a hedge of Pomegranate, which is loaded both with fruit and blossom.

"Every body has some tragical history to give of that night of horror, but none more than the poor Doctor. His house was laid in ruins, his canes burnt up by the lightening, his orange orchards, Tammeran Walks and Cocoa trees torn from the roots, his sugar works, mills and cattle all destroyed yet a circumstance was joined, that rendered everything else a thousand times more dreadful . . . it happened in a moment when a much loved wife was expiring in his arms, and she did breathe her last amidst this War of Elements, this wreck of nature; while he in vain carried her from place to place for Shelter. The hills behind the house are high and often craggy, on which sheep and goats feed, a Scene that gives us no small pleasure."

< >

On June 13, 1750 Samual Walkins Kerr and William Mackinnon were complainants against Charles Dunbar, defendant, for redeeming certain lands. The "Chancery Division of Kerr & Others filed against Charles Dunbar on May 22, 1751, claiming £104. 10s. 3d." The complaint runs several pages. To put this in perspective, Charles Dunbar must have been one of the heirs of Colonel Thomas Walker referenced in the Ownership Chronology.

Ashton Warner was manager of Dunbar's in 1791, when John Dunbar owned the plantation. In the mid-1830s, the British Parliament awarded the estate £861. 18s. 7d. (Antigua 21) as payment for granting freedom to 66 enslaved workers. The awardees were William Dunbar, Charles Henry Okey, and Elizabeth Cosby, listed as "other association." Unsuccessful were Anne Stevens and William Kent Thomas.

< >

Two indentured servants on the plantation, were married in St. John's Cathedral, in 1844/45, by Curate Samuel Ashton Warner, probably the son of the former manager. John and Mary Copperthite had a son, Henry, born in Antigua on December 4, 1846, and the family immigrated to New Haven, Connecticut, in 1848, when Henry was eighteen months old.

As a young adult, Henry went to Washington, D.C., penniless and without a friend and any sort of aid or comfort. He became the proprietor of the Connecticut Pie Company, the largest pie industry in the District of Columbia. He began by making pies for himself; his first day's sales were only ninety-five cents! During the Spanish/American War, Henry sold 19,000 pies in one day to soldiers stationed at Camp Alger in nearby Virginia. The term "doughboy" was the name attached to the troops who purchased his pies!

Henry also owned a 243-acre farm in Virginia where he raised most of the fruits and vegetables used in his pies, as well as the milk, eggs, butter, etc. He was a self-made man, and amassed a fortune. His one hobby was a good trotting horse, and he became well known for the trotting horses he raced. Michael Copperthite, a relative, visited Antigua several times to trace his genealogy and obtain records from Antigua's Archives.

Dunbar's combined with the Langford's estate (#6) and Mount Pleasant (#7) when Langford's converted its sugar mill to steam power. Aubrey J. Camacho assumed ownership of Dunbar's in 1933 together with Langford's (#6) and Mount Pleasant (#7). His father arrived in Antigua in 1878, and by 1891 owned several sugar plantations totaling over 2,000 acres (see Langford's #6).

< >

1950-1970: Dunbar's held the official rain gauge records for the island as the Government Agricultural Station, which was gazetted (Government paper) on a regular basis.

#9 - Marble Hill Plantation

The Ownership Chronology

1750: Samuel Nibbs.

1787: A document states "James Nibbs...leaves his Marble Hill estate to Sarah Willett Otley containing 171 acres, to have and to hold for one full year." *"History of the Island of Antigua"* by Vere Oliver, Volume II.

1790: James Nibbs. Baptized 1752. d. 1822. 1777/78 Luffman map.

1790: James Langford Nibbs. d. 1822.

1791: A letter dated November 13, 1791, says Peter Murray was manager of the estate owned by James Langford Nibbs, Esq.

1806: Reverend George Nibbs, the only surviving son of James Langford Nibbs.

1822: Mrs. Nathaniel Humphrey. She was the only sister of James Langford Nibbs, and "had a life interest in his plantation of Marble Hill." James' will gave Mrs. Humphrey the plantation upon his death in 1822, and she gave her nephew management responsibility for the "property and house at Marble Hill." The nephew announced her death in 1824.

1840: Bertie Entwhistle Jarvis. d. 1846.

1843: Mrs. Bertie Entwhistle Jarvis. d. 1862. She inherited the 172 acre estate from Mr. Nibbs. She had written a letter dated June 2, 1823 complaining that Peter Murray, the estate manager appointed in 1791 by James Langford Nibbs, "had for many years shamefully neglected this property by his infirmities, that his funeral was on the 17th and he was very much esteemed." *"History of the Island of Antigua"* by Vere Oliver, Volume II.

1872: Mrs. M. E. Jarvis. (See Hart's & Royal's, #3, re Thomas Jarvis, same year.) 172 acres.

1891: Mrs. Bertie Entwhistle Jarvis.

1921: Amelia Gonsalves.

1933: A. H. Stamers. 1933 Camacho map

1957: Antigua Syndicate Estates

1976 – 1983: Dominic Habsburg.

1980c: Molwyn Joseph.

1994: Drug Rehabilitation Centre, destroyed by fire and hurricanes.

2016: Residential area.

A photograph of the Gonsalves family 1920, at Marble Hill, showing
the mill works in the background.   Gonsalves Family.

The sugar mill of this estate is still intact, but more recent construction surrounds it so it no longer commands the landscape it once did. The ruins of the estate house are also still visible, but a recent fire burnt the building to the ground. The neighbouring estates were Dunbar's (#8), Weatherill's (#5) and McKinnon's (#10).

The Jarvis family owned Doddington Hall in Lincolnshire, England. (See Thibou/Jarvis plantation #34 for additional information on the Jarvis family.

< >

Top – The Marble Hill
House in 1976 prior
to being renovated by
Dominic Habsburg.

Bottom – An interior
picture of the living room
filled with leaf debris.
Rosemary Magoris.

The Marble Hill mill 1999
Agnes C. Meeker

The estate house had been partially restored in 1976/77 by Dominic Habsburg, who left Antigua in 1983 after leasing the estate to Molwyn Joseph. It is understood that the Antigua Government earmarked EC $129,000 to repair the historic house, but it remained closed and later fell into disrepair due to theft and the ravages of free-range goats.

An American Naval Construction unit (Seabees) completely refurbished the house (un-historically) in 1991 as a gift from the U.S. Government, so it could be used as a drug rehabilitation and halfway house. Shortly after the opening ceremony in 1995, Hurricane Luis pounded Antigua with 140-mile an hour winds for 36 hours, and the Marble Hill estate house was completely destroyed. Today only the mill is visible.

< >

The Marble Hill plantation received a Legacy award from the British Parliament of £2,482. 16s. 2d. (Antigua 38) for 199 freed slaves when Parliament abolished slavery in 1833 and set aside £20 million to compensate plantation owners for the loss of their indentured labor. The awardees were Reverend Henry Joseph Barton, William King, Benjamin Travers and Joseph Travers. Sarah Willett Hocker (nee Ottley) was a beneficiary. Bertie Entwhistle and Martha Flemming Ottley were unsuccessful claimants.

< >

In 1941, the Antigua Sugar Factory Ltd. cane returns were estimated at 554 tons. There were 76 peasants on the estate.

#10 - McKinnon's (Dickenson Bay) Plantation

The Ownership Chronology

1700s: Daniel McKinnon. b. 1697; d. 1767.

1750:   William McKinnon.

1790:   Honorable William McKinnon. 80 acres, bounded east and north by land of James Weatherill.   1777/78 Luffman map.

1800:   Sir William Alexander Mackinnon, 1st Bart.

1829:   Messrs. McKinnon. 830 acres, 271 slaves.

1831:   Indenture between W. A. McKinnon and J. C. Symes.

1843:   William Alexander McKinnon. b. 1787; d. 1870.

1851:   Messrs. McKinnon. 830 acres.

1870:   William McKinnon. b. 1823; d. 1893.

1872:   Edward Beckett. 633 acres, and was designated a Steam Works.

1891   James C. Lewis.

1933:   I. E. Dyett, Major. b.1865 d.1935   1933 Camacho map

1950s: Fred Abbott. b. 1891; d. 1973.

1975:   Heirs of Fred Abbott.

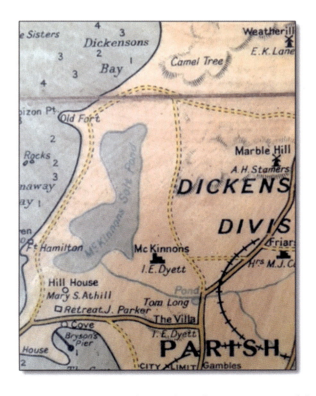

McKinnon's plantation was located on the west coast of Antigua
1933 Camacho map.

There is no sugar mill left on this site; in fact, all traces of the estate have been eradicated by modern residential construction. Most of those homes now enjoy the view facing west over McKinnon's swamp, Dickenson Bay and Runaway Bay.

In 1708 "Governor Parke writes..."*There is one Daniel Mackinin* (sic)*, that twenty years ago was a chyrurgeon to a Little Merchant ship, has drove off the island near 100 Men; all the Land where he lives was inhabited by poor people that lived upon some three, some five, some 10 Acres of Land."*

"History of the Island of Antigua" by Vere Oliver, Volume II.

George French, in his 1718 book *Answer to A Libel,* says that in 1716 *"Daniel MacKennon (sic), a Scots Apothecary, who laid the Foundation of a large Fortune he acquired on a corrupt unwarrantable Practice in Physick, whereby he became Heir, Executor and Administrator, to the unfortunate wretches fall'n into his Hands; and afterwards eminent for depopulating the island, by driving off a great many poor Families, to enlarge his ill got Possessions, in Revenge for his not being admitted of the Council....This man was violently suspected to have poison'd Sir William Mathews, Colonel Parke's Predecessor, who dy'd in the operation of a Dose of Physick of his Prescription and Preparation."*

In 1720, Mr. Oliver states: *Dr. Daniel Mackinen* (sic) *(d. 1720) age 62. It is stated that Daniel MacKinen immigrated to Antigua between 1678 and 1688 and perhaps received grants of estates called Drapers, Golden Grove (#23) and Dickensons Bay from (King) Charles II. I have in my possession an original deed by which it appears that Golden Grove Plantation was held in 1678-88 by Col. Edward Powell, Governor of Antigua 1716 to nephew Henry Powell. It was leased to Dr. Daniel McKinnon for 99 years.*

Mr. Oliver notes that as early as 1760, the property then known as Dickenson Bay Plantation, was *"indentured to Richard and Richard Jnr. Oliver....contained 80 acres bounded E(ast) & N(orth) with lands belonging to the heirs of Colonel James Weatherill* (Weatherill's #5) *dec(eased), S(outh) heirs of Henry Knight, dec(eased), now in the possession of Samuel Nibbs* (Marble Hill #9) *and W(est) which was heretofore the plantation of Nathaniel Knight."*

< >

William Alexander McKinnon was an absentee landlord until 1773, when he returned to Antigua. And, unlike his distant relative Daniel, who was accused of libel in George French's 1718 book, William did become a member of the island's governing Council, and he also owned Golden Grove (#23), 830 acres. In July 1787 the estate *"contained 80 acres bounded east and north with the land owned by James Weatherill."*

William Alexander McKinnon –McKinnon web site

A biography of William Alexander McKinnon states that he received part of the Legacy award paid to the estate for its freedom of its enslaved people. He was born on August 2, 1784 in Dauphine, France, the eldest son of William McKinnon and his wife, Harriet, daughter of Francis Frye of Antigua. Daniel McKinnon (b. 1791; d. 1836) was his younger brother.

By 1809, he succeeded his grandfather as the 33rd Chief of the Clan McKinnon and inherited his grandfather's estates. He was already wealthy from his father's success in the West Indies, and used some of his money to re-purchase the McKinnon lands in Scotland. He was a British politician (Tory MP), an absentee landowner, and Colonization Commissioner for South Australia.

On August 3, 1812, he married Emma Mary Palmer, the only daughter of Joseph Budworth Palmer of Palmerston, County Mayo. Emma was described as "a great beauty" and "an even greater heiress." She and William had three sons and three daughters, and on the death of Emma in 1835, he inherited the Palmer estates. He died in 1870 on one of his properties (Belvedere, Broadstairs, Kent) and was interred on another (Acrise Park, Kent). His estate was valued at £100,000.

His son William was a Liberal MP, and succeeded him as Chief of the Clan. Another son, Daniel Lionel, was killed at the Battle of Inkerman (Crimean War) on November 5, 1854; his grandson, Sir William Henry McKinnon, was an Army officer in South Africa.

In 1831, an *"Indenture between William Alexander Mackinnon of Hyde Park Place, Esq. and John Coles Symes of Fenchurch St....conveys to John Coles Symes all that 3rd part of all that plantation in the parish of St. John and Division of Dickenson's in Antigua, containing 771 acres ... bounded E(ast) with the highway and the lands now or formerly of John Dunbar and James Nibbs Esqs., N(orth) with the lands now or formerly of Anne Evanson and James Nibbs and S(outh) with the lands now or formerly of Eliz. Nibbs, John Taylor and Thomas Daniel Esq."*

< >

The artist Hogarth (1697 - 1764) painted a portrait of a Major General Daniel McKinnon (sic) in 1747. The portrait hangs in the National Gallery of Ireland. John Daniel McKinnon, son of William McKinnon, published a book entitled *"A Tour Through the West Indies in 1802 and 1803"*.

< >

As result of the abolishment of slavery by the British Parliament in 1833, the McKinnon's estate received a Legacy award (Antigua 35) of £3,942. 2s. 1p. in compensation for granting freedom to 278 enslaved workers. There were five claimants for the award: Reverend Henry Barnes and Louisa Barnes (nee McKinnon), John Daniel, Richard Davis, and Frances Keenan. Catherine McKinnon, Edmund Vernon McKinnon, and Rachel McKinnon see Yeamans) were unsuccessful. Samuel Boddington, George Cotsford Call, Reverend Thomas Cardale and William McKinnon were awardees Henry McKinnon was beneficiary and William McKinnon, beneficiary, deceased.

< >

Major I. E. Dyett was offered McKinnons estate, in 1933, by Attorney J. C. Lewis for £2,000 for 2,000 acres. At that time, the estate stretched from Back Street to Anchorage (Upper & Lower Gambles). Later that same evening Dyett *"was having dinner with a friend and recounted the story, saying he had no idea where he would ever get £2,000. His friend replied, why not, if he thought it* (the estate) *was worth it he'd lend him* (Dyett) *the money. After the first crop of cane Major Dyett decided to go into livestock and from the sale of the crop, cattle carts and other equipment, made more than enough to repay his debt."*

Quoted from Mr. Phillip Abbott, an heir of Fred Abbott.

Several years later, Fred Abbott was helping Major Dyett sort out the land for sale -- there were no surveyors in the 1940s -- and they agreed to a sale price of EC$100 per acre (EC$200,000 for 2,000 acres). The Major said *"he felt like a thief charging that much."*

Again, sourced from Phillip Abbott.

< >

#11 - Friars Hill (or Freeman's) Plantation
(aka: Walkins)

The Ownership Chronology

1679:   Dorothy Clarke, widow of St. Christopher, sold the 96 acres of "Fryers Hill in the Popeshead Division to Francis Carlisle."

1734:   Francis Carlisle, merchant.

1745:   Thomas Walkin.

1750:   Heirs of Thomas Walkin.

1790:   Thomas Oliver.   1777/78 Luffman map.
        This was an indenture lease by Godschal Johnson, Esq., of London, and Samuel Eliot, Esq., late of Antigua but now of Harley Street.

1829:   Capt. Haynes, Royal Navy. 230 acres, 166 slaves.

1843:   Haynes.

1852:   Mary Thomas. 230 acres.

1872:   Lady Thomas. 327 acres.

1878:   Montague White.

1891:   Henry Ogilvie Bennett. Purchased solely as a residence.

1893:   Antonio Joseph Comacho. d. 1894.

1921:   Aubrey J. Camacho.

1933:   Mrs. Aubrey J. Camacho.   1933 Camacho map

1970 - 1975: Vere Cornwall Bird, Antigua's first Prime Minister (1981).

< >

The old estate house was demolished in 2002, no sugar mill stands at this site, and there is no evidence of the former sugar works. The road leading out of St. John's to the north side of the island carries the name Friars Hill Road, as does the hill, which rises past where the estate house originally stood.

"The road leading from Gambles Estate (#14) *in a northerly direction, runs in a straight line for upwards a mile, planted on either side with Cocos and Cedars, which by extending an agreeable shade, give an additional interest to the bright and animated scene of Friars Hill, the Houses of the North to the works and all the bustle of plantation business suddenly arrest the attention."*

"Historical & Descriptive Account of Antigua, 1830."

Photograph of the Friars Hill Plantation house just before it was demolished.
Agnes C. Meeker

The estate was abutted by Dunbar's (#8) to the north, Cedar Valley (#42) to the east, and McKinnon's (#10) to the west.

< >

Antonio Joseph Camacho owned A. J. Camacho & Co., an export and merchant business. His son, Emmanuel O. Camacho inherited the business and ran it until 1918. By the time Emmanuel died in 1894, he owned more than 1,600 acres of sugar cane under cultivation, having purchased several other plantations. He was the single largest landowner on Antigua besides the Maginley family. Emanuel was a staunch supporter of the Catholic Church.

In 1834, with the abolition of slavery by the British Parliament, the estate was awarded £1,984. 16s. 10d. (Antigua 37) for 137 freed slaves.

VIEW OF SAINT JOHN'S HARBOUR, ANTIGUA.

This is either Friars Hill Plantation or McKinnon's (#10) with the Villa mill in the distance near to Rat Island and entrance to St John's Harbour. The Beinecke Collection, Hamilton College.

In 1948, the Secretariat Office on the Government House property burned to the ground, and the office was relocated to the Friars Hill estate house while the government office was rebuilt. **

During the administration of George Walter (1970 - 1975), the Friars Hill estate house was the home of V. C. Bird, who purchased the property for $7,000 and had it repaired by Sam Benjamin, of the Public Works Department, for $21,000.

"Not A Drum Was Heard" by Selvyn Walters

Margaret White, an heir of Montague White, tells the story of driving through Cedar Grove and stopping to ask an old man on a donkey for directions. He asked her about her family, and upon hearing she was related to the White family he told her Montague White, who at one time owned Friars Hill, while living at Hodges Bay House, had a reputation for ill-treating his slaves.

The Antigua Sugar Factory Ltd. cane returns for the 1941 crop were estimated at 982 tons, 572 peasants on the estate, 16.08 tons per acre.

The estate house was demolished several years ago.

** Author's note: My grandmother, Margaret Conacher (nee McSevney) managed the Government Secretariat Office and I remember riding my bike up Friars Hill Road to meet her at the government offices after Girl Guides at the Antigua Girls High School. The offices were relocated temporarily after a fire demolished the office within Government House grounds.

1885-1892: Papers, Correspondence and Plans: Hopkins: Friars Hill, Antigua: No. 178. Held by The National Archives, Colonial Office.England. Reference No. CO 441/15/15.

#12 - The Wood Plantation
(aka: The Body)

The Ownership Chronology

1671:   John Wood.

1750:   James Langford. Will 1726.

1779:   Jonas Langford Brooke. Baptized 1730. Will 1758. 1777/78 Luffman map.

1820:   Peter Langford Brooke. d.1829.

1829:   Peter Langford Brooke. Baptized 1793. d. 1840. 280 acres, 190 slaves.

1851:   Thomas Langford Brooke.

1878:   Heirs of Thomas W. Langford Brooke.

1891:   Antonio Joseph Camacho. d. 1894.

1894:   A. J. Camacho & Bennett.

1933:   Mrs. Aubrey J. Camacho.

1938:   Millicent Suter Abbott Sutherland. b. 1885; d. 1974. The estate contained 280 acres; sold to her for £800.

1978:   Helen (Nellie) Agnes Abbott, b. 1911; d. 1985, & George Scott Sutherland, b. 1912; d. 1981.

1985:   Divided between five members of the Abbott family: Jackson, Helen, Edward, Peter & Phillip.

< >

The large Wood plantation's estate house, built approximately 200 years ago, is still in its original condition and is the home of Phillip and June Abbott, heirs of Nellie Abbott. They continue to run a working farm and a small store selling feed and other livestock needs to farmers and homeowners.

Phillip and June are proud owners of one of the few remaining estate houses left in Antigua. They own an abundant collection of old maps, photographs, furniture and other mementoes of their ties to their historic heritage. Phillip is an avid researcher of genealogy, and can provide a detailed history of the Abbott, Sutherland, Goodwin and Maginley families to whom he is related. He also has considerable information on other families he has encountered in his research. The Abbott family immigrated to Antigua in the early 1800s from County Leitrim, Ireland.

A 1920's view of The Wood estate house, with an old Ford parked in front
Abbott Family

The house design is typical of many of the old estate homes, with steps leading up to a veranda on the second story, which opened into the living and dining rooms. Bedrooms were located on either side, each with a dressing room later converted into bathrooms. A kitchen was added upstairs to the rear of the dining room. It had previously been located in the back yard, separate from the main house, because of the danger of fire when it was customary to cook with wood or charcoal.

The second story of this home is constructed of wood set on a first story of stone, which contained the storerooms. This construction permitted the second story living space to be cooled by trade winds, while the thick stonewalls below helped maintain a cooler temperature.

The manager's house, which no longer exists except for foundations, was south of the bluff house on a small rise. Neither the sugar mill itself nor the extensive works exist today, but some of the out buildings, old cisterns and ponds can still be seen.

< >

House of Lords, 20th March, 1671: *"Holdsworth vs. Lady Honywood.Petition of Wm. Holdsworth, son-in-law and administrator (with the will annexed) of the goods and estate of John Wood, complaining of a discussion of his Bill in Chancery in 1646 concerning some estates of John Lamont."* Parliamentary Archives, Ref. HL/PO/JO.

< >

In 1779, when Jonas Langford Brooke owned the estate, there is a document reference to "Langford's Body Plantation in St. John's", hence the alternate name (rarely used) for this estate. By 1816, it was clearly identified as "The Wood estate in St. John's division containing 325 acres," according to Vere Oliver's Volume II. He cites a second reference which clarifies that the estate had two names: "The Body or Wood Estate . . . containing 28 acres, 3 roods" which was "indentured on 19 April 1816 between Thomas Langford and Johnathon Dennet for one year."

By 1825, there were three estates owned by Peter Langford Brooke, an obvious relative of the Langford family (see Langford's #6). According to Phillip Abbott, documents show *"P. L. Brooke was the owner from 1829 and then his heirs to 1878. He died in England in 1840 by drowning while skating on a frozen lake and the ice broke. The three estates were Langford's (#6), The Wood (#12) and Jonas (#85). I (Phillip Abbott) now live at The Wood. The house is about 200 years old and I was lucky enough to acquire a plan of the house and estate drawn by Peter Langford Brooke, in about 1825. There are also plans of Langford's, Jonas and Hodge's (Bay #34) Plantations available from the Library of Congress, US."*

< >

"PETITION. A Petition of Mary Prince or James, commonly called Molly Wood, was presented, and read, setting forth, That the Petitioner was born a slave in the colony of Bermuda, and is now about forty years of age; That the Petitioner was sold some years ago for the sum of 300 dollars to Mr. John Wood, by whom the Petitioner was carried to Antigua, where she has since, until lately resided as a domestic slave on his establishment; that in December 1826, the Petitioner who is connected with the Moravian Congregation, was married in a Moravian Chapel at Spring Gardens, in the parish of St. John's, by the Moravian minister, Mr. Ellesen, to a free Black of the name Daniel James, who is a carpenter at Saint John's, in Antigua, and also a member of the same congregation; that the

Petitioner and the said Daniel James have lived together ever since as man and wife; that about ten months ago the Petitioner arrived in London, with her master and mistress, in the capacity of nurse to their child; that the Petitioner's master has offered to send her back in his brig to the West Indies, to work in the yard; that the Petitioner expressed her desire to return to the West Indies, but not as a slave, and has entreated her master to sell her, her freedom on account of her services as a nurse to his child, but he has refused, and still does refuse; further stating the particulars of her case; and praying the House to take the same into their consideration and to grant such relief as to them may, under the circumstances appear right. Ordered, that the said Petition do lie upon the table."

< >

In the following text, Mary (aka Molly Wood) describes her life as a slave in the Wood household, as excerpted from *The History of Mary Prince* (her own words):

"Mr. Wood took me with him to Antigua, to the town of St. John's, where he lived. This was about fifteen years ago. He did not then know whether I was to be sold; but Mrs. Wood found that I could work, and she wanted to buy me. Her husband then wrote to my master to inquire whether I was to be sold? Mr. D____ wrote in reply, 'that I should not be sold to any one that would treat me ill.' It was strange he should say this, when he had treated me so ill himself. So I was purchased by Mr. Wood for 300 dollars, *(or £100 Bermuda currency).

"My work there was to attend the chambers and nurse the child, and to go down to the pond and wash clothes. But I soon fell ill of the rheumatism, and grew so very lame that I was forced to walk with a stick. I got the Saint Anthony's fire, also, in my left leg, and became quite cripple. No one cared much to come near me, and I was ill a long, long time; for several months I could not lift the limb. I had to lie in a little old out-house, that was swarming with bugs and other vermin, which tormented me greatly, but I had no other place to lie in. I got the rheumatism by catching cold at the pond side, from washing in the fresh water; in the salt water I never got cold. The person who lived in next yard (a Mrs. Greene) could not bear to hear my cries and groans. She was kind, and used to send an old slave woman to help me, who sometimes brought me a little soup. When the doctor found I was so ill, he said I must be put into a bath of hot water. The old slave girl got the bark of some bush that was good for the pains, which she boiled in the hot water, and every night she came and put me into the bath, and did what she could for me: I don't know what I should have done, or what would have become of me, had it not been for her -- My mistress, it is true, did send me a little food; but no one from

our family came near me but the cook, who used to shove my food in at the door, and say; 'Molly, Molly, there's your dinner.' My Mistress did not care to take any trouble about me; and if The Lord had not put it into the hearts of the neighbors to be kind to me, I must, I really think, have lain and died.

"It was a long time before I got well enough to work in the house. Mrs. Wood, in the meanwhile, hired a mulatto woman to nurse the child; but she was such a fine lady she wanted to be mistress over me. I thought it very hard for a coloured woman to have a rule over me because I was a slave and she was free. Her name was Martha Wilcox; she was a saucy woman, very saucy; and she went and complained of me, without cause, to my mistress, and made her angry with me. Mrs. Wood told me that if I did not mind what I was about, she would get my master to strip me and give me fifty lashes; 'You have been used to the whip,' she said, 'and you shall have it here.' This was the first time she had threatened to have me flogged; and she gave me the threatening so strong of what she would have done to me, that I thought I should have fallen down at her feet, I was so vexed and hurt by her words. The mulatto woman was rejoiced to have power to keep me down. She was constantly making mischief; there was no living for the slaves -- no peace after she came.

"I was also sent by Mrs. Wood to be put in the Cage one night, and was next morning flogged by the magistrate's order, at her desire, and this all for a quarrel I had about a pig with another slave woman. I was flogged on my masked back on this occasion; although I was in no fault after all; for old Justice Dyett, when we came before him, said that I was in the right, and ordered the pig to be given to me. This was about two or three years after I came to Antigua."

In the same book, John A. Wood is quoted in an August 18, 1828 court document as follows:

"The paper which Mr. Wood had given her (Molly) before she left his house, was placed by her in Mr. Stephen's hands. It was expressed in the following terms:-

"I have already told Molly, and now give it her in writing, in order that there may be no misunderstanding on her part, that as I brought her from Antigua at her request and entreaty, and that she is consequently now free, she is of course at liberty to take her baggage and go where she pleases. And, in consequence of her late conduct, she must do one of two things -- either quit the house, or return to Antigua by the earliest opportunity, as she does not evince a disposition to make herself useful. As she is a stranger in London, I do not wish to turn her out, or would do so, as two female servants are sufficient for my establishment. If after *this she does remain, it will be only during her good behavior; but on no condition will I allow her wages or any other remuneration for her services.*

"John A. Wood, London, August 18, 1828."

< >

Following the 1833 ruling by the British Government abolishing slavery in the British Empire, the British Parliament made a legacy award (Antigua 105) to Peter Langford Brook of £2,461. 7s. 7p. for granting freedom to 190 enslaved workers on the plantation.

< >

By 1852, Thomas Langford Brook owned Langford's (#6) 404 acres and The Wood's (#12) 280 acres, both in St. John's Parish, as well as Jonas's (#85) 325 acres in St. Peter's Parish, and Laroche's (#135) 231 acres in St. Paul's Parish. Ten years earlier, two other estates were sold, the whole of the Antigua property, totaling about 1,700 acres, for £10,000 to Aubrey J. Camacho. As noted in previous estate descriptions, by 1891 Mr. Camacho owned eight plantation estates, including Bellevue (#36), Briggin's (#22), Langford's (#6), Mount Pleasant (#7), Dunbar's (#8), Otto's (#16), The Wood (#12) and Jonas's (#85). All but the last were located in St. John's Parish.

Helen Abbott, who is part owner of The Wood as of 1985, remembers her grandmother Millicent Sutherland, who owned it in 1938 and had grown up there with her siblings:

"Granny Sutherland always kept cows and sold milk. She also worked at the Sugar Factory weighing cane for the Syndicate Estates and would walk from The Wood to the Factory through the back roads. Millicent Sutherland rented the land at The Wood in one acre lots (grounds) or more to peasants who grew cotton, sugar cane or vegetables. Where the Epicurean now stands there was a large field of tomatoes. I used to help our maid, who had a ground, pick cotton, and she would roast sweet potatos in the ground to feed us."

< >

In 1941, the Antigua Sugar Factory Ltd. had cane returns of 1,060 tons for The Wood. The 106 acre estate was worked by peasants who delivered 752 tons of sugar cane to the factory.

< >

In 1958/59, the "bluff" was rented by a young U.S. Navy Lieutenant and his wife, Woody and Anne Barnes. There was no housing on the Navy Base at the time, and they thought it romantic to be living in an old plantation house. The cane fields almost abutted the house, and Woody recalls an afternoon when a cane field caught fire, causing considerable anxiety about the safety of the home. Several people arrived and assisted the fire department in cutting a cane break to contain the fire. Woody and Anne also benefited from the friendship of old Fred Abbott, Phillip Abbott's father, who lived next door in the manager's house and who acquainted them with some of Antigua's history.

< >

A photograph of The Wood House as it appears today with plumbago hedge in full bloom. 2016
Agnes C. Meeker

The Woods Mall was constructed on The Wood estate land, hence retention of the name.

#13a -- Cassada Gardens Plantation
(aka: Cassava or Cassavia)

The Ownership Chronology

Early ownership by John Sampson.

1651:   Major General Sydenham Poyntz. Baptized 1607.

1671:   Samuel Jones, 500 acres in North Sound Division to Jonas Langford. In that same year, Francis Sampson of Antigua, "in consideration of 70,000 lbs. of Muscovado sugar, hath sold to Jonas Langford a moiety of a plantation about 1,000 acres in St. John's division called Cassava Gardens, bounded E(ast) by land of Timothy Snapes, N(orth) by Capt. Giles Blizard, W(est) by Sir Sydenham Poyntz, S (outh)by Col. Bastian Bayer."

1679:   John Sampson of London sold to Captain Samuel Jones, "a plantation granted by William Lord Willoughby to my father of 500 acres in New North Sound."

1679:   Jonas Langford. He purchased the land, 1,000 acres, from John Sampson of London for £10,000.

1701:   Nathaniel Sampson. d. 1701.

1709:   William Redwood, inherited one-half of Cassada Gardens plantation from his grandfather, Jonas Langford. d. October 31, 1709.

1750:   Honorable Abraham Redwood.

1788:   Abraham Redwood. b. 1709; d. 1788. 1777/78 Luffman map.

1829:   J. Langford L. Redwood. d. 1844.

1851:   Heirs of J. L. L. Redwood. 598 acres.

18xx: Mr. Ledeatt inherited from his Godfather Redwood.

1862:   Francis Shand. b. 1800; d. 1868. 699 acres.

1868:   Charles Arthur Shand. b.1855; d. 1910.

1891:   Heirs of Francis Shand.

1921:   Dubuisson & Moody-Stuart.

1933:   Dubuisson & Moody-Stuart.   1933 Camacho map

1940:   Antigua Syndicate Estates

1958:   Antigua Government

1969:   Lapp & others, The Buff

The original windmill is in excellent shape and still stands in front of the old estate house. The house itself is in disrepair, is currently referred to as "The Stables" and is used as both a bar and a house of ill repute. The land surrounding the house and mill was extremely flat, ideal for the cultivation of sugar cane. Today, the only reference to Cassada Gardens is the nearby horse racing track and housing development.

The name Cassada appears to be a derivative from "cassava", a plant, which produces large green leaves and a tuber that has long been a source of food from Aztec and Amerindian times. In the 1960s, a cassava factory in the south of Antigua (adjacent to the Claremont estate, #177) produced cassava flour and a coarser variety used to make farine, and bambula, a local sweet bread with coconut, and cassava bread or cakes   In *"Journal of A Lady of Quality"*, the author describes cassava cakes and the process to make them: *"Cassava (commonly called Cassada) is a species of bread made from the root of a plant of the same name, by expression. The water, or juice, is poisonous, but the remaining part after being dried, pounded and baked on thick iron plates, is both wholesome and palatable, it is eaten dry or toasted, and it also makes excellent puddings which they send up buttered. I eat it, not only without fear, but with pleasure"* (despite its poisonous reputation).

< >

1651: *"King Charles II appointed Major-General Poyntz, a former deserter from the Parliamentary power, to act as Governor of Antigua, which situation he filled until 1663, when Lord Francis Willoughby, of Parham, obtained a grant of the entire island from Charles II as a reward for his eminent services in the cause of that monarch; and Major-General Poyntz retired to Virginia. During the period this latter gentleman resided at Antigua as Governor, he owned and planned an estate called by him Cassada Garden, a title which it still bears."*

"Antigua & The Antiguans" by Mrs. Lanahan.

There also exists a 1702 affidavit of John Wilson, a 60-year-old planter, confirming that on July 25, 1701, he began working as overseer on the plantation of Nathaniel Sampson, a merchant, called Cassada Garden. He worked at the plantation *"two years and four months and planted five pieces (fields) of cane between the death of N. Sampson and that of his infant daughter Codrington Sampson."*

"History of the Island of Antigua" by Vere Oliver, Volume II.

< >

Abraham Redwood inherited one-half of Cassada Garden, in 1747, from his father, William Redwood, who had inherited the same property from his grandfather, Jonas Langford, in 1709. Abraham's property apparently was in St. George's parish. The other half of the original Cassada Garden estate was divided into quarters inherited by other members of the Redwood family.

Abraham was from Rhode Island in the American colonies, and is famous for founding Newport, Rhode Island's, historic Redwood Library in 1747 with 46 other Colonials, all of whom signed the Charter granted by George II. Mr. Redwood was President of the library from 1747 to 1788. The Redwood is the oldest continually operating lending library in the United States and is still in its original building, completely renovated and modernized.

The architecture of the Newport, Rhode Island, library building was admired by U.S. Secretary of State Thomas Jefferson when he visited Newport in 1790 in the company of President George Washington. Jefferson had been championing classical architecture as the model for government buildings in the new American Republic. Interestingly, the Court House in St. John's, Antigua -- now the Museum of Antigua & Barbuda -- was designed by the very same architect, Peter Harrison, in 1750.

Nearly 135 years earlier, in 1613, Robert Redwood, *"a good old Puritan, gave his house on the city wall (in Bristol) for a library. Alterations were finished in 1614 and Richard Williams, the Vicar, was appointed as the first librarian; the books were free to all citizens. This was, we believe, the first free library ever established in England."* "History of the Island of Antigua" by Vere Oliver, Volume III.

The British Government abolished slavery in 1833, and the British Parliament awarded a legacy payment to Cassada Gardens (Antigua 103) of £2,856. 18s. 11p. for granting freedom to 197 enslaved people who had worked the plantation. The awardees were Langford Redwood, John Henry Roper, and James Trecothick the younger. Unsuccessful claimants were Abraham Redwood (the previous owner), William Cokes, and Francis Thwaites.

However, subsequently, Parliament awarded £636. 16s. 10p. (Antigua 104) to Abraham Redwood, of Newport, RI, and Langford Redwood for freeing another 33 slaves.

< >

A typical example of an old plantation owner is the Shand family, which first owned Cassada Gardens in 1872, when Francis Shand took title to the property. The Shands were the quintessential example of the successful planter family. Francis Shand was a prominent estate owner in the 1830s: as a member of the Antiguan Assembly he was vocal in his argument against apprenticeship and, like other large land owners at the time, was also a merchant, ship owner, and owner of an estate on Montserrat. His prominence enabled him to testify before the Select Committee in 1848 as to the healthy state of sugar production in Antigua.

The Shand "empire" had grown substantially. In the early 1860s, Francis and Walter Shand owned ten estates, totaling 2,400 acres, scattered across Antigua. They had called upon the Encumbered Estates Court to acquire three additional estates -- Cassada Gardens, Donovan's (#65) and Gunthorpe's (#64) -- and then bought two more, Tomlinson's (#17) and Paynter's (#61), directly from an individual owner. They also leased the Diamond (#87). Then, they hit hard times.

By 1868, he was living in England; it is assumed another member of the Shand family remained in Antigua to look after the family's interests. After Francis died, his son, Charles Arthur Shand, assumed management responsibilities. In the tradition of wealthy planter families, Charles was educated at Harrow, in England, worked for a large Liverpool merchant company, and then came (or had been sent) to Antigua to look after the family's plantations.

By 1878, the Shand's owned only two of their original ten estates -- Fitche's Creek (#67) and Cedar Valley (#42). They retained ownership of the other five they had purchased through the Encumbered Estate Court as an individual owner, giving them ownership of more than 3,700 acres of agricultural land, enabling the Shand's to remain the second largest land owners on Antigua.

As the island's economy continued to decline, Charles Shand petitioned the court in 1888 to sell all seven remaining estates, which was completed in 1892. The seven estates were bundled as a package and sold for only £10,000, a trifle of their value mindful that Cassada Gardens, Donovan's and Gunthorpe's alone had sold for £6,500 during their first pass through the court a few years earlier.

The package of seven Shand estates, was purchased by G. A. Macandrew, a merchant based in Liverpool. He was, apparently, the Shand's agent. He also had long ties to Antigua; had replaced the Shands as lessor of the Diamond estate by 1878 and owned it by 1891. However, the Shands apparently did not relinquish total control because the estates were still listed as Shand properties in 1897, when they went into receivership.

Charles Arthur, meanwhile, became a member of the local Legislative Council and was appointed one of Antigua's representatives to the Leeward Island Legislative Council. He also was on its Executive Council as of March 1895, and listed himself as manager of Fitches Creek in 1897 and as proprietor in petitions signed in 1898 and 1899. However, by 1902 Fitches Creek was listed as owned by the Macandrew heirs.

In 1940, ownership of Shand properties shifted to a new line of estate owners. According to recorded minutes, a new company called Antigua Sugar Estates reissued 18,000 shares at £1 apiece to three members of the DuBuissons family: James Memoth DuBuisson, Mrs. Edith Manus DuBuisson, and William Herman DuBuisson, as well as Alexander Moody-Stuart and Judith Gwendolyn Moody-Stuart. George Moody-Stuart was offered shares, but declined.

The estates to be controlled by the new company were Gunthorpe's (#64), Cassada Gardens, Paynter's (#61), Tomlinson's (#17), Fitche's Creek (#67), Donovan's (#65), North Sound (#66), Cedar Valley (#42), Galley Bay (#30) and Five Islands (#31).

< >

Colin Spencer attired in his riding outfit as Overseer for the estate - Elsie Spencer

"In 1941/42 the U.S. Base hired many Antiguans and they would pass Cassada Gardens on their way to work early in the morning. On their way they would each pick up an armful of cane off the pile awaiting loco transfer to the factory. Mr. Colin Spencer who was slight in stature and the manager, recently arrived from Barbados, told them to stop stealing the cane and they in turn threatened him. Mr. Spencer went to the police and the next day, under Rupert James, the police hid in the cane fields and jumped the men when they attempted to pick up the cane. They were able to catch four of them whom they took to jail. In those days the pay in the fields was $65 dollars a month and one pound was the equivalent of $4.80 and there was big money to be had at the Navy Base."

Elsie Spencer

August 1, 1943, Gunthorpe's Estates Ltd. was restructured into a new company renamed Antigua Syndicate Estates Ltd. The original company had purchased for £30,700 Cassada Gardens, Cedar Valley, Fitches Creek and North Sound. Delap's was bought for £7,734.

< >

By 1945, Cassada Gardens *"had an excellent breed of horses, and the stables were one of the best on the estates. Races were held at the Cassada Gardens race track at least four times a year: Easter Monday, Whit Monday, August Monday and Boxing Day. The Gomes boys from Betty's Hope were the leading jockeys. Two to three times a week it was my job as a boy to ride a donkey to Parham for fresh fish and I would mount it off the gallery which was raised without a railing. One day I leapt off only to find the donkey had moved and I landed flat on my 'arse'. This did not stop the donkey. It took off straight to Parham without me that day."*

Lawrence Royer

Three-to-four races continue to be held annually by the Antigua & Barbuda Turf Club (2016)

< >

Other interesting facts:

Labour riots in 1918 prompted bands of men to stop cane cutters from working on Cassada Gardens as well as Morris Looby's (#141), Donovan's (#65) and Millar's (#59).

In 1941, the Antigua Sugar Factory's returns were estimated at 6,362 tons from 317.5 acres, with 98 acres of peasant land on the Cassada Gardens estate. Total: 5,363 tons, estimated at 16.30 tons/acre.

In 1969, Lapp & Others are listed as the owners of Cassada Gardens. Lapp & Company consisted of V. C. Bird, Antigua's first Prime Minister, Eustace Cockran, Bradley Carrott and Austin Lapps. *"Not A Drum Was Heard"* by Selvyn Walters

Top – One of the small outbuildings
maintained and used today 2006.

Bottom - The sugar mill
today showing several of the
openings closed in and last
used as a store room.

Agnes C. Meeker

Fore-go
by Mary Geo Quinn

In the days when sugar was king, the post of Fore-go
Was a prized and coveted one on each estate.
Not given out of favour or for vain show,
But to the one who could cut cane at the fastest rate.
To the Fore-go fell the vital task of setting
The pace at which work was to be done.
The Fore-go had to have the knack of getting
Workers to work steadily in hot sun.

Mary's poem goes on to state how Millie was sent with a crew to clean out an estate house and among the rubble found a gun, which she kept in her pocket. The Antigua Trades & Labour Union were agitating for everyone to strike against a new way of paying cutters (by weight instead of by row), and when the AT&LU arrived at Cassada Gardens brandishing placards and tools, Millie stood up to the picketers. They forced their way into the fields, but Millie brandished her gun and the frightened men fled. The gun, however, was a mere toy discarded by a child.

Papers, correspondence and plans, Redwood Cassada Gardens,
Antigua No. 29. Held by the National Archives (UK) Colonial
Office. Ref #C)441/6/9.

#13b - Clare Hall Plantation
(AKA: Oliver's, Nugent's, Skerrett's)

The Ownership Chronology

1700: Richard Oliver. d. 1716. 520 acres in St. John's Division.

1710: Edward Chester.

1716: Richard d.1763, and Rowland Oliver d. 1768.

1737: Oliver Nugent. d. 1802. 500 acres.

1758: Walter Nugent.

1765: Robert Skerrett Nugent. Married to Robert' Skerrett's sister Antoinetta. d. 1771.

1774: John Kirwan. d. 1806.

1777: Sir Peter Parker.   1777/78 Luffman map.

1790: Charles Warner Dunbar. b. 1743; d. 1794.

1800: Joseph Liggins. d. June 22, 1800.

1806: Nicholas Nugent.

1820: John Lynch.

1829: Nicholas Nugent, MD.

1851: Sir. W. C. Codrington. 613 acres.

1872: Henry Liggins. 613 acres, leased to a Dr. Edwards as a grazing farm.

19xx: Sir C. Bethel Codrington.

1921: Colonel R. S. G. Cotton. b. 1849; 1925.

1913: Clare Hall model village.

1933: Colonel Dyett. d. 1937.   1933 Camacho map.

1945: Bob Smith, brother-in-law of Colonel Dyett and Alice Smith.

1960c: Ellis Dowe. He later turned the buff house into apartments.

< >

The mill no longer exists on this site, but there is a detailed plan of the estate's entire layout. Robert Skerrett Nugent, who took possession of the estate in 1765, was Irish and owned property in County Clare, Ireland. He considered himself a "near relative" of Walter Nugent, who owned this estate seven years earlier. He married a Miss Craggs, and obtained the title of Baron Clare.

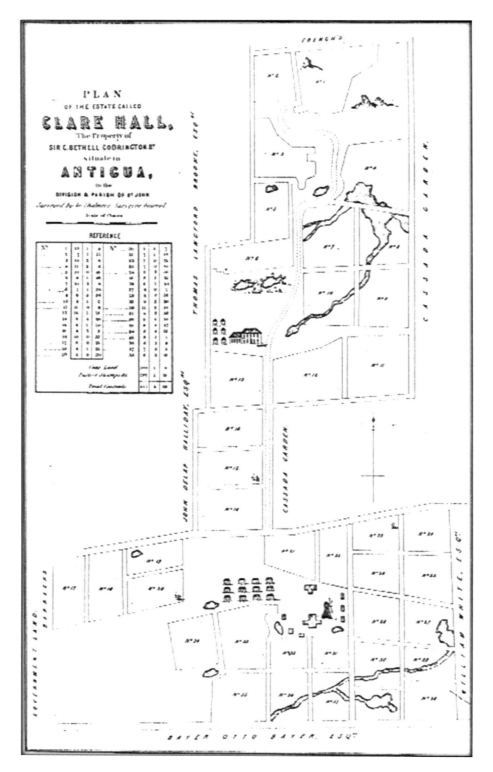

Detailed plan of the original plantation's 500 acre layout.
Codrington Estates

"My father, having about this time built a house on his estate in Antigua, obtained His Lordship's consent to call it Clare Hall, by which name I always heard it called while I had connection with a hope from it."

An excerpt from a letter dated December 27, 1844, written by a Major Nugent-Dunbar to his son states: *"Walter Nugent was the first Nugent to settle in Antigua following the family's forfeiture of lands in Drumcree, County Westmeath, Ireland, around 1720. He acquired two portions of land at St. John's town. The Robert Baker map of 1740 shows four plots of land to the north and east of St. John's belonging to Walter Nugent."*   *Nugents of Antigua.*

Two views of the old
Clare Hall
main house barely standing. 1999
Agnes C. Meeker

In 1721, Robert Skerrett, of Nugent's, sold the 500-acre estate in St. Philip's Parish. He died in 1771. Oliver Nugent, first son and heir in his family, was baptized May 22, 1737 at St. John's. He is credited with building the Clare Hall manor house. He was a member of the Council, sold his estate to Robert Skerrett, a resident of Dominica, in 1773. Oliver went bankrupt in 1777 and died in North America in 1802.

According to an October 22, 1936 circular of the West Indies Committee (and subsequently published in the *Antigua Star*), the Nugent estates were sold in 1765 by Oliver Nugent, the son of Walter Nugent and grandfather of Sir Oliver, to Robert Skerrett, who had married his sister, Antoinetta, the daughter of Walter and Antoinetta Skerrett. This created the Skerrett estates.

By 1768, the Skerrett family had relocated from Galway, Ireland and, like the Nugent's, were one of the original Irish families to settle in Antigua. Robert and Antoinetta Skerrett had no children, so some of the estates owned by the family, variously known as "Skerrett's" or "Nugent's", reverted in due course to Nugent ownership. This same year, a small part of the estate called Dunning Hill (#190) was sold to the island's Assembly for £2,000 to erect Government House. The sale was completed by Antoinetta Nugent, the widow of Walter Nugent, and her grandson, Nicholas Nugent.

Oliver and Bridget (Lynch) Nugent's second son -- Nicholas Nugent -- became a doctor and lived most of his life in Antigua. He became Speaker of the Assembly, and in 1829 he either bought or inherited the Nugent/Skerrett estates from his cousin, John Lynch, Antoinettea Skerritt's nephew.

Nugent's of Antigua, and Vere Oliver, Volume III.

John Kirwan secured possession of the numerous Nugent's estates in 1774 as mortgagee, and held them for 24 years until his death in 1806. He had amassed a fortune of £150,000; was known as "a rough Irishman noted for his blunders."

"History of the Island of Antigua" by Vere Oliver, Volume II.

Joseph Liggins lived in London, and was absentee proprietor of Clare Hall, Lyons (#123) and Ffrye's (#118) estates. He was buried at Kensall Green Cemetery.

St. Phillip's Anglican Church, Antigua.

< >

The Clare Hall estate, alias Nugent's alias Skerrett's, runs almost a mile on the road past the barracks on the edge of St. John's. It was described by Ms. Janet Shaw, author of *"Journal of A Lady of Quality"* as a plantation *"belonging to a Lady, who is just now in England. From her character I much regret her absence, for by all accounts she is the very soul of whim. Her house, for she is a widow, is superb, laid out with groves and delightful walks of Tamarind trees, which give the finest shade you can imagine.*

"Here I had an opportunity of seeing and admiring the palmetto tree with which this Lady's house is surrounded and entirely guarded by them from the intense heat. They are in general from forty to sixty feet high before they put out a branch, and as straight as a line. If I may compare great things with the small, the branches resemble a fern leaf, but are at least twelve or fifteen feet long. They go round the boll of the tree and hang down in the form of an Umbrella; the great stem is white, and the skin like Satin.

"Above the branches rises another stem, of about twelve or fourteen feet in height, coming to a point at the top, from which the cabbage springs, tho' the pith or heart of tree is soft and eats well. The stem is the most beautiful green you can conceive, and is a fine contrast to the white Boll below. The beauty and figure of this tree, however, rather surprised than pleased me. It had a stiffness in its appearance far from being agreeable as the waving branches of our native trees, and I could not help declaiming that they did not look as if they were of God's making.

"We walked thro' many cane pieces as they term the fields of Sugar-cane and saw different ages of it. We returned from our walk, not the least fatigued, but the Musquetoes had smelt the blood of a British man, and my brother has had his legs bit sadly. Our petticoats, I suppose, guarded us for we have not as yet suffered from these gentry."

< >

The British Government abolished slavery in 1833, and the British Parliament made a Legacy payment to Antigua plantation's as compensation for freeing unpaid slaves. Clare Hall received (Antigua 101) £4,442. 2s. 0p., paid to the owners for granting freedom to 296 enslaved.

In 1847, the estate was sold at public auction, according to Vere Oliver. *"Particulars of a freehold plantation called Skerrett, otherwise Clare Hall, situate in the Parish of St. John's . . . which will be sold . . . at the Public Sale Room of the said Court, at Gray's Inn Coffee House, Holbourn, London, on Monday, the 13th day of September, 1847.Containing about 612A 3R 39P of land, more or less, of which 320 acres are cane lands and the remaining pasturage and swamps . . . together with the messuage or dwelling house thereon, managers' and overseers' houses, labourers' cottages, windmil boiling and airing houses, still with their fittings and appurtances, stills, coppers, worm tubs, clarifiers, coolers and all other matters and things there to belonging, store rooms, Stables, and cattle sheds, also farming utensils, carts, harrows, agricultural implements, cattle, horses, mules and asses, with harness, saddles, bridles and other gear, and other matters and things of the said estate. Sir Oliver Nugent."*

"History of the Island of Antigua"
by Vere Oliver, Volume II.

Five years later, in 1852, Skerrett's 314 acres was described as *"a boys' home very near Clare Vue Hospital ("crazy" house) that dealt with truant boys."* Nearby was also Lady Nugent's Cemetery, which was the pauper's burial ground, later moved out of town to the site that the new Market now stands. A nearby street still bears the name of Lady Nugent.

"In 1902, the Botanic Garden was transferred from Clare Hall to Victoria Park immediately east of St. John's, now known as the Botanical Gardens. It was argued that Clare Hall was too exposed to hurricanes, etc. . . . and a sheltered spot was found in an abandoned quarry thirty feet deep that was about half an acre in size. Along with the environs the area composed of some nine acres.

"The settlement known as Clare Hall was, in 1913, laid out as a model village. It was clean and exhibited as the prime example of what a rural development ought to be. Because of its proximity to St. John's, Clare Hall became one of the early land settlement schemes.

"Prior to 1913, Clare Hall and Skerritt's represented the prime agricultural land, so fertile, that in October 1899 the first Botanical Station in Antigua was established there. Two supplementary Botanic Stations were established, one at Cobbs Cross and the other at Body Ponds. Clare Hall was the headquarters. Nearby in Skerrit's a sugar cane experimental station was established to deal with the ravages caused by sugarcane diseases, particularly the Rind fungus that affected the Bourbon cane which was the most popular variety of cane grown in the island at the time."

"Not A Drum Was Heard" by Selvyn Walters

< >

In 1941, the Antigua Sugar Factory's return from the sugar cane crop at Clare Hall and Golden Grove was estimated at 1,240 tons; actual tonnage was 1,247.

#14 - Gamble's Plantation (Upper & Lower)

Ownership Chronology

1668: Honorable George Gamble. 50 acres, surveyed July 18, 1668. Mr. Gamble, a merchant, had increased the acreage to 127 plus four portions of land in St. John's, according to a land grant dated July 2, 1689, by Sir N. Johnson.

1710: Edward Chester.

1710: Governor Daniel Parke. b. 1664; murdered 1710.

1723: Lucy Chester. d. 1770.

1770: Charles Dunbar. b. 1743; d. 1794.

1790: John Halliday. 1777/78 Luffman map.

1829: Rear Admiral John Halliday Tollemach.

1843: John Tollemach (nee Halliday). By 1852, 300 acres.

1872: Viscount Combermere. 290 acres.

1891: Lord Combermere & C. I. Thomas. Lord Combermere was the son of Viscount Combermere, who purchased the estate from John Tollemach in 1872.

1921: Colonel R.S. G. Cotton.

1933: Colonel Dyett. d. 1937. 1933 Camacho map.

1945: Bob Smith, brother-in-law of Colonel Dyett, and Alice Smith.

1990: Dr. Ivor Heath, Bluff house only.

< >

No mill has survived on either Upper or Lower Gambles, but it is confirmed that in combination with the Daniel's estate (The Villa #15) the original mill had been converted to steam by 1872. Lower Gambles apparently operated the "works", which is depicted in the 1830 drawing featured as a postcard below, and Upper Gambles was where the buff, or estate house, was located.

The Wood estate (#12) was directly north of Gamble's, the city of St. John's was south, Lower Gamble's was west and Clare Hall (#13b) was east. The old estate house on top of the hill is currently (2002) the home of Dr. & Mrs. Ivor Heath.

The old Upper Gambles estate house currently the home of Dr. & Mrs. Ivor Heath
Patti Heath

In 1689, merchant George Gamble secured 127 acres and four "proportions" of land in St. John's town, granted July 2nd by Sir N. Johnson. The Honorable George Gamble, age 44, was in considerable debt in 1710, owing the Assembly £2,000, so he mortgaged the estate's 316 acres to Governor Daniel Parke for £6,000.

The estate was then bounded on the east by the property of Captain Giles Watkins, south by the common road leading to Parham, west with the common road leading to Dickenson's Bay and Popeshead, and north by the estate of Jonas Langford (#6) and Jacob Leroux. There is a portrait of Governor Parke painted by Sir Godfrey Kneller and engraved by G. Vertue "with his arms".

"History of the Island of Antigua" by Vere Oliver, Volume II.

Edward Chester (probably Lucy Chester's husband) subsequently purchased the estate, and in 1720 turned it over to the Royal African Company. Lucy is listed as owner as of 1723.

In 1721, the planter Joseph French and his wife Ann sold to Richard Oliver (Clare Hall, #13b), also a planter, their moiety of the Gamble's plantation for £150 and quit claim. Then, in 1723, the merchant Sidney Rodney, executor of the estate of the late Governor Daniel Parke, gave to Thomas D. Parke and his wife Lucy, the Governor's estate of 316 acres, formerly mortgaged by Colonel George Gamble.

"History of the Island of Antigua" by Vere Oliver, Volume II & III.

Gambles plantation in full work order.   Museum of Antigua & Barbuda

Lord Combermere, the son of Viscount Combermere, a British cavalry commander in the early 1800s, distinguished himself in several military campaigns. Combermere Abbey, in Cheshire, England, was founded by Benedictine Monks in 1133. They were evicted from the Abbey in 1540 by King Henry III. The Abbey later became the Seat of Sir George Cotton KT, Vice Chamberlain to the household of Prince Edward, son of King Henry VIII. In 1814, Sir Stapleton Cotton, a descendent of Sir George, took the title "Lord Combermere" and in 1817, became the Governor of Barbados. As Governor, he ordered a professional investigation of "Moving Chase Coffins" located inside a sealed vault. The coffins were said to have been "moved about by unnatural forces." There is a well-known photograph of Lord Combermere's library, taken in 1891 by Sybell Corbet, while the Lord's funeral was underway a few miles distant. He had died after being struck by a horse drawn carriage. The photograph shows Lord Combermere sitting in a chair.

"I remember Colonel Cotton - he was the owner of Gamble's estate and a war man like my boss, Affie Goodwin. He got crippled in the Boer's War. The Colonel was the first man I ever see knit like a Granny."

"To Shoot Hard Labour" by Keithlyn and Fernando C. Smith

In January 1866, there was an exchange of lengthy letters between Viscount Combermere in the U.K. and a Mr. Hartman, who was sent to assess the estates recently purchased by the Viscount. They included Gamble's (#14), Weatherill's (#5), Delap's (#137), Lucas (#135) and Glanville's (#97). To review the detailed correspondence, refer to Weatherill's (#5).

< >

A legacy award of £19,961. 4s. 5p. (Antigua 123) was paid by the British Parliament following the abolition of slavery in 1833 for Gamble's freedom of 115 enslaved. Daniel Hill, deceased, was the primary beneficiary; Vice Admiral John Richard Delap Tollemach (nee Halliday) and John Tollemach (nee Halliday) also were successful claimants. Both Daniel Hill and George Wickham Washington Leadeatt were unsuccessful.

Selvyn Walters, author of *"Not A Drum Was Heard",* remembers being sent to Gamble's by his mother to buy milk. He and his friends also played a game called "Putian" (Lilliputian), a form of cricket played on one's knees using golf balls found in the bushes of Gamble's Golf Course.

Land was acquired from the Gamble's estate by the government for use as a public cemetery, and when someone died it was often referred to as "passing on to No. 10", the number of the field when sugar cane was grown there. Upper Gamble's was turned into Antigua's first nine-hole golf course, and later became a housing development. Rumors claim there supposedly are two ghosts at Gamble's, one being a groom for horses and the other Major Dyett, who wanders around the grounds.

"Major Dyett [he was really a Colonel] *came from near Cheshire, England, and came out to Antigua to manage the Cotton estates* [about 1933]. *One of the Cottons lived at Gambles* [Colonel R. S. Cotton] *and shot someone around the back steps leading people to say the place was haunted. The Major was also haunting the place -- one of our cooks saw him very clearly. At one time Major Dyett lived at Belvedere Estate (#38), which is out in the foothills beyond Greencastle. He died on 15th May 1934 shortly after marrying his second wife, Alice Smith. Major Dyett was not related to the Abbotts, but left McKinnon's* [#10] *to John Abbott (son of Fred Abbott) who died in 1942.* Mary Evelyn Smith.

< >

During Bob Smith's ownership, which began in 1945, Gamble's owned and trained a fine stable of racehorses. It was not unusual, when arriving at the estate house, to see saddles draped over the balcony rail with the currying brushes nearby. Bob ("Whiffy") Smith was an excellent horse trainer. His wife worked at the Antigua Girl's High School and also was the house manager for the Beach Hotel. They had one daughter, Mary Evelyn, who married and settled in Canada.

Lower Gamble's, also known as the Buff House Gamble's, was the domicile of Carlton Moore and his family in the 1950s. He was a Senator, and was very active in the now defunct West Indies Federation. Helen Abbott (see McKinnon's, #10) is certain that Senator Moore purchased Lower Gamble's from the Abbott family after the death of her grandfather, W. J. Abbott. At one time there was a circular "bread and cheese" hedge, planted by Helen's grandfather, in which the Moore children's birthday parties were held. The ruins of the old buff building are still visible to the east of Joseph's Lumber Yard. Mrs. Moore ran a small shop in St. John's, called Moore's, in which she sold cloth and sewing items.

< >

A map drawn by Geoffrey Owen in 1952 shows a sugar mill called "Willows" at the Gamble's site. His map is based on information dating from 1884 - 1891.

In 1872, the Horseford Almanac lists another Gamble's Estate in Five Islands; 157 acres owned by J. E. Anthonyson.

In 1941, the Antigua Sugar Factory Ltd. had cane returns estimated at 1,213 tons: 101 acres under peasants on the estate; 782 tons of cane delivered.

#15 - The Villa Plantation
(aka Daniel's or Morgan's)

The Ownership Chronology

1667:   The first mention of the name Morgan: Rice Morgan, was given a grant of 180 acres in Bermudian Valley on April 17, 1667; registered as a planter in 1672.   *"History of the Island of Antigua"* by Vere Oliver, Volume II.

1722:   Samuel Morgan. Baptized in 1711.

1742:   William Lindsey. d. 1748. 290 acres.

1743:   Jacob Morgan, who died this year: *"I granted to Edward Chester and Peter Horgall my plantation of 216 acres in St. John's Parish."*

1767:   John Lindsey. 231 acres, 114 slaves.

1788:   Thomas Daniel. d. 1806. 1777/78 Luffman map.

1790:   Godschal Johnson, of London, and Samuel Eliot, *"late of Antigua, now of Harley Street* [London] *for 5/- lease those two plantations called Morgan's of 74 acres and Walkins of 93 acres, for one year."*

1806:   Earle Lindsey Daniel. Will: 1813.

1811:   William Lindsey. Will: 1811. Sold two plantations in Antigua to Thomas Daniel. The plantations are not named in his will.

1813:   Earl Lindsay (sic) Daniel. Will: July 9, 1813, forfeited his estate in Dominica *"to pay encomberances on my Villa Estate in Antigua."* He was a Lieutenant in the 12th Dragoons.

1820:   T. Blackburn. 1829: 290 acres, 42 slaves.

1833:   Philip Lyne Thompson.

1851:   Heirs of T. Blackburn.

1878:   Lord Combermere.

1891:   Lord Combermere & C. I. Thomas.

1921:   Colonel R. S. Cotton.

1933:   I. E. Dyett.   1933 Camacho map

1940s: Millie Este or Brysons.

1960s: Dr. Noel Margetson. Site of the plantation house.

2012:   Winter Clinic on the bluff house site.

< >

The estate house was beautifully situated on a knoll to the north of St. John's with a charming view toward the west, overlooking St. John's harbour and Fort

James. The Villa Estate, combined with Gamble's (#14), converted the sugar mill operations to steam around 1872. There is no mill left on this estate, nor any remnants of the old stone works or machinery.

This area was still considered country until the 1950s. One of the locomotive lines crossed Fort Road at the location of the current Kentucky Fried Chicken fast food outlet. Even in the fifties, this was a residential area, which has become very commercialized with the encroachment of St. John's.

<>

Anne Lindsey (b. March 5, 1759), the only daughter of Earl Lindsey Daniel, became the Attorney General of Dominica. She died in 1806. Lord Baronet, or Viscount Combermere, was a title granted to Stapleton Cotton and his family of Combermere Abbey in England. Sir William Stapleton, the first Baronet, laid the foundations of the Stapleton lands and interest in the Leeward Islands, West Indies. At the time of his death in 1688 he had an interest on four islands.

Stapleton Cotton manuscripts, held at Bangor University, Ref. GB0222 STAP

<>

With the abolishment of slavery by the British in 1833, the owner of the Villa, Philip Lyne Thomson, was paid £702. 5s. 2p. (Antigua 106) for granting freedom to 41 enslaved. An additional £1,241. 12s. 3p. (Antigua 107) was paid for the release of 81 enslaved, but records do not indicate the awardee.

<>

"My mother used to visit Millie Este in the 1940s when she lived in the Buff house. In 1951 the old Buff house which was situated off Whapping Lane between Back street and Alfred Peters street, was turned into the Rialto Club which provided a place for table tennis, warrie, dominoes and games for young people. It was also in the Rialto Club that the famous debate on Christianity vs Islam took place in 1951 between Dean Baker, Arnold Chambers and Al Haji Talib Dawud. Islam prevailed that night.   Selvyn Walter, *"Not A Drum Was Heard".*

"Tom Henry, one of the first ALP [Antigua Labour Party] *founders, owned quite a bit of land near the old Buff house, known as Cassie Pasture. Around 1951 he started selling lots in Cassie Pasture."*

In the 1950s/1960s *"The Villa Buff House as I knew it was on the hill behind Barrymore Hotel and a Mr. Fane last lived in the house. The estate used to raise animals, and Mr. Fane managed the property for Brysons, which sold the meat. The house was demolished when Dr. Noel Margetson bought the property and built on the site around the late 50s, early 60s."*   Margaret White.

Dr. Margetson's home (2010), beautifully constructed with Antigua green stone from the Liberta area, is now the site of the Winter Clinic, in near proximity to the Adelin Clinic. The Villa, as we know it today, is a village north of Dickenson Bay Street.

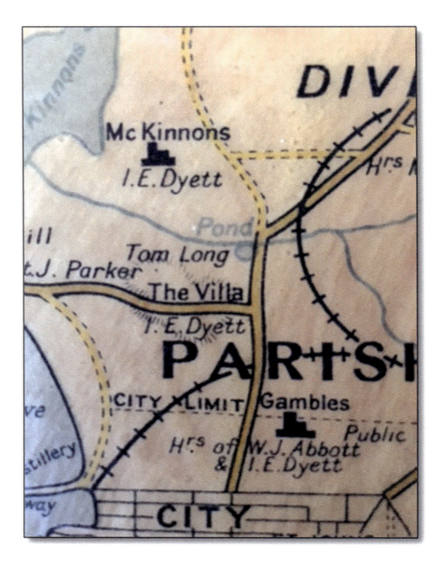

1933 Alex Camacho map showing The Villa owned by I.E. Dyett just below McKinnons (also owned by Dyett) and not far from the City Limit of St. John's.
Agnes C. Meeker

#16 - Otto's Plantation

The Ownership Chronology

1600s: Colonel Sebastiaen Baijer. d. 1704.

1701: Colonel John Otto Baijer. d. 1725.

1790: John Oliver Baijer. d. 1790. 1777/78 Luffman map.

1800: John Otto Baijer. d. 1816.

1829: John Otto Baijer. 678 acres, 165 slaves.

1852: Langford Lovell Hodge. b. 1808; d. 1862. 578 acres.

1856: Daniel Burr Garling. b. 1785; d. 1857.

1860: Samuel Henry Garling. b. 1836; d. 1892.

1872: F. Garraway.

1878: S. Dobee & Sons.

1891: Antonio Joseph Camacho. d. 1894.

1921: John J. Camacho.

1933: W. T. Malone. 1933 Camacho map

< >

The sugar mill on this estate is no longer in existence, but it is known that the estate converted to steam in the mid-1800s under the ownership of F. Garraway.

Horseford Almanac.

Progress and time have obliterated any trace of this estate; however, the area continues to retain the name.

Colonel Sebastiaen, whose signature is conspicuous on the capitulation document ending the French and British war, as well as letters which passed between the two after the war, was of Dutch extraction. He immigrated to Antigua from Holland early in the island's colonization; died in London in 1704. His will, dated 17 June 1701 (proved 26 October 1704 by the executors, recorded at Antigua 17 June 1705), stated *"To my nephew, Bastiaen Otto Baijer, eldest son of my nephew John Otto Baijer, a moiety of my plantation of 588 acres in St. John's Division at 25, and the other moiety to his father."* *"Antigua & the Antiguans"* by Mrs. Lanahan.

His will also specified that his remains should be interred in the vaults of the Dutch church in Austin Friars. Many of his descendants died without issue, and he left his property to the individual who assumed his name. They usually resided on the island for a year or two. The William Crosbie Estate Papers (#2) contain letters from John Otto Baijer, who was the agent/manager for the Crosbie estate (1792-1816).

A print of the Otto's Plantation showing the Buff House, Mill, Works and slave huts.
Jake Underhill

< >

Otto's Buff was situated above Garling's land, south of St. John's, on the hill known as Michael's Mount, where the Mt. St. John Hospital sits today. It overlooked Country Pond. The following quote refers to the area as Otto's Dam or Dam Gutter, names used prior to the actual building of Country Pond:

"Otto's Dam, on what is now called Camacho Avenue, or Dam Gutter as it was back then, was another supply of water in St. John's in times of drought, but Otto's Estate owners never did like to give the city people water. Sometimes the governor have to dip mouth in there for them to get water."

"To Shoot Hard Labour" by Keithlyn and Fernando C. Smith

"Otto's Pasture was where they executed the slaves. Bodies stretched from Gallows Hill, where the archives are now, down past Vivian Richards Street and Temple to Green Hill Bay. Crosses, gibbets and stakes, where slaves were burnt

to death. There is a large tree in the yard of the 'Ah We Soup Shop' near Temple Street, which young children did not want to pass by. Slaves hung from that tree and it was said to be an evil place. Otto's Pasture was a place later where black people met to gamble and fight, a lawless den of iniquity."

"Not A Drum Was Heard" by Selvyn Walter

A 1904 view of the Otto's Plantation works with its unusual square chimney - Foote family album.

The Scottish Kirk, a place of worship, was built on the estate hill where the Archives and Library of Antigua and Barbuda are now located. It was never considered a particularly outstanding building architecturally. *"The half finished Kirk of the Scotchmen, the foundation stone of this place of worship was laid with the usual ceremonies by Sir William Colebrooke, the late governor, on 9th of April, 1839. It is situated upon an ascent the eastern outskirts of the town, and from it may be seen many a lovely landscape. It progresses but slowly. In its present form I can say but little about it, except that the same fault cannot be found with it as there has been with the Methodist chapel - the small size of the windows - for the Scotch kirk appears to be all windows and doors."* "History of the Island of Antigua" by Vere Oliver, Volume I.

The Scottish Kirk about where the Archives is today – Museum of Antigua & Barbuda.

The church was destroyed in the mid-1800s and was never rebuilt, seemingly due to little interest in the Presbyterian religion at that time. The bell was given to the Anglican Cathedral, and is most likely still located in its North tower, which houses a collection of 13 old bells that comprise the carillon, including one from the Golden Grove estate (#23). One large bell enables the clock to strike the hour. It is inscribed: "Presented by W. H. Thompson and A. Coltart to the Presbyterian Church, Antigua, Thomas Mears Founder, London 1842." That bell from the Scottish Kirk is approximately 30 inches high not including the bracket on top, with a diameter of 40 inches at the base.

It is cast in bronze. The South tower has two bells: one for weddings and one for funerals.

< >

Otto's was paid a Legacy award (Antigua 108) by the British Parliament, in 1833, of £2,549. 6s. 1p. for freeing 175 enslaved. The only awardee was Langford Lovell, who owned the estate at that time.

Also in 1843, Antigua experienced a very severe earthquake between eight and nine in the evening. *"There were twenty-one distinct shocks felt between twelve at night and five in the morning. A fire broke out at Otto's estate, which was supposed by many to have been occasioned by a meteor striking a wooden building. Credence was leant to this when the attorney of Otto's estate witnessed a meteor descend upon a branch of a coconut tree, which grew near his house, and set it on fire."* "History of the Island of Antigua" by Vere Oliver, Volume I.

An 1844 census shows Richard Abbott as manager at Otto's Plantation; the overseer was Alfred Nanton. Phillip Abbott, memories of . . .

< >

Daniel Burr Garling appears to have arrived in Antigua around 1804, if not before. Blue Books show that Daniel was Assistant Superintendent at Skerretts (#114) in 1804; Acting Assistant Superintendent of Agriculture that same year; 2nd Outdoor Officer in the Treasury in 1805; and Acting Harbourmaster and 1st Outdoor Officer in the Treasury in 1807 and 1809. At the time of his death he had served for 27 years. The Government recommended an annual allowance of £50 for his wife, which the Colonial Office approved.

Between 1818 and 1856, he wrote 59 letters from Antigua for the Bible Society and was very involved with the Wesleyan-Methodist Church and the preaching of Nathaniel Gilbert. He attended the laying of the corner stone in 1837.

"Six Months Tour of Antigua & Jamaica" by James Thomas & Horace Kimball

Daniel's name appears on the 1822 Committee for the English Harbour Sunday School Society for Boys and Girls. The Vice Chairman was John Gilbert, Esq., and the Superintendent of the Girl's School and Book Steward was Mrs. Gilbert.

In 1849, Daniel was listed as the attorney for thirty-nine estates. His letters from 1830 show his support for emancipation and state *"in the year 1833 the Gang of Slaves which were at Crawford's are to be free -- about 150 people old and young, & I believe a patch of ground will be purchased for them to live & maintain themselves upon. So Antigua is likely to be first honoured with a free peasantry. Hitherto no free persons will work in the field & this makes a great difficulty in the planter's way -- but often these people will occasionally hire themselves out as a Gang to hole by the acre or do other work to which they have been accustomed, surely some facilities will be given to a new and better order of things. I hope you pray for Slaves & for the inhabitants of Antigua generally at times -- you ought, as most of your ease & comfort spring from thence."*

Daniel Burr Garling, prior to his ownership of Otto's estate in 1858, was an attorney for several of Antigua's sugar plantation owners. He left the estate to his son, Samuel Henry Garling, whose wife was Harriet Maria (nee Caddy) and his daughter was Caroline Sophia Garling. He was the author's great-great-great-grandfather, and several letters have been found which he wrote to a Mr. Charles Curtis (see sample). It is a quaint mixture of business and idle chatter, while the use of words such as "cuten" and "quire" are no longer in today's vocabulary.

"April 19th 1808

"Dear Sir:

You wrote for paper. I have sent you some of two sorts cuten. Use the receipt of the best quire (foolscap) in the Plantation Journal the other is good enough for a sick house book. You have omitted to charge Geo Buttery's Board which to 31st December last at £40 the annum amounts to £28-11-11½ - being 8 months & 18 days. Mr. Hill paid you £18 on 22nd December in this respect. I believe your account is right. The Fleet is gone or going -- They endeavour to get away at twelve O'clock. Twas well you found Capt Head as old Drysdale is so grumpsious he may fret himself to death in the passage. - Neighbour Altus writes me that his disappointment with Miss Fanny has laid so heavy on his heart that he had the fever all night and is very unwell today -- I have half a mind to send her a billet with the distressing information -- poor fellow. The mail just arrived. I have not yet heard the News.

Yours sincerely, Daniel B. Garling"

An excerpt from Daniel's December 1857 will reads: *"I give and bequeath to my dear wife for and during the term of her natural life and in lieu of and bar of Dower all that my Estate of Plantation called The Otto Estate situated lying and being in the Parish of St. John on this island containing 6 hundred and Seventy seven acres of land or thereabouts together with the Mills sugar works Mansions and other buildings and premises thereon belong with all their uses mules cattle sheep and other live and dead Stock though subject nevertheless to the lease of certain lands to Robert John Barton and afterwards to my son Samuel Henry Garling and subject also to annual sums of payment to be made to our dear children namely the sum of One Hundred and Eighty Pounds to our dear son Samuel Henry and the sum of Eighty Pounds to our dear daughter Caroline Sophia payable to each one half every six months the first of such half yearly payments to be made and become due one month after the day of my decease."*

< >

Samuel Henry Garling, Daniel's son, became a merchant in St. John's, and gambled away the family's fortune and the estate until there was just a narrow strip of land between Mt. Saint John Medical Center and the harbor known as "Garling's Land". Title to that land was transferred to his wife, Harriet Maria Garling.

Samuel left Antigua on a ship in 1868 and was never heard from again. A death notice of Samuel Henry Garling was listed in the Post Office Directory at Grevilles, 258 miles north of Sydney, Macquarie (Index 10851/1892), District of Parramatta, a suburb of Sydney. It lists "parents unknown." The author's grandmother, Margaret Furlong Conacher (nee McSevney) remembers as a young girl having to accompany her grandmother, Harriet Garling, every Saturday in a buggy c.1914 as she collected rent from the poor residing in Garling's land. The rent was only one or two shillings at the time, but people were hard pressed to pay it. *"My grandmother did not look forward to collecting it, but the income was necessary for the family's survival after the disappearance of her grandfather, Samuel Garling."*

The last of the land, sold to individuals in 1948, settled the Garling's estate, £3,870 was divided between heirs Mrs. Goodall, Mr. N. Garling, Mrs. A. Goodwin, Mrs. Duncan and Mrs. M. Conacher. On the sale of the property, there was mention of Lot 10, which sold for $890; Lot 11A sold for $1,200; and Lot 11B sold for $1,440. At the time, the dollar in Antigua was equivalent to 100 English halfpennies, or £0. 4s. 2p.

< >

1918: *"The Contract Act and wages were being renegotiated which caused much unrest within the labour force of the sugar industry when Colonel Bell was Chief of Police. Cane fires were set at Otto's estate and in the early morning hours at Gamble's (#14), just outside St. John's. The next morning, the cane cutters at Otto's refused to cut the damaged canes and the owner sent in cutters from another of the estates, under police protection.*

"At this time (Chief) Bell thought he had everything under control and that night another field was set alight very close to Government House. Four men were identified in the crowd as the ringleaders and Bell was determined to arrest them: Joseph Collins, George Weston, John Furlong and 'Sonny' Price. They not only lived in the city, but lived in the Point area considered a law unto itself. Upon arrest Furlong escaped but was later killed that afternoon.

"At this point a large crowd gathered from Popeshead and Newgate down to Point with the rallying cry 'no payment by the ton' and the militia was called in

to disperse them. Several bayonet charges were attempted and then an order to fire. Fifteen people were injured, two or three subsequently died. Thirty-eight were arrested and at least half of them were women who had all been throwing stones. A curfew was set but the unrest continued and Col. Bell called in reinforcements, which included a British patrol boat. However, all was quiet by the time they arrived. A large rock in the sidewalk on the corner of Popeshead and Newgate streets commemorate the riots."   *"Antigua History"* by Susan Lowes

"The family loved Ottos Estate. The manager and my grandfather were 'tinkin kin' friends and not even the wind could blow between them. At that time most people wanted to live in the capital, St. John's, or close to it. Ottos Estate was only a few yards away. The midwifes were close by, so too were the Women Healers, the market, milk for the baby and tobacco for my grandfather."

Aunty Dood in *"Symbol of Courage"*.

< >

Antonio Joseph Camacho (d. 1894), owned Otto's as of 1891, plus several other plantations, as noted in previous plantation descriptions.

In 1941, the Antigua Sugar Factory Ltd. cane returns from Otto's were estimated at 1,585 tons from 68 acres. Tons of cane actually delivered: 822 at 9.72 tons per acre.

Additional information on Otto's estate can be found at the National Archives, Kew Gardens, England, as referenced below. These records are not digitized but are available to researchers visiting on site. **
* 1855-1876 Papers, Correspondence, Plans and Deeds: Garroway: Otto's: Antigua; No.102. Held at The National Archives (UK) - ColoniaL OFFICE REF. #CO441/11/1.
** 1855 - 1876 Papers, Correspondence, Plans, Deeds: Garroway: Otto's Antigua No. 102. Held at the National Archives (UK) - Colonial Office Ref. #CO 441/11/4.

A water colour painting of the mill at Ottos.
Jake Underhill

#17 - Tomlinson's Plantation

The Ownership Chronology

1708: Walter Philips. In 1709, he granted 264 acres and 16 slaves to John Tomlinson, the second husband of Elizabeth Philips.

1709: Major John Tomlinson. d. 1739. He was granted 106 acres by Governor Parke. In 1744 Tomlinson was Chief Baron of Exchequer, a member of the Council in 1745 and Deputy Governor of Antigua in 1753.

1750: John Tomlinson, Jr. d. 1758.

1758: John Tomlinson, Esq. d. 1761.

1790: Heirs of John Tomlinson.   1777/78 Luffman map.

1802: Penelope Tomlinson. b. 1735; d.1806. see codicil of her will, 1805: *"Power to trustees to let my plantation called 'Tomlinson's' and houses in High St., St. John's.* 2nd codicil: *All my real estate to my kinsman Wm. White of Antigua free and simple, and not in trust.*
"History of the Island of Antigua" by Vere Oliver, Volume III.

1812: William White.

1830: Elizabeth Montgomerie (nee White).

1843: John Osborne. 600 acres, 149 slaves.

1872: Francis Shand. d. 1868. 600 acres. The sugar mill was steam powered.

1891: Heirs of Francis Shand.

1921: DuBuisson & Alexander Moody-Stuart. b. 1899; d. 1974.

1943: Antigua Syndicate Estates, Ltd.

1969: Antigua & Barbuda Syndicate Estates, Ltd. (Vesting Act).

1981: Vere Cornwall Bird. b. December 9, 1910; d. June 28, 1999. Prime Minister's residence.

< >

The sugar mill still stands on this estate, one of those converted to steam in the mid-1800s. The house is not the original, which was riddled with wood rot. It was replaced in 1948 by Sir Alex Moody Stuart who raised his family there until his retirement, when he returned to London. A few outbuildings and the garden wall can be seen. Surrounding estates would have been Paynter's (#61), Potter's (#47) and Cassada Gardens (#13a).

The plantation's sugar mill was converted to steam in mid-1800s.
- Agnes C. Meeker.

The home was occupied, in 1981 by Antigua's first Prime Minister, Sir Vere Cornwall Bird Sr. (December 9, 1910 - June 28, 1999). He and Sir George Walters (the second Prime Minister) were both interred in the walled front garden. V. C. Bird is considered The Father of the Country because he was Antigua's first Prime Minister after it received its independence from England in 1981. He designated the Tomlinson estate house as the Prime Minister's official residence. His son, Lester Bird, was elected to succeed him as Prime Minister in 1994.

V. C. Bird was declared a national hero. He was unique from other West Indian politicians, lacking in any formal education except primary school. He attended St. John's Boys School, now known as the T. N. Kirnon Primary School. He was an officer in the Salvation Army for two years, interspersing his interests in trade unionism and politics. He gave up the Salvation Army and decided to leave his post to campaign for the freedom of his people because of the way the local Antiguan and Barbudan landowners were being treated. This he succeeded in doing.

In 1943, he became President of the Antigua Trades & Labor Union (ATLU). He achieved national acclaim politically for the first time when he was elected to the Colonial Legislature in 1945. He formed the Antigua Labor Party (ALP) and became the first and only Chief Minister, and first Prime Minister, an office he held from 1981 to 1994. He resigned due to failing health and internal issues within the government. V. C. Bird died in 1999.

In 1985, Antigua's international airport, which was first named Coolidge, was renamed V. C. Bird International Airport in his honour. There also is a large statue of him, created by a Cuban artist, which stands near the public market in St. John's, as well as a small bust of him across from the Central Post Office. The lands surrounding his burial place have been declared the Hero's Park Cemetery, and the home became a museum after his death, but suffers from a lack of upkeep. The Tomlinson's estate property is located on a small rise, which afforded a 360-degree view of the surrounding flat land, and access to cooling breezes from the trade winds.

< >

Major John Tomlinson held the post of Chief Baron of the Exchequer in 1744, was a member of the Council in 1745, and Deputy Governor of Antigua in 1753. His will, dated 29 May 1758, states:

"To my dau(ghter) Lydia 2 negroes & 1000 pounds st. To my dau(ghter) Jane 3 negroes & 1000 pounds st. To my dau(ghter) Eliz(abeth) 2 negroes & 1000 pounds st. To my dau(ghter) Alice 2 negroes & 1000 pounds st. to my dau(ghter) Penelope 2 negroes and 1000 pounds st. To my said 5 dau(ghter)s. My title to the house, now in the possession of John Hoskins. All residue to my son John, he and William McKinnon & Harvey Webb, Esqrs. & 20 pounds c. each. Witnessed by Thomas Fraser, Ashton Warner, Dr. William Millar. Codicil. My Ex'ors to repair my said dwelling house in St. John's. To my 5 daus. Equally my furniture, linen, plate, china, wine, sheep & 30 pistoles. Witnessed by James Scott, Thomas Fraser 13 ---- 1753." "History of the Island of Antigua" by Vere Oliver, Volume III.

The 1802 will of Penelope Tomlinson, and a codicil dated 1805 states: *"Power to trustees to let my plantation called 'Tomlinsons' and houses in High Street, St. John's. 2nd codicil - all my real estate to my kinsman Wm. White of Antigua in fee simple, and not in trust."* "History of the Island of Antigua" by Vere Oliver, Volume III.

By the time Penelope wrote her will in 1805, she was the sole surviving sister, and names no nieces, nor nephews. She left legacies to various MacKinnons, the children of her first cousin on her mother's side, and to various Whites, the children of her eldest first cousin on her father's side.

She left Tomlinson's estate in Antigua to William White, the eldest son of her first cousin Michael White. However, the compensation for Tomlinson's was awarded to the executors of Marie White for a mortgage of £10,000 and upwards. The initial claimant for Tomlinson's was John Osborn as owner-in-fee. His relationship to the Tomlinson family has yet to be established.

< >

A Legacy payment of £2,220. 8s. 11p. (Antigua 111) was made by the British Parliament to Tomlinson's in 1833 for granting freedom to 145 enslaved. Elizabeth Montgomerie (nee White) was the awardee. Crisp Molineaux Montgomerie was the awardee's executor. J. H. Forbes is listed as "other association." Unsuccessful were Thomas Tomlinson, Crisp Molineaux Montgomerie, Elizabeth Hamilton White, Lydia White, Maria White, Michael White and William White.

< >

The sailing vessel *Clara* left Hong Kong in 1881 with 128 Chinese men, arriving in Antigua on February 1, 1882 with only 100 passengers, the others having died on board, according to the captain. The 100 who arrived were not greeted with enthusiasm, according to an article published in the *Antigua Times.* They also did not settle well in Antigua, engaging in a dispute over the payment of wages with the Chinese doctor and interpreter who came with them, accusing them of having been *"in collusion with the enlisting agent to mislead them."*

Almost a year passed without further incident, but the *Antigua Times* reported on Wednesday, January 17, 1883: *"Chinese from several estates congregated at Tomlinson's on Sunday, and consulted with each other . . . and they decided that some 9 planters against whom they hold some ill feeling, should be subject to death."* Mr. Look Lai referred in the news article to *"burning properties"*. In an excerpt from Colonial Correspondence, Look Lai states that the Governor, Sir J. H. Glover, reported that two Chinese labourers, Lee Sung and Ah Kung, were executed on January 29, 1883 within the walls of the gaol for the murder of Mr. Augustus Lee, the manager of Green Castle Estate (#163).

"Chinese in the West Indies 1805-1995" by Walton Look Lai

< >

In 1940 the Antigua Sugar Estates issued 18,000 shares of stock, at £1 each to three members of the DuBuisson family (James Memoth DuBuisson, Mrs. Edith Manus DuBuisson, and William Herman DuBuisson) as well as Alexander Moody-Stuart and Judith Gwendolyn Moody-Stuart. George Moody-Stuart declined the shares he was offered. Antigua Syndicate Estate minutes of January 4 and May 1, 1940.

This was a watershed event, signaling the final shift to the next generation. The estates which would be controlled by the company included Gunthorpe's

(#64), Paynter's (#61), Tomlinson's (#17), Fitche's Creek (#67), Donovan's (#65), North Sound (#66), Cedar Valley (#42), Galley Bay (#30) and Five Islands (#31).

Gunthorpe's Sugar Estates Ltd., however, was restructured into a "new" company on August 1, 1943. This firm was called Antigua Syndicate Estates, Ltd., dropping the word "Sugar" mindful that Antigua's sugar refining business was essentially non-existent by the 1940s. Over the next year, this new firm purchased the original estates owned by Antigua Sugar Estates, including Tomlinson's and the tractor workshop from Gunthorpe's Estate.

George Moody-Stuart CBE (1851 - 1940), who declined shares in the firm Antigua Sugar Estates, first came to Antigua and St. Kitts in 1890. He never resided in Antigua, but visited the island for several weeks annually between New Years and Easter. He was responsible for establishing the central factories for the Antigua Sugar Estates firm in 1904 and St. Kitts in 1911. The factories were owned by London-based companies and managed by Henckell DuBuisson & Company.

George remained Chairman of these companies (Antigua Sugar Estates, which became Antigua Syndicate Estates, and Henckell & DuBuisson & Company) until 1937. He was succeeded by oldest son, Mark. His youngest son, Sir Alexander Moody-Stuart, came to Antigua in 1942 to manage the Gunthorpe's group of estates as well as the Codrington (#77a/b) and Tudway (#77a/b, #93) estates which had been acquired by his father and associates in 1944. His goal was to bring higher standards of agriculture to more of the sugar cane area, and he formed the firm Antigua Syndicate Estates Ltd., which he managed until his retirement in 1961. His firm was eventually acquired by Antigua Sugar Factory Ltd.

Sir Alec Moody-Stuart
Margaret Moody-Stuart Groom

He was born in Wimbledon, England, in 1899, attended Cambridge for his Masters after serving in World War II as a teenager. He was wounded three times and received a Military Cross. He was in the first class of the School of Tropical Agriculture in Trinidad (now University of the West Indies). In 1925 he married Judy Henzell, the daughter of Len and Lena Henzell who built the Gunthorpes Sugar Factory in 1905 and managed it until 1937. Sir Alexander Moody-Stuart was an agronomist, and with other cane farmers founded the Syndicate Estates, where he was a manager and director. He also was the local agent for PanAm Airlines, which made its first flight into Antigua in 1929. Alec was knighted in 1960 cited for services to agriculture in the Caribbean, especially education. The residents of Antigua had raised more per capita for the college in Trinidad than any other island. Sir Alexander's son, George Moody-Stuart (named after his grandfather), managed the Antigua factory for the London firm of Henckell DuBuisson & Co. from 1961 until 1968, when it became obvious that sugar production on the island was no longer economically worthwhile. The island's government under V. C. Bird then stepped in to purchase Antigua Sugar Factory Ltd., struggled to run the firm for a few years, then closed it.

Memoirs of George Moody-Stuart.

Moody-Stuart children and
their famous donkey cart.
Margaret Moody-Stuart Groom

The Moody-Stuart children in their
famous donkey cart at Tomlinson's.

Margaret Moody Stuart Groom.

The Moody-Stuart children were famous for their donkey cart, which provided them with hours of fun. It was also used at the annual Government House fancy dress parties to provide attending children with rides around the gardens. And it was a hit at Bishop Mather's school room (across from Country Pond) and Anglican fetes, and at the Antigua Girls's High School celebrations. The donkey cart was eventually given to the Spencer family who were living at Lavington's (#121).

In her memoirs, Margaret (Moody-Stuart) Groom wrote: *"At Tomlinson's old house there was a big store underneath in which they kept tallow, rope and coffins of plain white wood. They were there in case someone on an estate died on a Saturday night in which case the mule cart would be sent on Sunday to pick up the coffin. Burials took place on the same day and the workshop was always closed on Sunday. The new house was built by Terry Peters who was a Seventh Day Adventist and who had ten daughters. Every Saturday morning they would walk to town in 'Sunday best' in a series with the little ones first. Mrs. Peters used to weave our hats out of date palm that we wore to ride in. The stone that is cut at an angle by the doors of the new house came from the ruins at Betty's Hope. The architect who designed the house was a Mr. Mitchell, who drew the plans for a lot of the estate houses and also the new Potters School. That school had sloping sides, more room at the top than at floor level and I was told it was because you needed lots of oxygen to learn!*

"The workshop grew immensely. There was a large mahogany tree which was down in the yard that was used for shade for the carpenters with the blacksmith's shop down below. This later died when they stored barrels of weed killer under it that leaked. They made the mule cartwheels there, then put the steel band around the wheel and put it in the water pit to cool. I can remember it well as we spent hours watching. Later they put up a huge lumber store and eventually a 6ft. fence - probably to stop us bugging the men for wood and nails."

Memoirs of Margaret (Moody-Stuart) Groom.

The Moody-Stuart name was again popularized during the fight with the Antigua Workers Union, headed by V. C. Bird, in the early 1950s. This was thirty years before Antigua achieved its independence and Mr. Bird became Prime Minister.

Lawrence Royer, in his 1948 memoirs, wrote: *"The Syndicate workshop was situated below the buff house at Tomlinson's and J.C. Webster was shop manager in 1948. He built 'Baron Villa' across the road. He raised chickens in a fenced area where the gas station is now on the corner, but nearly every night someone would steal a fowl and he gave up in disgust and turned it into a cane field.*

"Electricity still depended on batteries but at Tomlinson's they were charged by a Delco generator and it was my job to check the oil daily at age 11. It was also used to pump the water from the pond and catchments. After school I knocked around the shop and often went out on the road with Eddy Barnes who was the chief mechanic. There was King the welder, Mr. Moore was the shopkeeper and Mr. Lake was on the lathe. There was a Wheelright who made the cart wheels out of greenheart and banded them right there. This work shop was very crucial and maintained all the syndicate mechanical equipment such as the ploughs, tractors, trucks, etc. They could make any part in that workshop. There was a Giant tiller (rota tiller) that my father used to be the night watchman for in 1938 before he returned to Dominica."

Memoirs of Lawrence Royer, 1948

"Douglas Luery, who is very interested in machines, locomotives, etc., apparently has been searching for the rota tiller for several years. It was huge: so large the ground shook as it rumbled over the ground tilling the soil. Only a few were built, and were sent to various places in the Colonies, India, etc."

In 1969 the lands of the Antigua & Barbuda Sugar Factory Limited and the Antigua & Barbuda Syndicate Estates Limited (Vesting Act), 30th December 1969, were described as *"all that piece or parcel of land forming part of Tomlinson's, approximately 4,946 acres as contained in Certificate of Title No. 6211951 dated 15th September 1951 and registered in Register Book J Folio 157."*

< >

Pam and Terry Tyrrell arrived in Antigua in 1952, early ex-pats, when Terry was hired to manage the Syndicate Estates machine work shop at Tomlinson's. The house they were to live in at the estate was not ready for them so they were housed in the Beach Hotel. That first night, Pam viewed the moonrise over the water and the waving coconut trees and vowed she would never leave Antigua. She never did. She founded a Toy Shop on High Street in 1955, then moved it onto Long Street, and finally Redcliffe Quay where the shop is still operating today in 2016.

Tomlinson's had a terrific garden, which included sweet peas and asparagus among other vegetables. Pam kept it liberally watered. She had no fridge so Terry made her an ice-box which they stocked weekly from the fisheries. Pam was amazed at the huge influx of expats moving to Antigua expecting creature comforts such as air conditioning, washing machines and refrigerators.

Terry devised a cane-cutting machine. It was never put into operation, but he continued searching for a more efficient mechanical way to harvest the cane crop. He was, however, very successful with T. J. Wolfe & Co. (Pam's father), which produced a fun, run-about car called the Hustler.

Top – the old estate house destroyed in the late 40's.
Margaret Groom nee Moody-Stuart
Bottom – the new Tomlinson's estate house.   Agnes C. Meeker

Pam recalled that when the crop was finished all of the island's locomotives would be decorated with boughs of flamboyant flowers.

Elsa Hollander was an agent for Pan Am and one day told Pam she had dreamed that the flight Pam had booked her children on was going to crash. Pam immediately pulled her children, Mike and Nickie, off the flight, which did crash into a mountain on Montserrat, something Pam could never forget.

Memories of Pam Tyrrel.

#18 - Drew's Hill Plantation

The Ownership Chronology

1700s: Samuel Morgan. b. 1711.

1742: William Lindsey. d. 1748.

1748: Reverand William Lindsey. Baptized: 1758. d. 1812. A complicated indenture relating to the relationship between Thomas Daniel and the Lindsey family.

1750: Captain William Mathew. b. c1684; d. 1752.

1777: John Conyers. 1777/78 Luffman map.

1811: Thomas Daniel. Will, 1806.

1829: Heirs of Thomas Blackburn. The estate contained 290 acres and 42 slaves.

1840: Thomas Blackburn,

1852: Honorable Burnthorn Musgrave. b. 1823; d. 1894. 253 acres.

1872: Mrs. Emma Purvis. She also owned Belmont (#19) and Herbert's (#20); total acreage, 788. The mills had converted to steam.

1878: Lord Combermere. (Stapleton-Cotton family, UK).

1891: Lord Combermere & C. I. Thomas.

1921: Colonel R.S. Cotton.

1933: I. E. Dyett.   1933 Camacho map

1940s: Millie Este or Brysons.

< >

Drew's Hill (aka "Drew's Gift") combined with the Gamble's Estate (#14) when Gamble's converted its sugar mill from wind to steam power in the mid-1800s. There is no mill left on this site, but there is an undated map of Drew's Hill which identifies its borders abutting the Belmont Estate (#19) on the north, the Potter's Estate (#47) and Potter's Village on the west, the Briggin's Estate (#22) on the east, and the Otto's Estate (#16) on the south.

The first mention of the last name Morgan appears when a Rice Morgan, an Antiguan planter, was given a grant of 180 acres in Bermudian Valley on April 17, 1667 (registered in 1672). Samuel Morgan, obviously a relative, sold "Morgan's" (more often called the Villa Estate, #15) to William Lindsey in 1742.

"History of the Island of Antigua" by Vere Oliver, Volume II.

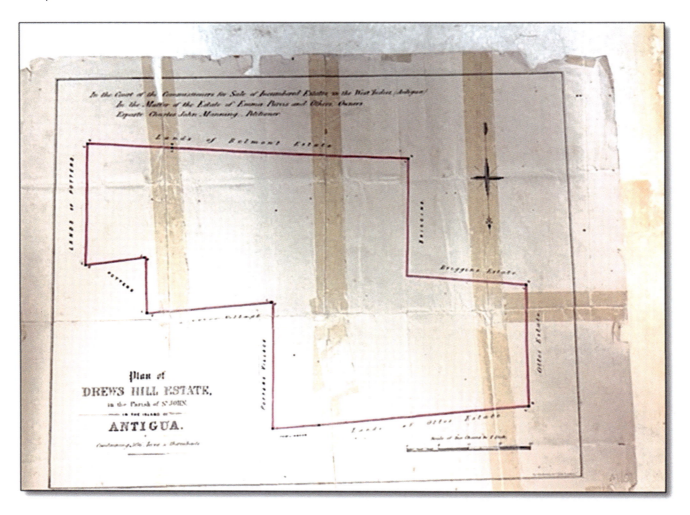

An old plot map shows the boundaries of the Drew's Hill Plantation.
Museum of Antigua & Barbuda

Mary Elizabeth Murray, wife of Andrew Murray, held a moiety by the will of a John Drew in 1716. In that same year Andrew and Elizabeth sold, for 7 shillings, "150 acres and a boiling house" to Archibald Cochran, Esq. and Frances Delap, merchant, both of Antigua. Then in 1724, Andrew Murray is listed as possessing 175 acres "of Drew's Gift".

By 1752, Captain-General William Mathews, of the Leeward Islands, *"charged with 1,500 pounds for my grandson William payable at the termination of Colonel Gilbert's lease of Drew's Hill . . . whereas I own 5 rocks called the 5 islands* (Five Islands, #31) *close by Antigua and Crabb Island and the 2 little islands near by called the Great and Little Passage. I give the 5 islands to go with Drew's Hill and the other to go with Peitenny and Cupid's Garden in St. Kitts. The schedule of Negroes on Drew's Hill: 97 men, 17 boys, 75 women, 6 girls, 32 infants."*

"History of the Island of Antigua" by Vere Oliver, Volume II.

Then in 1761 a John Murray, obviously a relative of Andrew and Elizabeth, is identified as the occupant of Drew's Hill, *"bounded North by the land now or late of His Excellency William Mathew, Esq, East by the lands now or late of Thomas Nicholls, Esq., and John Williams, Esq., and West by the lands now or late of the said Edward Chester.*   *"History of the Island of Antigua"* by Vere Oliver, Volume II.

It is clear that the Murray clan occupied Drew's Hill Estate for many years, but never actually owned the property.

William Lindsey, who owned the estate as of 1742, noted in his will dated 1811 that he had sold his two plantations in Antigua and Dominica to Thomas Daniel, Esq., the father of Earl Lindsey Daniel, Esq., and was still owed £1,500. Ms. Lindsey, the only daughter of John Lindsey, married Thomas Daniel of the Villa's Estate (#15) in 1788. He was the Attorney General of Dominica, and died in 1806.   *"History of the Island of Antigua"* by Vere Oliver, Volume I.

< >

Anthony Musgrave, MD, was born in Antigua in November 1793, educated in Edinburgh, Scotland, and became a doctor in 1814. He married Mary Harris Sheriff and they had thirteen children. Dr. Musgrave served as an Assemblyman of Antigua in 1817, the same year he published a book about the history of yellow fever, which was regularly prevalent on the island. He also authored many articles for medical journals abroad.

He served as Treasurer of the Island's government from 1824 to 1852 and passed away in Antigua on February 24 of that year.

In 1852, when Burnthorn Musgrave, a descendent of Dr. and Mrs. Musgrave, assumed ownership of Drew's Hill with 253 acres in St. John's Parish, he also owned Gaynor's (#108) with 67 acres, and Wickham's (#105) with 216 acres, both in St. Philip's Parish. Burnthorn Musgrave was first a sugar planter in Antigua, and then became a clergyman of the Reformed Episcopal Church of America. He was born on the island on March 11, 1823, and married Frances Albony on June 30, 1847. Frances was the daughter of John Adams and Margaret (Albony) Wood. They had six children. Burnthorn settled in "Holworth" at, King's County, England, in May 1870, and died there on July 19, 1894. Frances died there in 1893.

Fanny Wood Musgrave (1850 - 1947) another descendent of Dr. Anthony and Mrs. Musgrave's, spent her early years on Antigua, where her grandfather and great-grandfather had held public office.

< >

The Stapleton-Cotton family held the title of Viscount Combermere. Further information on the Combermere-Cotton family may be found at Bangor University, Great Britain, 0222 STAP Manuscripts 1701-1884.

The Drew's Plantation was granted a Legacy award by the British Parliament, in 1833 (Antigua 114), of £2,159. 13s. 1p. for granting freedom to 144 enslaved in 1833. Robert Grant was attorney; Joseph Weston (deceased) and Mary Weston were the awardees.

In 1860, Drew's Estate was involved in a legal petition by John Manning, Petitioner: *"In the Court of the Commissioner for sale of encumbered estates in the West Indies (Antigua). In the matter of the Estate of [Mrs.] Emma Purvis and Other Owners. Exparte Charles John Manning, Petitioner.* Mrs. Purvis is listed as the owner of Drew's Hill in 1872.

#19 - Belmont/Murray's Plantation

The Ownership Chronology

1667:   Lieutenant Colonel Sebastian Baijer. d. 1704.

1701:   Captain Sebastian Otto-Baijer. d. 1724. White marble tomb in St. John's Church yard.

1790:   John Otto-Baijer. b. 1703. 1777/78 Luffman map.

1829:   John Otto-Baijer. 678 acres, 165 slaves.

1843:   Langford Lovell.

1857:   Daniel Burr Garling. b. 1785; died 1875.

1870:   Samuel Henry Garling. b. 1836; d. 1892.

1872:   Mrs. Emma Purvis. She owned 788 acres, which included Belmont, Herbert's (#20) and Drew's Hill (#18). Belmont's sugar mill also had been converted from wind to steam power in the mid 1800s.

1878:   S. Dobee & Sons.

1891:   Antonio Joseph Camacho. d. 1894.

1894:   John J. Comacho. d. 1929.

1921:   Aubrey J. Camacho.

1933:   J. Dew & Sons Ltd. 1933 Camacho map

< >

The Belmont Estate was located off All Saints Road, but there is nothing left of it except for the name given to the area. As noted above, the sugar mill had been converted to steam power, along with several other estates in the mid-1800s, when it was owned by Mrs. Emma Purvis. The Belmont Clinic, located on All Saints Road, is one notable business in the area.

Lt. Col. Bastian Baijer, the original owner, was granted 500 acres in the St. John's Division by then Governor Austin. He also was granted an additional 18 acres by Governor Keynell, and obtained 728 acres in Popeshead Division and another 140 acres (location not identified). A surveyor determined that St. John's had "run out" 25 feet of the Colonel's land on the south side, which he had owned since April 11, 1688. His counsel (W. Hinde, Esq.) proved he had the land from Robert Hollingworth.

The elder John Otto Baijer was baptized in St. John's in 1703, and grew to own Belmont, Otto's Estate (#16), Five Islands (#31) and Cooke's Estate (#26). Both Belmont and Otto's were later sold to Daniel Burr Garling.

"History of the Island of Antigua" by Vere Oliver, Volume I.

In his book *"Five of the Leewards"*, author Douglas Hall includes a table of sugar crop production for the six Estates owned by a Mr. Shand: (Belmont/ Murray's, Belle Vue/Stoney Hill (#36), Cedar Valley (#42), Will Blizzards (#54), Blubber Valley (#168) and Rose Valley (#216), for the years 1832 through 1847, as follows:

Year	Avg. Labor Cost/cwt.	Avg. Total Cost/p.cwt.	1 as % of 2	Comment
1832	-	11/4d	-	slavery
1833	-	8/1d	-	slavery
1834	-	5/2d	-	slavery
1835	3/10d	8/7d	44.7	(1st yr wage labour)
1836	5/11d	16/2d	36.6	(hurricane)
1837	10/7d	29/1d	36.9	(drought. Contract Act in operation.)
1838	4/5	7/8d	58.7	
1839	4/-	7/11d	50.5	
1840	7/3d	15/1d	48.1	(Severe drought)
1841	10/11d	12/6d	80.7	(Daily wage 6-9d)
1842	12/5d	15/9d	78.8	(Ind. villages forming
1843	8/11d	15/10d	56.3	(Earthquake Feb.)
1844	11/1d	23/1d	48.0	(Repairs in progress
1845	11/5d	19/7d.	58.3	(Severe drought/fld)
1846	20/9d	35/6	58.5	(Imports Madeirans)
1847	9/6d	17/11d	53.1	(Madeirans at work)

Mr. Shand lived in Antigua from 1832 to 1841. It is interesting to note the years of slavery vs. the first year wages were paid (1835); the years of severe drought; the year that villages started to be built (1842); and the year (1846) when many Portuguese arrived from Madeira for a five-year indentureship.

S. Dobbee & Sons and W. Parker & Co. were small firms that also purchased estates through the court: W. Parker & Co. bought Hawse (#79), Mercer's Creek (#78), Big Duers (#89), Little Duers (#90) and Lower Freeman's (#82); S. Dobbee

& Sons bought Belmont, Otto's (#5) and Blackman's (#63). The two companies sold off these properties to individuals, and both firms were gone by 1891.

"Sugar and Empire" by Susan Lowes.

< >

Belmont received a Legacy award from the British Parliament (Antigua 128) of £2,386. 2s. 4p. for granting freedom to 160 slaves. The awardees were William Musgrave, William Shand and Charles Wollaston. Meade Horne Daniell was unsuccessful.

Admiral Tollemach (Weatherill's #5) sent his nephew William Bertie Wolseley (d. 1881) to run his estates of Weatherill's, Gambles (#14), Delaps (#137) and several others. Bertie first resided at Weatherill's, then moved to Belmont/Murray's in 1828 and may have owned and received compensation in 1835 of £159. 3s. 3p. for granting freedom to 11 slaves.

The Antigua Sugar Factory's returns from the 1941 sugar crop were estimated at 813 tons from 200 acres under peasants on the Belmont/Murray's Estate; 569 tons of sugar cane were delivered.

See Langford's (#6) for a history of the Camacho family.

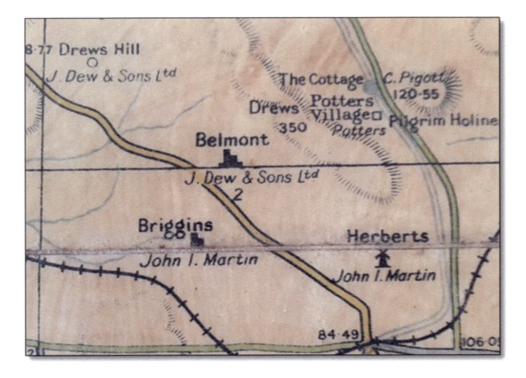

1933 Camacho map shows Briggins in relation to Belmont and Herberts.
Agnes C. Meeker

#20 - Herbert's Plantation

The Ownership Chronology

1733:   Colonel Thomas Williams. d. 1733.

1742:   Edward Williams. b. 1710; d. 1784.

1773:   Sir Richardson Herbert.   1777/78 Luffman map.

1790:   John E. Herbert. b. early 1700s.

1829:   William Burnthorn. b. c1732. 305 acres, 197 slaves.

1843:   Anthony Musgrave, MD. 305 acres.

1872:   Mrs. Emma Purvis.

1878:   Charles J. Manning. b. 1799; d. 1880, age 81.

1880s: Robert Goodwin. b. 1874; d. 1950. 100 acres.

1891:   John MacDonald.

1900:   George Alan, b. 1869, and Kathryn Dora Macandrew.

1921:   Emmanuel O. Camacho.

1933:   John I. & Eldina Martin (rented only).

1945:   Sid & Norma Turock (the house only).

1986:   Raymond Raeburn (UK), the house and 3 acres.

2000:   Marina MacLean, the house and 3 acres.

< >

There is no longer a sugar mill nor any of the works or outbuildings of this estate, but the very large estate house still stands and is privately owned and lived in. It has a full lower story constructed of dark stone (not lime stone), with a double-edged staircase in front, which leads to the second story, also built of stone. The house is said to have been built in 1742, and is often referred to as "William's" instead of Herbert's by neighbors residing on the surrounding Potter's Estate (#47), the Renfrew's Estate (#21) and the Briggin's Estate (#22).

Colonel Thomas Williams was one of the first settlers in Antigua, in the mid-1600s, and lived in Old Road in St. Mary's Parish. Colonel Rowland Williams was the first white male born on the island. He married Elizabeth, first daughter of Samuel Winthrop, who was Deputy Governor of Antigua. Rowland died in 1733. The Williams family subsequently owned Tom Moore's (#175), the Cistern Estate and the Claremont Estate (#177) as well as Herbert's. The Herbert family first settled in Nevis before locating to Antigua in 1773, when Sir Richard Herbert took possession of the Williams estate and re-named it Herbert's.

Top – Herbert's with old Ford in front in 1942 – Macandrew family
Bottom – Herbert's in 1999 – Agnes C. Meeker

John E. Herbert was born in the early 1700s and became owner of the estate in 1790. He had two brothers, Thomas and Joseph, who became Members of the Council in Nevis. Thomas Herbert and his wife Mary had a daughter, Frances, who married William Woolward, Esq. They, too, had a daughter, Frances (Fanny) Herbert Woolward, who was born in 1761 in Nevis, and was only two years old when her mother died giving birth to a son, William.

The Caribbean custom at the time among governors and sugar plantation owners was to educate their sons in England, but keep the daughters at home. Fanny grew up as her father's constant companion. He was the Senior Judge in Nevis and a partner in an export business. The West Indies was under English rule and trade was brisk and profitable.

Fanny received a good education from an English governess, became accomplished in French (the court language), painting, drawing, playing the harpsichord, singing, and dancing; everything to make her desirable, attractive and pursued by the island's bachelors. She promised her father to never marry anyone of whom he disapproved.

Her first husband was Josiah Nisbet MD, in Nevis, a friend of her father's and an eccentric doctor with whom she had one son. She was widowed at the age of 22, and subsequently married Rear Admiral Horatio Nelson, Captain of His Majesty's ship *Boreas,* on March 11, 1787. She was Nelson's wife for 18 years, of whom he said *"I find my domestic happiness perfect. I am possessed of everything that is valuable in a wife."* However, he fell in love with Lady Emma Hamilton, became estranged from Fanny, who never ceased to love Nelson. She supposedly slept with a miniature of him under her pillow which she kissed every night. Excerpted from caribbean-beat.com/issue-32/lord-nelsons-west-indian-widow-fanny-nesbit

< >

British Parliamentary Papers P. 309, describe a claim (T71-877) made by William Burnthorn, owner of Herbert's at the time (1829-1843) as owner in fee. His claim was counter claimed (T71-250) by John Ewart & Co., brokers and commission merchants in Liverpool. Their claim shows William Burnthorn as a resident proprietor in the 1832 return, and an agent for Earl Crawford & Lindsay. In the Burnthorn ancestry site, there is a list of slaves, by name and age, owned by William Burnthorn. He is listed as *"born about 1732, residence 1817, Antigua."*

Also in 1829 (September 12) there was another counter-claim (T71-1230) filed by Charles John Manning, dated 09/22/1829: *"indenture registered in Antigua April 17, 1830, made between GHR, W. S. Rose, Frances Theodora Rose and*

Charles John Manning: Little Duers (#90) conveyed to Charles John Manning. The name of Charles John Manning used by Manning and Anderdon as trustee in purchase, estate and slaves conveyed to the said Charles John Manning without his knowledge or consent."

Manning was a West Indian merchant and received compensation T71-877 (noted above, Antigua claims No.69), for Lower & Upper Walrond (#79) and Little Duers (#90) estates. Little Duers conveyed to Charles John Manning. Manning and Anderdon ultimately went bankrupt, and their creditors brought suit vs. Charles John Manning in Antigua for supplies.

< >

In 1833, when the British Parliament abolished slavery, the Herbert's Plantation received a Legacy payment (Antigua 116) of £1,137. 15s. 6p. for granting freedom to 56 enslaved. William Burnthorn was the awardee; John Ewart was unsuccessful. The Plantation received an additional Legacy payment (Antigua 117) of £622. 15s. 1p. for freeing 34 enslaved. William Coles, John Henry Roper, Francis Thwaites, Esq., and John Trecothick the younger were owners-in-fee.

< >

"At a meeting of the Council of Antigua held this day, Dr. Anthony Musgrave presented his diploma from Edinburgh University, dated June 24th, 1814, and received a license to practice." Source unknown.

Dr. Musgrave became owner of the Herbert's Estate in 1843, as listed above in The Ownership Chronology.

An 1860 petition was filed with *"the Court of the Commission for Sale of Encumbered Estates in the West Indies (Antigua). In the Matter of the Estate of Emma Purvis and Others, Owners. Exparte Charles John Manning, Petitioner."* The map provided by the Commission shows Potter's and Gunthorpe's on the northern boundary, St. Clare's and Belmont Estate to the east, and on the western boundary the lands of Walter Watkins and lands called "The Grove." Nothing appears on the map regarding the southern boundary of Herbert's Estate.

By 1872 Emma Purvis owned this estate along with Drew's Hill (#18) and Belmont's (#19) for total acreage of 788. The Herbert's sugar mill also had been converted from wind power to steam.

When John MacDonald took possession of the Estate in 1891, it was producing annual revenue of £200, but by 1892 the revenue had declined to only

£50. The estate passed from MacDonald to George Alan and Katherine Dora Macandrew. George was the City's, or Tomlinson's estate agent. Douglas, son of George & Katherine and his wife Mary Macandrew, rented Herbert's from John I. Martin in the 1940s, and their daughter, Marguerite, supplied the photograph of the plantation house.   Wendy Gardner and Antigua newspaper extracts.

< >

In 1918, Emmanuel O. Camacho was the sole owner of A. J. Camacho & Co., a merchant business formed by his father Antonio Joseph Comacho. Emmanuel owned Briggin's (#22), Herbert's (#20) and Dunning's (#190), presumably inherited from his father.

Sid Turock, who occupied the estate house in 1945 with his wife, Norma, was *"a master furniture builder and joiner. He restored antiques and had a wonderful personal collection. Herbert's was a show place in his time."*
                                              "Not A Drum Was Heard" by Selvyn Walter.

Raymond Raeburn, from the U.K., purchased the old estate house plus three acres of land in 1986, to be joined later by Marina MacLean. Upon Raymond's death Marina continued the upkeep of the historic building, which was featured in a BBC television documentary when the producers were searching for an estate house dating from the mid-1700s, the time of England's Industrial Revolution. The documentary showed how the revenue from sugar helped to fuel England's industrial revolution.

The Antigua Sugar Factory Ltd. estimated cane returns in 1941 from Herbert's and Briggin's (#22) at 1,060 tons; tons of cane actually delivered, 1,581.

An old Plan of Herbert's estate made during the sale of the Encumbrance Act showing buildings in centre off road. St Claire and Belmont estates are on the West, Lands called The Grove on the East, Potters and Gunthorpes on the North.

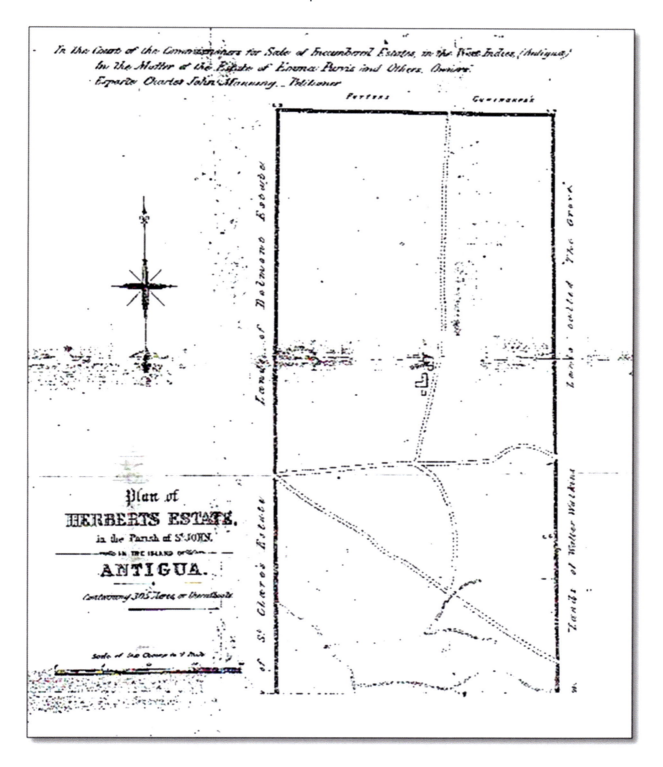

#21 - Renfrew's Plantation

The Ownership Chronology

Early history is unknown. The only mention of "Renfrew" that could be found appears in Vere Oliver's *History of the Island of Antigua Vol. I,* and on the Nugent family web site (#13b, Clare Hall).

1777: An estate called Murray's was located in this area owned by Sir John Laforey. It is unclear if they owned the land or merely lived at Renfrew's. 1777/78 Luffman map.

1831: Edward Emerson. 17 acres.

1872: M. Chambers of Dickie Hill; rented from the owners of Renfrew's.

1900: Harper. (The Harper family does not give dates.)

19xx: Miss Bessie Harper's family.

1933: George Alexander Henry.

1940: Dennis Gabriel.

1944: John Barreto. 144 acres. b. 1909; d. 2007.

1962: Dr. Locker. The sugar mill and house only.

2000: Residential area.

2015: Dickie (Dickey) Hill for sale as part of Renfrew's.

< >

The sugar mill on this small estate still stands, but the estate house purchased in 1962 by Dr. Locker burned to the ground in the 1980s. The mill is now surrounded by a housing division and no longer commands the landscape it once did. Some of the land still belongs to the family of John Barreto.

The estate buildings were severely damaged by an earthquake on February 8, 1843. There were 172 sugar mills on Antigua at that time, and 35 were entirely leveled, 82 were split from top to bottom, and virtually all of the remaining 55 suffered considerable damage, including Bellevue, the various Shand's estates, Renfrew's, Belmont's, Bath Lodge, among others.

Renfrew's with mill in full sail – Museum of Antigua & Barbuda

The Horseford Almanac of 1872 shows that the owners of Renfrew's rented the Dickey Hill 26-acre estate from M. Chambers and others. Dickey Hill later became part of the Renfrew's plantation. In fact, in 1944, when John Barreto purchased the land it was comprised of only 64 acres, which included Dickey Hill. He later purchased an additional 80 acres, known as Hunts Pasture, from John I. Martin, expanding the Renfrew Estate to 144 acres.

Dickey Hill was a small estate in its own right prior to being incorporated into Renfrew's. Another old map shows this as the area where Government House was once located when Richard Oliver was in residence, right across from Clarke's Hill, the acknowledged site. By 2015, the land was being cleared for sale and an elderly man named Fredricks, who tethered his cows in the area, identified a burial site on the south side of the main hill. A wall, which most likely surrounded the site, is still visible, along with three or four broken and weather beaten headstones. The writing on one stone remains fairly legible but no date can be seen: "the Baby of _____ William_____ Horsford_____". In Vere Oliver's Volume II he shows, under Horsford, a William Edward Yeamans Horsford, baptized August 4, 1746 at St Paul's of Grenada 1780 and a William Entwhistle Horsford baptized June 1771 at St. Paul's.

On top of the hill there are many large stones suggesting there might have been a residence there, with a beautiful view of the surrounding countryside. There also are broken bits of pottery and china. Most of the old plantations buried their people, both slaves and owners, on the estate property prior to churches establishing graveyards. Regrettably, most of these private burial grounds have been destroyed by backhoes as the land has been reclaimed.

"From Caribeanna 1774, an article states that the residence of Richard Oliver was on Dickey Hill, according to 1746-48 Baker map. The article says that at the burial ground at Dickey Hill, most of the accompanying headstone inscriptions are illegible and the stones badly broken. There are a few inscriptions intact, but most of the accompanying headstone inscriptions are illegible and the stones badly broken. There are a few inscriptions that can still be read:
* *"Here lies the body of Mary Camron, who departed this life July 2nd, 1809, aged 8 years 2 months 21 days."*
* *"Sacred to the memory of Henrietta Horsford who departed this life 17th March"* (rest is illegible)
* *Here lies the body of Mary Darby who departed this life June …"* (rest is illegible).

Also, standing up on the pasture about 150 yards from the little graveyard in which these and another six or eight stones stand or lie, is another clearly marked "My Elizabeth departed May 12th 1805." This headstone faces northeast, so it may have been the grave of a slave or animal rather than a family member.

Archbishop Spooner.

< >

Excerpts from the bill of sale dated May 4, 1944, between George Alexander Henry and John Barreto's memories make for interesting reading:

"AND WHEREAS the Vendor has agreed to sell the said hereditaments to the Purchaser at the price of Eight hundred fifty Pounds . . All that estate called 'Renfrew' situate in the Parish of Saint John in the Island of Antigua containing seventeen (17) acres or thereabouts and bounded on the North by lands called 'Hunt's Pasture' on the South by lands called 'Laws Land' and 'Dickey Hill' on the East by 'Hunt's Pasture' and on the West by lands commonly called 'Herbert's' or however otherwise the same may be butted and bounded lying and being."

Top – Renfrew house – Nugent Family web site

Left – Francis & Gwen Nunes on their honeymoon – Nunes family

Right – Inside mill – Agnes C. Meeker.

"In the early 1940s John and Angelo Barreto leased Willock's Estate from Dennis Gabriel which was planted in sugar cane, while John Barreto lived at Renfrew's and raised cattle, race horses, guinea fowl, chickens, pigeons in the old mill, and at one time had over 100 ducks. Just about every Sunday they had duck for lunch! The ducks went down to the large pond towards Lightfoot and when they returned they formed a 40-foot line of waddling ducks!

"There was a big black bull called Confusion who, when young, used to walk right into the house. He later became very mean and because he would chase everyone was kept on a 100-foot chain - everyone was frightened of Confusion. It was a wonderful time to live and grow up on an estate, which was totally self-sufficient. The windmill generated electricity, the cisterns contained enough rainwater which was tediously hand pumped to an overhead tank to provide gravity feed and you raised your own livestock and vegetable garden.

"The four Barreto children were allowed full range of the estate picking tamarind, cashews, mango, ginnip, cherry, plums and guavas when in season. They played by the pond, which contained as all ponds did, leaches, lilies and collie fish. They hunted ground and turtle doves with hand made catapults and BB guns, played cricket or rounders and were told stories about jumbies and jack o'lanterns at night by the servants which scared the daylights out of them. Life was simpler and slower paced."

< >

The Harper name comes from the Kingdom of Delriada in ancient Scotland. It was the name of a person who occupied the role of "harper", an important figurehead where the elegance and music of the harp deserved noble status. Harpers were first found in Lennox, Scotland. There is a record of a William Joseph Harper, born in 1790 in Antigua, died in America in 1847.

The Royal Bank of Canada, in 1915, opened for business in a two-story wooden building owned by the Harper family in St. John's, proprietors of Harper's Drug Store. Elizabeth (Miss Bessie) Harper established a scholarship foundation so students lacking funds could attend the Antigua Girls High School which at that time was private.

Renfrews Mill and Works from the North – Museum of Antigua & Barbuda

< >

Renfrew's was known for the quality of clay for making coal pots, yabbas, flower pots, etc… and as far back as the slave days vessels produced in the village of Seaview Farm were made with Renfrew clay. Samuel, known as 'Captain', an old man who worked for Mr. Barreto, walked up to the Seaview Farm once a week to collect money from the potters for the clay they used. It usually amounted to eight or ten shillings, but after Captain died, it was a "free for all!"

Memories of John Barreto.

Hyacinth Hillhouse still runs her mother's business, "Elvie's", in her backyard at Seaview Farm, using clay from Renfrew's. She produces flowerpots, yabbas and candle holders in the age-old manner of slavery days, shaping her products by hand, and firing the pots under boughs of coconut palm in the back yard. It is a dying art.

< >

Elvie fashioning pots in her back
yard at Seaview Farm – Museum
of Antigua & Barbuda.

In 1941, the Antigua Sugar Factory, Ltd., reported estimated cane returns from Renfrew's of 2,518 tons from the 120 acre estate; 26 acres under peasants on the estate; 2,567 tons of sugar cane delivered at 19.26 tons per acre.

< >

#22 - Briggin's Plantation
(Little Zoar)

The Ownership Chronology

1661: Captain Harvey Keynell. He was granted 100 acres by the crown, with another 300 acres added in 1676. d. 1681.

1678: Colonel Edward Powell, the Governor of Antigua, 1683-1688. The plantation owner until 1688.

1688: J. Robert Weir

1708: Edward Chester (?). May have been the owner until 1743.

1716: Henry Powell, the Colonel's nephew.

1777: Berg Ireland, Esq.   1777/78 Luffman map.

1780: Granado Hodgson, plus many shares awarded to heirs through 1828.

1782: Mare Seager, owned 1/12th of Briggin's; passed to Granado Chester.

1790: Benjamin Ireland.

1828: Ann Hodgson Lenaghan & Reverend James Lenaghan.

1829: William Gregory. 426 acres, 50 slaves.

1851: Heirs of William Gregory. 426 acres.

1872: Dr. Jesse W. Thibou, MRCSE. 440 acres.

1891: Antonio Joseph Camacho (d.1894) & Emanuel O. Camacho.

1894: Emanuel Oliver Comacho. Estate reduced to 392 acres

1940s: John I. Martin.

2003: Heirs of John I. Martin.

< >

Perusing the Ownership Chronology it is evident that there is some confusion over the shifting ownership of this estate, especially when, in 1780, when we know of at least 12 shares. Estates often were divided as part of the inheritance by large families, most of whom lived abroad as absentee landowners. The estates, whole or partial, were managed by a resident property manager and an overseer.

The view towards the West from the top of the hill where the estate house was likely
located, looking down towards the works with chimney. Agnes C. Meeker

The sugar mill was converted from wind power to steam in the 1880s. It no longer exists, but a tall, square chimney stands on the site with the inscription "J. W. T. AD 1876" (Jesse W. Thibou). Old machinery from the factory dots the landscape, and on the hill above there are the remnants of a stone wall, which most likely marks the site of the bluff house.

Harvey Keynell's father was Colonel Christopher Keynell, who accompanied Sir George Ayscough's fleet to the West Indies in 1651. The Colonel was commissioned by Oliver Cromwell as Governor of Antigua, and served from 1653 to 1660. His widow, Joan, married John Hall, who owned Betty's Hope. Widowed for the second time, Joan fled Antigua during the French occupation for safety in Nevis. She returned in 1668 and repaired the estate's buildings, but the plantation was taken away from her and given to Colonel Codrington (see #13b - Clare Hall) because it was felt the Betty's Hope estate was "too great a quantity of land" for Joan to handle.

It is believed that a Dr. Daniel Mackinen immigrated to Antigua between 1678 and 1688 and may have received grants from King Charles II for the estates Draper's, Golden Grove (#23) and Dickenson's Bay (#10 - McKinnon's). Dr.

Mackinen died in 1720, age 62. An original deed shows the Golden Grove estate was held from 1678 to 1688 by Colonel Edward Powell, the Deputy Governor of Antigua. Ownership passed to his nephew, Henry Powell, in 1716, who leased the estate to Dr. Mackinen for 99 years.
"History of the Island of Antigua"
by Vere Oliver, Volume II.

Mare Seager's 1/12th ownership, which he passed to Granado Chester in 1782, is typical of the divided estate inheritance described above. Also owning 1/12th was Ann Hodgson Lenaghan and the Reverand James Lenaghan.

Left – the chimney still stands tall with a plaque inserted at the bottom (right) which reads "J.W.T. AD 1875". Machinery still littered the hillside.
Agnes C. Meeker

The 233 acres of "Little Zoar", in St. John's Division, was purchased by Robert Weir in 1704. He already owned Briggin's and combined the two into a single estate with 426 acres; the amalgamation was accomplished by Robert Chester, who paid £16,092. 10s. 0p. for 220 acres at £20/acre including 60 negro men, 52 negro women, 14 boys and 3 girls.
"History of the Island of Antigua"
by Vere Oliver, Volume I.

An excerpt from the 1743 indenture of Edward Chester reads:

"Elizabeth, Mary and Sarah Carbery grant and convey to Robert Smith in his actual possess being . . . all that boiling house and one fifth of 24 negro houses standing upon the plantation called 'Briggins' in the Parish of St. John's, Antigua, and all those 10 slaves (names given) and 5 head of horned cattle, 1 ox, 2 cows and 1 calf and all that undivided fifth of all that windmill . . . ."

"History of the Island of Antigua" by Vere Oliver, Volume I.

< >

In 1833, when the British Parliament abolished slavery, the Briggin's estate was given a Legacy award (Antigua 118) of £731. 55s. 9p. for granting freedom to 49 enslaved. Awardees were Anna Jane Gregory, Elizabeth Gregory, George Murray Gregory, Mary Gregory and Thomas Smith. The Gregory family members were owners of the estate at that time.

< >

Dr. Jesse W. Thibou, MRESE, was a medical officer in St. John's Parish in 1872, and a member of the Assembly for St. John's Division as well as the owner of Briggin's.

An excerpt from *"Symbol of Courage - Aunty Dood"*, by Keithlyn Smith, describes a group of people who left Hatton's and stopped at Briggin's because they saw empty rooms. They were not aware that if they stayed they would be required to work without pay. *"They turned eastward to Briggin's Estate one mile and a half way (from Hatton's Estate). To their surprise, Briggin's had empty rooms and plenty of it. They decided to rest their heads for a while but a hard lesson was to be learnt at Briggin's. That meant that whoever lived there had to work for the estate, but would not be paid."*

Emanuel O. Camacho, who assumed ownership in 1894, was the sole owner of the business, A. J. Camaco & Co., an export and merchant business, founded by his father, Antonio Joseph Camacho. Emanuel owned Briggin's (#22), Herbert's (#20) and Dunning's (#190), presumably inherited from his father. Aubrey J. Camacho had assumed ownership of Briggins in 1878, and by 1881 had amassed ownership of several estates totaling over 2,000 acres.

< >

An 1816 letter from Robert Jefferson to his brother provides interesting insight into the management of a plantation by an absentee landlord:

"I have got nothing definite done here yet I'm sorry to say. Gibson is advancing wages & last week actually bought stock which so far I am glad of as I expect to get a cash settlement from him for our account in some shape or form & this must tend to facilitate it & he has made sundry offers but as yet such vague ones I have not entertained them, but this next week will I do hope bring matters to a close as by Action comes in to force the week after & I fancy Gibson may be brought to terms to prevent proceedings going on — the owners seem to me to care little about matters & have turned him over to battle with me.

"Davis is not too clever or too sharp but he is attentive and looked up to & now that Sheriff has given up business he is a kind of protege of his & benefits by his advice — he was in reality the only man I could get & sharp though Woodcock may be I have been here long enough to know he is an old scoundrel — He has not one farthing to rub against another, he was a sort of decoy check for Wright in the Bank in his frauds as through his instrumentality the victims were induced to endorse the notes & the other day he endeavoured to take me in with some molasses — the man's appearance is enough for me — Davis wants sticking up to — he is soft & I spoke rather sharply to him only yesterday for ever entertaining one of Gibson's offers that he should quietly work the Estate & pay our account in three yearly installments the first to begin in November next!!!

"The fact is everyone here is so interwoven with each other had I the opportunity of getting a man I know from any of the Islands I would do so at once — I must however battle the watch as I am doing & Nugent still agrees with me it was the most judicious step to bring an action at once as I did whatever turns up — I hope my next will report satisfactorily."

"An Antigua Trading Company" by Mary Gleadall.

< >

In the 1940s, Briggin's owner John I. Martin operated a fleet of buses on Antigua. His son, George, would collect the fares, dropping them into a canvas bag *"which he held very tightly."* The bus routes were mostly in Liberta. It was said that Mr. Martin made his money in New York, and when he returned to Antigua he acquired as much land as possible. At the time, land was very cheap.

"Not A Drum Was Heard" by Selvyn Walter

"John I. and George would come into Royal bank every week for the money which they put in a big bag. It was said that George could put the money in but only John I. could take it out. The tellers all received gifts from them at Christmas."

Helen Abbott, Memories

What was the Briggin's estate formerly was the site of the John I. Martin IV Grounds, a drag strip for racing cars. That racetrack is now located adjacent to Sir Vivian Richard's Cricket Ground and Lower Cedar Hill.

< >

In 1941, the Antigua Sugar Factory, Ltd., estimated sugar returns from Herbert's & Briggin's of 1,060 tons from 1,581 tons of cane delivered, a combination of estate and peasant-worked land.

John I. Martin.
The Observer Newspaper

#23 - Golden Grove Plantation
(Paull's)

The Ownership Chronology

1650: Elinor Paull.

1660: William Milder (Mildon). Became Deputy Governor of Antigua in 1667. Will: 1669.

1669: Jacob Hill.

1683: Boyd sold to Edward Powell, Deputy Governor.

1684: Colonel Edward Powell, Deputy Governor of Antigua. Will: 1667.

1702: Dr. Daniel Powell.

1710: William McKinnon. b. 1658; d. 1720.

1720: William McKinnon. d. 1809.

1717: Callaghan McCarthy.

1740: William Buckley.

1790: Bertie Entwhistle. d.1803.   1777/78 Luffman map.

1829: Bertie Entwhistle leased to F. Shand & Co. 254 acres; 458 slaves.

1843: Heirs of Bertie Entwhistle.

1878: Reverend Thomas Peters leased to G. Bennett. 254 acres.

1891: Heirs of Reverend Peters.

1921: T. E. Peters.

< >

There is no longer a sugar mill or not any other buildings standing on this plantation. Colonel Edward Powell was granted a patent on December 27, 1684, for 380 acres in St. John's Division, formerly called Paull's and now known as Golden Grove. He was the Deputy Governor of Antigua in 1667, and according to his 1687 will he also owned The Road Plantation. *"History of the Island of Antigua" by Vere Oliver, Volume III.*

The will of William Milder, dated 1669, states: *"To my son Jacob Hill half of my plantation called 'Paul's' in Antigua recently purchased from the widow Elliner [sic] Paull, together with 12 or 13 negroes. To my friend John Travers the other half of my plantation also my moiety of the sloop 'Martha' and half of the ship 'Charles' of Nevis'."* In this same year, Thomas Ayson of Bristol, England, bequeathed to his kinsman 50,000 pound of muscavado sugar from his plantation in Nevis, and

William Mildon of Bristol and Nevis referred in his 1669 will to his estate called "Paull Plantation" on the island of Antigua. It recently had been purchased by Elliner Paull.

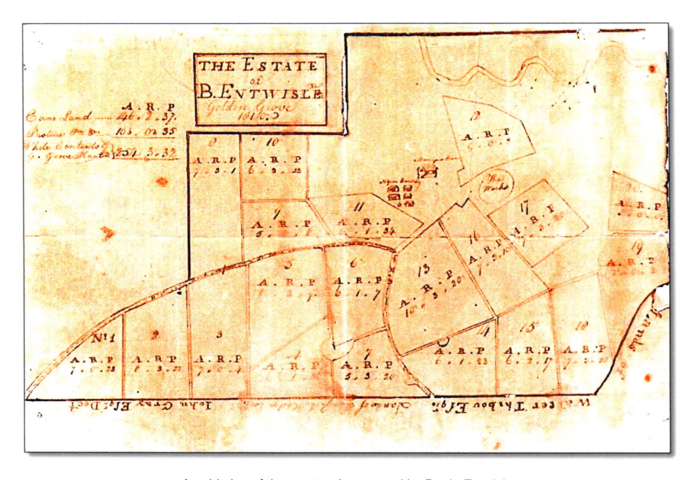

An old plan of the estate when owned by Bertie Entwisle -

In 1698, there was a petition from William McKinnon stating that William Bridges, Esq, was holding the Golden Grove Plantation in trust for Thomas Trant, a Roman Catholic (deceased) *"by his letter of attorney dated November 1698 appointed Mr. Garret Trant of Montserrat, Mr. David Rice and Mr. Thomas Trant, Jr., of London to sell or let that estate, and two of them accordingly in 1702 granted a lease of it for 99 years to Dr. Daniel McKinnon at £100 per year."*

"History of the Island of Antigua" by Vere Oliver, Volume III.

William McKinnon was an absentee planter for many years. He returned to Antigua in 1773 and became a member of the Council. He owned both Golden Grove and McKinnon's (#10), an estate of 830 acres.

In 1716, Captain John Gamble, indentured to William and Elizabeth Bridges, *"seized of certain plantations . . . one called Golden Grove, the other the Road Plantation, formerly Rakes Bay.* *"History of the Island of Antigua"* by Vere Oliver, Volume II.

Charles Curtis managed this plantation for Samuel Martin from about 1801 to 1812. When Bertie Entwhistle died in 1803, Samuel Martin was his trustee, and through that connection Mr. Curtis became manager of Golden Grove, Barnacle Point (#58) and Jolly Hill (#167). Mr. Curtis returned to England in 1822. A distant relative of his, Janet Richards, discovered a box of correspondence between her relative and Samuel Martin, including 41 pages of accounts for the Bertie Entwhistle Trust for these estates between 1812 and 1822.

< >

Initially, people of colour were refused internment in the church yard at the St. John's Cathedral. The bell, which normally tolled to honour the demise of plantation owners and their families *"was prohibited from being used to perform that service for those degraded ones whose veins flowed the least drop of Africa's tarnished blood. Accordingly, a smaller bell (which still hangs in the belfry) was obtained from the estate called Golden Grove, and which was regularly kept for the sole use of persons of colour."* "History of the Island of Antigua" by Vere Oliver, Volume II.

< >

In 1833, when the British Parliament abolished slavery, Golden Grove was granted a Legacy award (Antigua 96) of £2,363. 5s. 9p. for granting freedom to slaves. The sole awardee was Ralph Peters.

< >

During World War II, Flying Horse Hill operated a bar called Flying Horse. It was located near where Wendy's sits today. There was considerable action all through the war between Flying Horse and Allie's Bar owned by Con White, Sr. Four photographs were prominent in Allie's Bar, Stalin, Churchill, Roosevelt and Chiang Kai-Shek. Mr. White also owned a night club in Golden Grove, where the State College is now located. That club featured 'brams', a cheap dance somewhat on the rough side. Flying Horse Hill sold the land at this site to the government for construction of the State College. *"Not A Drum Was Heard"* by Selvyn Walter

< >

In 1941 the Antigua Sugar Factory, Ltd. estimated its returns from Golden Grove and Clare Hall (#13b) at 2,518 tons from 2,567 tons of cane delivered at 19.26/ton; 120 acres; 26 acres under peasants.

#24 - Grays/Turnbull Plantation

The Ownership Chronology

1750: Merrick Turnbull. He was a doctor who served on the Assembly during the trials of the 1736 rebellion.
1790: Honorable John Gray.   1777/78 Luffman map.
1829: John Gray. 100 acres, 48 slaves.
1843: John Gray. 100 acres.
1872: Heirs of John Gray, leased to Otto's Plantation (#16). 71 acres.
1891: Heirs of William Odlum.
1892: Antonio Joseph Camacho. d. 1894.
1894: John J. Camacho. d. 1929.
1920: Edna Edwards, the bluff house only.
1923: J. Drew, et al. 230 acres in 1921.
2006: The bluff house was sold.
2014: The Gray's Hill estate house is again for sale.

< >

The sugar mill and outbuildings at Gray's/Turnbull no longer exist, but miraculously the wooden estate house has survived. However, it is surrounded by the encroaching expansion of the city of St. John's. The entrance to the property is marked by an iron gate between two stone gateposts.

The bluff house was called Mayfield and is situated on the same hill as the Gray's Hill reservoir, which at one time was a major source of collection and purification of water for the city of St. John's. In 2011, the reservoir was completely renovated by the Chinese to include a new roof and pump house, and the reservoir is back in service today.

"I recall my father, Robert Bell, working at the upper and lower reservoirs during the time we lived there, the buildings were well maintained and the surrounding areas (lawns and trees, etc.) were trimmed and tidy. Workers, full, part-time and casual, kept the filter beds clean. The lower reservoir was always covered with thick sheets of galvanize. These were painted dark red. There are two filter beds, which formed part of the filtration system for the water that was pumped into them. I am sure you are still able to see the west filter bed but I do not believe that the filter beds are in use today. The top of the reservoir is paved

and they are now covered with grass. There were few houses at the top of the hill in those days and we walked back and forth to school up that hill which was covered in fruit trees. Growing up it was a children's paradise."

Florence Bell, *Memories of . . . .*

The Gray's Turnbull bluff house known as "Mayfield", listed as one of three houses in Antigua to have 100 windows – Agnes C. Meeker

The "Mayfield" house is one of three large houses in Antigua known as "a house of 100 windows"; the other two were Millar's and the Camacho town house, which is now Bishop's Lodge owned by the Catholic Church. London's Buckingham Palace apparently has 100 windows, so in order not to convey the impression that the plantation owners were putting themselves on a par with royalty, they opened only 99 windows at any one time!

"Not A Drum Was Heard" by Selvyn Walter

< >

An agreement was struck between John Gray, Esq., and Alexander Willock, Esq., on April 29, 1771, for the Turnbull's Plantation of 120 acres, including *"all negroes and other slaves,"* to be leased for one year.

< >

With the abolition of slavery in 1833, the British Parliament granted a Legacy award (Antigua 716) to Turnbull's of £716. 13s. 10p. for granting freedom to 42 enslaved. Successful was John Adams Ward. Unsuccessful were Hardman Earle, Elizabeth Grace Gilchrist, John Gray, Charles Turner, John Hayward Turner and Samuel Athill Turner.

< >

The old gate posts still stand at the entrance to Mayfield.
Agnes C. Meeker

John Ogden was an officer at the Navy Base in the late 1950s. There were many nightspots and houses of ill repute around the island that provided a social outlet for men "cooped up" on the base. One by one, most of them were eventually declared Off Limits. Here is part of Ogden's report on a night club in Gray's Farm:

"Sick Call" by John Ogden

"I'm going to put that abomination off limits," stated the Commanding Officer. He was referring to a nightspot I will call the Castaway, (and you'd have to stretch to call it a nightclub), located way back in hill country of the sub tropical island of Antigua in the British West Indies.

The story goes on to tell of the raid one night by the Commanding Officer.

#25 - Denfield's or Hutchinson's Plantation

The Ownership Chronology

1777:   John Otto Baijer, Esq. d. 1796.   1777/78 Luffman map.
1933:   Mrs. M. T. Camacho.   1933 Camacho map
1940s: John I. Martin.
2000:   George Martin.

< >

Very little is known of this estate. The sugar mill still stands, and the surrounding area on the brow of the hill is littered with cut stone and the foundations of buildings. To the west is a magnificent view towards Five Islands with The Union (#27) directly north. New homes are being constructed below and along the ridge which affords beautiful views.

In 1787/88 John Otto-Baijer, Esq. was owner of a plantation on Five Islands Division, as well as Denfield's (#25), Cook's (#26), Dewitt's and Otto-Baijer's (#16) *"History of the Island of Antigua"* by Vere Oliver, Volume I.

Denfield mill in 1975 with Dr. Reg Murphy – CVE Mill Project

George Martin mentioned to this author that he had heard that somewhere on the hill there is a stone marking a spot where slaves were once hung but was unable to identify the site, but it also could have been at Union (#2).

A 1777 map by John Luffman shows an estate he labeled "Domfield" owned by Otto-Baijer, Esq. It is almost surely a misspelling of Denfield's.

#26 - Cook's Mill Plantatiion

The Ownership Chronology

1700s: John and Lady Elizabeth Cook.

1716:   Houses and wharf sold to James Nesbitt.

1722:   John and Edward Otto-Baijer.

1750:   Honorable Edward Otto-Baijer. Baptized: 1709; d. 1779.

1790:   John Otto-Baijer. d. 1796. 1777/78 Luffman map.

1829:   Heirs of Lovell Langford Hodge.b.1806
           604 acres, 253 slaves.

1843:   Langford Lovell Hodge.

1851:   Langford Lovell Hodge.

1872:   John C. Anthonyson. 500 acres, plus 10 held by R. S. Heagan.

1891:   John Joaquin.

1921:   F. A. Joaquin. 474 acres.

< >

A landfill now occupies the site of this former planation. It services the entire island, with garbage filling it at an alarming rate. The sugar mill is still perched on the side of the hill, with many machinery parts scattered around the property. It was converted from wind power to steam in the 1880s, and a chimney built at that time also is still standing. Most of the sugar mill machinery was shipped back to England as scrap iron during World War II to aid the war effort, but that activity seems to have been abandoned in mid-collection.

In 1716, James Nesbit purchased Lady Cook's houses and wharf, and on July 16, 1722, the Cook's plantation and other moiety of 118 negroes was sold to John Otto-Baijer. *"History of the Island of Antigua"* by Vere Oliver, Volume I & III.

Bastian Baijer was the first Baijer to settle in Antigua, arriving from The Netherlands. He was accompanied by a friend, Peter Coone, who received 500 acres, in St. John's Division.

By 1787, John Otto-Baijer owned a plantation in the Five Islands Division as well as Denfield's (#25), Dewitt's, Otto-Baijer's (#16) and Cook's. In the early 1800s, John Duer Cranstoun was manager of both Union (#27) and Cook's estates.

The Cranstoun family later went on to own Potter's (#47), Cochrane's (#83) and Thomas's (#138). (The Cranston family history will be found under Cochran's Bethesda (#139), in Volume III.)

The mill and chimney at Cook's attesting to first, wind power and second, the chimney which denotes switching to steam in the mid 1800's. Agnes C. Meeker

The British Parliament abolished slavery in 1833, and Cook's Plantation was granted a Legacy award (Antigua 97) of £4,103. 18s. 7p. for freeing 254 enslaved. the only awardee was Elwin.

In 1941, the Antigua Sugar Factory, Ltd. estimated cane returns of 900 tons from 513 tons of cane delivered; zero acres of peasant land on the estate.

< >

In 2011, Prime Minister Baldwin Spencer praised the contribution of MSP Management & Development Company and the Royal Bank of Trinidad & Tobago as they broke ground on a $10 million affordable housing project at Cook's estate. *"Not only will this project increase the housing stock in this community but during the construction phase . . .many people will receive employment. The contribution to the construction sector by this project will be significant,"* the Prime Minister said. The project, called Eldina Gardens, planned to build 120 affordable homes.

Cook's mill 2004 with abandoned machinery both inside and outside the mill. Agnes C. Meeker

#27 - The Union Plantation
(Haddon/Hatton or Weekes)

The Ownership Chronology

1678:   Captain John Haddon, granted 274 acres.
        d. 1723. Passed 250 acres to Dr. John Haddon,
        b.1690; d. 1738.
1678:   Richard Haddon, granted 250 acres.
1738:   John Weekes, Esq., d.1738. Bequeathed his
        estate to James Nibbs, of Popeshead.
1738:   James Nibbs. d.1751.
1751:   Jonas Ian Nibbs.
1777:   James Langford Nibbs. Baptized 1738; d. 1795. 1777/78 Luffman map.
1792:   James Langford Nibbs. Baptized 1738; d. 1795.
1817:   James Lovel Hodge. 1817.
1829:   Heirs of Langford Lovell Hodge. b. 1807.   514 acres, 208 slaves.
1843:   Heirs of Hodge.
1872:   Robert W. Dobson. b. 1861; d. 1918. 483 acres.
1891:   Robert Dobson.
1921:   F. December. 460 acres.
1933:   Mrs. M. T. Camacho.   1933 Camacho map.
1940s: John I. Martin.
2000:   George Martin.

< >

This plantation started in 1678 with 250 acres of land, expanded to 514 acres by 1829 and then began to shrink. In 1921, it consisted of only 460 acres. The decline was undoubtedly the result of the higher cost of labour after the British Parliament abolished slavery in 1833, and the decline of Antigua's sugar business in the late 1800s and early 1900s.

The former plantation site is littered with the remaining foundations of old buildings and abandoned and broken machine parts from the original sugar mill, which somehow escaped the World War II steel reclamation program. The mill was converted from wind power to steam in the 1800s. The chimney is in excellent shape even today but the mill was recently destroyed.

Antigua W. I. „Union" Estate.

Jose Anjo, Photo Studio, St. John's, Antigua W. I. No. 149.]

The Union estate showing main house, mill and works in the background beyond the shade of a large tree. Chimney denotes the use of steam. Jose Anjo postcard.

Although best known as the Union the 1777/78 map by cartographer John Luffman identifies it as "Weekes", presumably in recognition of the owner John Weekes, who died in 1738. The estate was originally known as "Haddon's"; it was owned by Richard Haddon, then his son Dr. John Haddon, who left it to Mr. Weekes. The first mention of the name "Union" appears in Vere Oliver's second volume of Antigua's history, where he notes that Langford Lovell Hodge (b. 1807) owned the Cook's (#26), Union (#27) and Hodge's Bay (#4) estates. Today the area continues to be called "Hattons", a derivative of "Haddons".

"He was able to place my mother and family at Hatton Estate. Hatton and Grays abutted and bounded on the west. There they stayed for some weeks until the Manager and my grandfather fell out. I was told that they could not see horse at all (eye to eye) and so the family had to leave."

Keithlyn Smith on Aunty Dood in *"Symbol of Courage"*.

In 1772 the estate was indentured *"between Thomas Turner Wise (son of John Wise), William Livingston and the Honorable Francis Farley, witness that in consideration of 5 shillings paid to Wise and Livingston grant to Francis Farley all that plantation, late of John Wise, containing 156 acres and dwelling house and all slaves, horned cattle and living stock for one whole year that Francis Farley may be in actual possession."*   *"History of the Island of Antigua"* by Vere Oliver, Volume III.

In this 1970's image of the Union sugar mill and chimney some of the wood appendages still exist and the road which is now paved, still runs by unpaved, and made of marle.
Picture taken for Antigua & Barbuda tourist magazine.

Francis Farley of Farley Bay, Antigua, has been the subject of DNA research as part of the Sauratown Project by Professor Charles D. Rodenbough in North Carolina. Professor Rodenbough is using DNA to trace the 100 slaves from Cameroon who worked on Farley's Antigua plantation. He subsequently relocated them to his tobacco plantation in Virginia and his cotton plantation in North Carolina.

John Duer Cranstoun was manager of both The Union and Cook's estates in the early 1800s, and his family went on to own Potter's (#47), Cochrane's (#83) and Thomas's (#138).

< >

In 2009, the complete works for crushing sugar cane could still be seen. They were one of only three remaining sets on the island, one of the others being at Betty's Hope, which was completely refurbished as a working showcase of the old plantations. The works at Betty's Hope actually came from the Thibou Jarvis sugar mill (#34) and were donated by the Shoul family.

Machinery inside the mill, removed in 2016 by "Tyre Master" destined to be part of a Museum on Sugar. Right shows the three rollers that crushed the cane to extract the juice, and left, the shaft that connected the rollers to the wind mill sails which provided the power to drive the machinery. Agnes C. Meeker

In the early 1940s most scrap iron on Antigua was shipped to the U.K. to aid the World War II military effort. This included all of the mill works no longer in use, with the exception of this mill and a few others. The mill at The Union is crumbling rapidly. However, the brick chimney from the days when the estate converted the mill to steam is still in excellent shape. This mill was one of the last to operate, not decommissioned until the 1920s. The ruins of the estate house also are visible further down the hill.

The mill was so damaged by 2013 it was partially knocked down to remove the iron works inside. Police launched an investigation to determine if the mill had been demolished by someone anxious to steal the iron works for salvage. Tyre Master, who had removed the works, publicly stated he would construct a Museum at the Antigua Sugar Factory, open for public viewing. That has not yet happened (2017).

George Martin says there was a stone marker on the estate where slaves were hung (also see Denfield's, #25), but it cannot be located.

< >

In 1941, the Antigua Sugar Factory, Ltd. estimated cane returns from The Union estate at 100 tons from 98 tons of cane delivered, 0 peasants land on the estate.

#28 - Creek Side/Thibou's Plantation

The Ownership Chronology

1730:   Isaac Thibou. d. 1758, approximately 80 years old.

1790:   Walter Thibou. Baptized 1741. Still living in 1774. <small>1777/78 Luffman map.</small>

1829:   Thomas Franklyn Nibbs. Baptized 1771. 367 acres, 187 slaves.

1843:   Nibbs.

1851:   Thomas Franklyn Nibbs. 367 acres.

1872:   John H. Moore. 396 acres; 180 in St. Mary's Parish.

1891:   James Davey.

1910:   Ernest Dew. Married Violet in 1918; then Millicent. The girls were the Maginley sisters!

1921:   Mrs. Ernest J. Dew.

1933:   Dew & Sons Ltd. <small>Camacho map</small>

1943:   Antigua Syndicate Estates

1958:   Antigua Government

< >

In 1739, during the ownership of Isaac Thibou, he, his wife Catherine (nee Field) and her spinster sister Sophia Field, contested the will of Catherine and Sophia's brother, Theophilus Field, who had stipulated that he wanted "his" estate to be used for charitable purposes. The legal document reads:

"Antigua: Isaac Thibou, Esq., and Catherine his wife (late Catherine Field) and Sophia Field, spinster, appellants: Ashton Warner, Esq., his Majesty's Attorney General of the Leeward Islands, at the relation of the parsons and vestries of the parishes of St. John and St. Mary in Antigua, respondents: the respondents case to be heard before the Right Honourable the Lords of the Committee of Council, at the Council Chamber at the cockpit, Whitehall, on Wednesday the 13th (i.e., Tuesday the 26th) day of February,1739 at six o'clock in the afternoon."

There is no mill or evidence of an estate in existence on this land, but the beautiful old Creek Side Bridge is still visible from the main road. It was constructed in the elegant triple arched design from old stone, reminiscent of a scene from the English countryside. It was built over the tidal inlet (Antigua has no flowing rivers), presumably at the time of the original estate. Water flows through a series of dams and ponds from the Body Ponds area, through Creek Side, and empties into the flashes and the sea by Seaforths.

Antigua. W. I. Creek Side.

José Anjo, Photographer, Antigua. W. I.

Creek Side bridge with buggy crossing, through which waters pass from
Body Ponds to the flashes at Seaforth.   Jose Anjo postcard

Thomas Franklyn Nibbs was a resident of Antigua and a Member of the House of Assembly. He claimed the Creek Side estate, having purchased it subject to a mortgage. Gibbs and Henry Moreton Dyer settled a division of the compensation between them. In 1805, Thomas appeared with William Baxter, a merchant, certifying the exchange rate of a document dated January 1, 1805 from John Cole, surgeon at HM Naval Hospital, Antigua, seeking payment from the Commissioners to Lord Lavington for Sick and Wounded Seamen in London for disbursements at the Hospital. Jane Austen's father, the Reverend George Austen, was trustee of James Nibb's Antiguan estates. Nibbs was godfather to Jane's brother, James.

< >

Creek Side was given a Legacy award (Antigua 125) by the British Parliament following the abolition of slavery in the 1830s. The award totaled £2,973. 15. 11p. for the freedom of 184 enslaved. The awardees were Henry Moreton Dyer and Thomas Franklyn Nibbs. Walter Thibou was listed as previous owner. Unsuccessful was Elizabeth Maria Thibou. Alexander Coates was mentioned as "other association."

< >

In 1941 the Antigua Sugar Factory Ltd. estimated cane returns from Creek Side of 2,008 tons from a 100-acre estate, from 1,988 tons of sugar cane delivered at 18.42/acre; 15 acres of peasant land.

< >

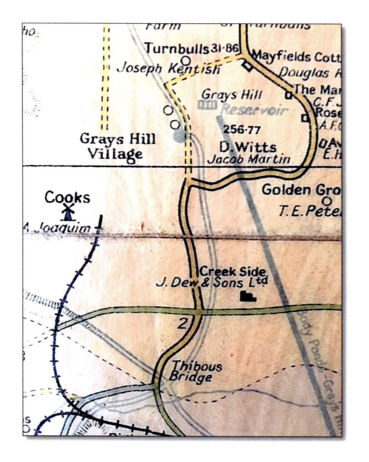

August 1, 1943, Gunthorpe's Estates Ltd. was restructured (see #64, Gunthorpe's) into a new company renamed Antigua Syndicate Estates, Ltd. The estates then held by the Dew's family included Gilbert's (#80), Pares/Cochrane's (#83/84) and Comfort Hall (#103) as well as Creek Side. Papers and correspondence between 1867 and 1892 for Moore, Creekside. Antigua No. 50 held at the National Archives (UK) Colonial Office, Ref. #CO441/7/12.

1933 Camacho map showing Creekside owned by J. Dew & Sons Ltd. not far from Cooks (#26) Agnes C. Meeker

#29 - Yepton's/Yapton Farm Plantation

The Ownership Chronology

1750:   Edward Otto-Baijer. Baptized: 1709; d. 1779.
1790:   John Otto-Baijer. d. 1796. 1777/78 Luffman map.
1800:   Sir George Thomas. d. 1815.
1821:   George White-Thomas
1829:   Messrs. Hyndman. 344 acres; 111 slaves.
1843:   Alex McDowell.
1851:   Ralph W. Baxter. 343 acres.
1878:   Alex Coltart.
1891:   Robert Warneford. b. 1862; d. 1938.
1921:   Rex A. L. Warneford. 290 acres. First man to shoot down a German Zeppelin in World War I.
1933:   Rex A. L. Warneford. d. 1938.   1933 Camacho map.
1940:   F. ("Frankie") Henry S. Warneford. b. 1892; d. 1980s.
1990s: Ralph Francis, the bluff.

< >

The name of this estate is believed to originate from the town of Yapton, near Arundel in Sussex, England. Sir George Thomas, who took ownership of the plantation in 1800, was a native of Yapton.

"The estate house enjoyed a beautiful view of St. John's harbour and the surrounding area. After the death of Frankie Warneford, the estate was sold to Ralph Francis but shortly thereafter the house caught fire and burned to the ground. The ruins are still visible today. Frankie was a friend of my grandmother's and was known for his talent in the theatre as a young man. He played the piano and was fond of entertaining in his home, which he did in grand style using the family silver and crystal. He was always a perfect gentleman, but never a family man.
Agnes C. Meeker.

The mill still stands on this site. It was repaired in 2001, by the owners of the Royal Antiguan Hotel, which is situated on a hill. A great deal of the acreage is hilly and was used to raise cattle when the estate was flourishing. The estate house was on the hill to the north of the mill works. The flashes below were very productive salt ponds from which salt was collected in baskets for sale in the market.

< >

In 1790, the Thomas Baronetcy of Yapton, in the County of Sussex, was created for George Thomas, Governor of the Leeward Islands from 1753-1766. The title became extinct on the death of the seventh Baronet in 1972, a prominent chess player.

In 1802, an indenture between Sir George Thomas and his son specified the same to Thomas Edwards *"and his heirs in fee simple a plantation therein described for the price of 22,000 pounds to be paid as follows . . ."*. George White-Thomas took the name Thomas upon inheriting Yapton from his grandfather, Sir George Thomas (d. 1821) and his memorial encryption is at Yapton's.

"History of the Island of Antigua" by Vere Oliver, Volume.

Messrs. Hyndman, who owned Yapton in1829, also owned several other estates on Antigua: Bendalls (#37), with 503 acres; Towerhill was owned by William Hyndman, Esq.; Belvedere (#38), with 361 acres, Yapton Farm with 343 acres, and Mathew's or Constitution Hill (#132), with 888 acres, were owned by Warrick P. Hyndman in 1852, as was Elmes (#109) with 158 acres and Sawcolt's (#174) with 234 acres.

< >

Slavery was abolished by the British Parliament in 1833, and Yepton's was awarded a Legacy payment (Antigua 1045) of £1,681. 4s. 1p. for granting freedom to 113 enslaved. The awardees were Boyd Alexander, Claude Neilson and William Maxwell Alexander. Unsuccessful was Robert Hyndman, and involved was the Honorable William Fraser.

Apparently, in the 1850's, the owner of Yeptons was Alex Coltart (although he listed historically as taking possession in 1878.) He was proprietor of Harney & Coltart, a firm which struck farthing coins -- a quarter of a penny in British currency -- for the collection of salt from the nearby salt ponds. As noted earlier, several ponds in Antigua yielded salt that was harvested in baskets, but the only source of salt currently is in Barbuda, where it is collected during the dry months and stored in large barrels for local use.

In the mid-1800s and well into the early decades of the 20th century, the Yepton's pond behind Deep Bay was a valuable source of salt. It was a coarse-grained type, ideal for salting fresh food or making ice cream. Sea water was introduced through a small channel at the north end of the pond, and during the hot dry months it was blocked from leaving so the sun's rays could evaporate the sea water, leaving behind a bed of salt crystals.

At the end of the drying season, village ladies from Five Islands and other villages would harvest the salt. They were paid in farthings, by Harney & Coltart, for every basket of salt they delivered. Currently, these tiny coins are sometimes found and brought to the Museum of Antigua & Barbuda.

"Heritage Treasures" by Desmond Nicholson

< >

According to shipping records a Henry Warneford arrived in Antigua from England on September 22, 1913, aboard the S/V *Giuina."* He was 21 years 6 months old. His relative, Francis "Frankie" Warneford (son of Rex Warneford and Nellie Blackmore) was associated with the Agricultural Department, ultimately becoming Superintendent of Science & Agriculture at Jepstones. He owned, lived and died at the estate. He was a good friend of the author's family, with a reputation of being strict and honest.

Rex Warneford was a merchant in St. John's. He sold his business to Jim Piggot in 1938, the year of his death. Piggot purchased the business for his daughter Kate.

In 1941 the Antigua Sugar Factory Ltd. had cane returns of 168 tons from an 18-acre estate, no peasants on the land; Tons of cane delivered 144 at 14.40 per acre.

Top - Yepton's mill c.1998
showing deterioration.
Bottom - c2005. after renovation.
Agnes C. Meeker

#30 - Galley Bay Plantation

The Ownership Chronology

1750:   Honorable George Thomas.
1790:   George T. Thomas. 1777/78 Luffman map.
1829:   Heirs of George T. Thomas. 447 acres;
        168 slaves.
1843:   Inigo Freeman Thomas.
1851:   Inigo Freeman Thomas.
1872:   Freeman Thomas. 447 acres.
1891:   C. I. Thomas.
1921:   Dubuisson/Moody-Stuart.
1933:   Dubuisson/Alexander Moody-Stuart.
1940s: Dr. J. W. Sutherland.
1960s: Galley Bay Hotel was constructed.
1990s: Residential area constructed in the surrounding hills.

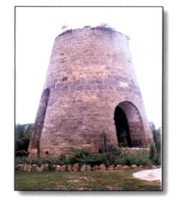

< >

The original sugar mill still stands on this plantation site, recently refurbished by the owners of the Galley Bay Hotel, which contains many artifacts found on the property during construction of the surrounding area. The mill serves as the main shore side entrance to the hotel, making a significant statement before guests are taken across the water of the pond to the hotel itself, which sits on the beach. The beach is one of Antigua's finest, but does feature heavy swells during the winter months. The Galley Bay Resort has taken over 40 acres of the hillside, offering terrific views of Deep Bay and the Caribbean Sea.

A rectangular stone above the main arch of the mill bears the date 1845, suggesting it must have been repaired following the earthquake which struck Antigua in 1843.

The estate was owned in 1843 by Inigo Freeman Thomas, who also owned Freeman's (Friar's Hill, #11), 365 acres and Winthorpe's (#56), 231 acres, as well as Galley Bay. In 1872, under the ownership of F. Thomas, the estate was used as a grazing farm for cattle.

From inside the Galley Bay Mill looking across the lagoon to the hotel. Agnes C, Meeker

In 1940, the Antigua Sugar Estates reissued 18,000 shares at £1 each to three members of the DuBuisson family (James Memoth. Mrs. Edith Manus, and William Herman. See Tomlinson's, #17), as well as Alexander Moody-Stuart and Judith Gwendolyn Moody-Stuart. This marked the final shift toward the next generation of ownership. George Moody-Stuart declined the shares offered to him (Antigua Syndicate Estates, minutes of January 4, 1940 and May 1, 1940.)

The firm continued to control Gunthorpe's (#64), Cassada Gardens (#13a), Paynter's (#61), Tomlinson's (#17), Fitches Creek (#67), Donovan's (#65), North Sound (#66), Cedar Valley (#42), and Five Islands (#31) as well as Galley Bay.

On August 1, 1943, Gunthorpes Estate Ltd. was restructured (see Gunthorpe's, #64) into a new company, renamed Antigua Syndicate Estates, Ltd. Five Islands and Galley Bay were the only two estates retained by the Moody-Stuarts.

< >

Deep Bay, the body of water in front of the Royal Antiguan Hotel and beach, has a long history dating to Archaic times in 1,400 BC. Many conch shell and stone hand axes have been found at the edge of the salt pond close to the Royal Antiguan Hotel's swimming pool. Those artifacts are in the Museum of Antigua & Barbuda in St. John's.

Fort Barrington, located on Goat Hill overlooking Deep Bay, was first captured by Royalist Prince Rupert during Oliver Cromwell's 1652 revolution. It was taken again by the French, in 1666, when they landed at Deep Bay and captured the eight guns at the Fort, routing the British troops. The French occupied Antigua for about six months; the English regained control of the island through the Treaty of Breda.

The submerged wreck in Deep Bay is the steel sailing barque "Andes". She displaced 866 tons and was carrying a cargo of 1,330 barrels of pitch, which she was transporting from Trinidad to Chile on June 5, 1905. The cargo caught fire, so the "Andes" put into Antigua off Sandy Island. She was later moved to Deep Bay to avoid obstructing shipping in and out of St. John's harbour. Two hundred barrels of the pitch were salvaged before "Andes" was consumed by flames. The tip of the boat's mast protrudes through the water surface at low tide, and is popular with snorkelers and SCUBA divers.

< >

In 1833, when the British Parliament abolished slavery, the Galley Bay estate was granted a Legacy award (Antigua 1042) of £25,351. 8s. 9p. for granting freedom to 180 enslaved. The awardee was Freeman Thomas. Inigo Freeman Thomas was unsuccessful.

It is believed that, at some point, Ellis Ferris, who managed the Five Islands estate (#31), may also have managed Galley Bay.

Colonel Martin also is mentioned in connection with this estate prior to the 1800s.

The mill at the entrance to the hotel. Inside are artifacts found on the site.
Agnes C. Meeker

#31a/b - Five Islands Plantations
(Upper & Lower: Pelican)

The Ownership Chronology

1660: Colonel Robert Carden, Governor of Antigua.
       1661- 1664; killed before 1668.
1678: Robert Carden.
1688: Colonel Robert Carden. d. 1697.
1700: Edward Otto-Baijer.
1720: John Otto-Baijer. d. 1817.
1750: Walter Sydserf. b. 1692; d. 1760.
1790: Sir George Thomas, Bart.   1777/78 Luffman map.
1829: The heirs of Sir George Thomas. 703 acres, 215
       slaves.
1833: Marmaduke Robinson. b. 1757; d. 1836.
1872: Sir Stephen J. Hill, C.B. b. 1809; d. 1891. Governor of the Leeward
       Islands in 1863. 703 acres leased to S. B. Johnson.
1921: Mrs. M. Abbott (leased).
1940: Antigua Sugar Estates restructured, leased to M. Abbott.
1943: Antigua Sugar Estates Ltd. (Moody-Stuarts).
1940s: Dr. Bill and Millicent Sutherland.
1950s: Henckell DuBuisson & Co.
1960s: Keith Edwards.

< >

Both sugar mills which stood on this estate still exist. The estate is currently operated by the Edwards family, which raises sheep, cattle and poultry. This is consistent with the history of the property, which was well known for rearing cattle and growing ground provisions. The site is very hilly, which made sugar production difficult.

The Ownership Chronology above tells only a partial story of the numerous people who owned, leased or inherited some or all of the lands identified as Five Islands Upper & Lower. A year before Robert Carden is listed as owner in 1668, Thomas Turner and John Bridges had been awarded 266 2/3 acres by then Governor Winthrop, presumably the same land located in St. John's Division.

Robert Carden was the son and heir of deceased Colonel Robert Carden, and in 1668 he was granted a patent for 360 acres at Five Islands. He sold 300 acres of the Five Islands plantation in 1678 for £14,000, and another 80 acres to Samuel Martin. A year later, he sold an additional 100 acres to Thomas Dipford and John Mitchell. Since none of these men are listed as owners of Five Islands, the land they acquired from Mr. Carden might not be considered part of the plantation. *"History of the Island of Antigua"* by Vere Oliver, Volume I.

Documentation has established that from 1707, citizens of Scotland were the largest group to migrate to Antigua, whereas in the seventeenth century arrivals were primarily from England and Ireland. Thirteen Scottish dynasties were established in Antigua during the first three quarters of the eighteenth century. Walter Tullideph was one of these enterprising Scots, as was his cousin Walter Sydserf, a doctor and planter, who is officially listed as the owner of the Five Islands Plantation in 1750.

Dr. Walter Sydserf appears to have purchased considerable acreage on Antigua in 1743. He is cited as having paid £32/acre for Witt's land at Belfast and £25/acre for Nicolas Hall's lands. *"History of the Island of Antigua"* by Vere Oliver, Volume II.

< >

William Thomas and his wife *"granted an indenture [in 1763] to Richard Oliver the younger [of] all that plantation late the estate of Walter Sydserf containing 450 acres in the Parish of St. John's and division of Five Islands Harbour.*
"History of the Island of Antigua" by Vere Oliver, Volume II.

The Ownership Chronology states that Sir George Thomas owned Five Islands as of 1790. His heirs assumed ownership in 1829 and held ownership until 1872, when the acreage became the property of Stephen J. Hill. In 1825, an indenture states *"the St. John's division of Five Islands, bounded E[ast] with the flashes and lands called Salt Ponds and part of the Five Islands Harbour, W[est] with lands belonging to Sir George Thomas (great-great-grandfather of Sir W. L. G. Thomas), N[orth] with the plantation formerly of James Gamball deceased, and afterwards Edward Otto-Baijer, Esq., and S[outh] with the sea.*
"History of the Island of Antigua" by Vere Oliver, Volume II.

Another 1825 indenture by *"Sir W. L. G. Thomas and Dame Lucretia his wife and Dame Sophia Thomas (mother) grant to Richard White all that plantation containing 450 acres in the Parish of St. John's and Division of Five Islands, bounded East with the flashes and lands called Salt Ponds."*
"History of the Island of Antigua" by Vere Oliver, Volume III.

By 1829, both Upper and Lower Five Islands totaled 703 acres with 215 slaves. Many mature tamarind trees grow on the estate, and at one time the fruit was harvested and shipped off island to be used in making soap and as a cooking ingredient excellent in curry dishes.

< >

In 1833, when the British Government abolished slavery, the Five Islands estate was awarded a Legacy payment (Antigua 1044) of £3,589. 15s. 1p. for granting freedom to 250 enslaved. The awardee was Marmaduke Robinson; unsuccessful was Sir William Lewis, George Thomas.

< >

By 1852, the heirs of Sir George Thomas owned both Upper and Lower Five Islands, consisting of 703 acres in St. John's Parish, plus the 602-acre North Sound Estate (#66) in St. George's Parish, which he sold to the late George Estridge about 40 years ago. The North Sound Estate is now vested in Mr. Estridge's daughter. The Horseford Almanac of 1872 shows Five Islands still consisting of 703 acres owned by Colonel Stephen J. Hill, C.B., but leased to S. B. Johnson.

In 1940 the Antigua Sugar Estates reissued 18,000 shares of stock at £1/ share to each of three DuBuissons (James Memoth, Mrs. Edith Manus, and William Herman), as well as Alexander Moody-Stuart and Gwendolyn Moody-Stuart (see Tomlinson's, #17). This signaled the final shift to the next generation, as George Moody-Stuart was offered shares but declined.

Antigua Syndicate Estates minutes, 4 January 1940, 1 May 1940.

The estates to be controlled by the new company were Gunthorpe's (#65), Casada Gardens (#13a), Paynter's (#61), Tomlinson's (#17), Fitches' Creek (#67), Donovan's, North Sound (#66), Cedar Valley (#42), Galley Bay (#30) and Five Islands (#31a/b). On August 1, 1943, Gunthorpes Estates Ltd. was restructured into a new company renamed Antigua Syndicate Estates Ltd. Five Islands and Galley Bay were retained by the Moody-Stuarts. During the DuBuisson tenure William Richard was an overseer.

< >

Five Islands estate house – Helen Abbott

During the 1930s, when Mrs. Mary Abbott was still leasing the Five Islands estate, her grandson, William (Bill) Sutherland, spent a lot of time on the estate, may have worked it, and as an adult felt a strong tie to it. Before leaving for college in Guelph, Canada, the last thing he said to his mother Millicent Sutherland was: "Ma, I'm going to come back and buy Five Islands." .Dr. William Sutherland worked for years as a veterinarian in Bermuda until he retired and sometime in the 1940's he purchased Five Islands. His ashes were returned to Antigua and buried below the buff house, marked by an eternal flame.

Once owned by Dr. Bill, he built a cottage at the bottom of the hill, where the sheep pen was formerly located. Mrs. Abbott lived in that cottage, cultivating a beautiful garden of fruits and flowers.

Millicent Sutherland, granddaughter of Mrs. Abbott, ran Five Islands for many years after her son bought it. She sold milk in town to someone who retailed it to customers on Nevis Street. With the help of another veterinarian, Dr. Thomas, a dam was built to the west of the sugar mill, which she named "Thomas Dam." Cattle and sheep were raised on Five Islands.

Helen Abbott, Memories

< >

Pelican Mill: Lower Five Islands

The lower sugar mill has always been referred to as Pelican Mill. It is located a short distance from the sea and what was formerly a nice beach.

Pelican Mill taken from the beach overlooking the flashes – Agnes C. Meeker

Sand mining has since destroyed both the beach and the land behind it, which adjoin the flashes. The sand mining will eventually permit heavy seas to flow through it, turning the point into an island. Cockles are still harvested in the flashes.

"*South of Gulf Point is land that was belonging to Massa Pelican, owner of the Pelican Mill that people claim to be the best in the area at one time. Massa Pelican rename Hawksbill Rock, the Pelican Rock. That new name slip away after time.*"

Pappy Smith in "To Shoot Hard Labour".

The mill known as Pelican Mill,
Lower Five Islands near the
beach and the flashes.
Agnes C. Meeker

#32 - Hawksbill Plantation
(aka Hanson's)

The Ownership Chronology

1710:   James Hanson. b. about 1680; d. 1715.
1713:   Richard & Robert Hanson.
1730:   Will Francis Hanson.
1738:   Thomas Harrison.
1750:   Eilias Ferris. d. 1754.
1790:   Elias Ferris.   1777/78 Luffman map.
1829:   John Billinghurst. 180 acres, 62 slaves.
1852:   John Allway.
1871:   Sarah Elizabeth Farr.
1878:   Reverend Peter Malone.
1800s: Late: William Jeffrey. (Born William Jeffrey O'Mard; died 1927.)
1964:   The Hawksbill Hotel leased the land from the Jeffrey family.

< >

The original sugar mill on this estate is still in mint condition, serving as the gift shop for the Hawksbill Hotel. The mill is located on a headland above the ocean and during the plantation's heyday it must have been a magnificent site. There is no sign now of the estate's great house which most likely was located where the hotel is situated currently, or any of the buildings mentioned in the book "To Shoot Hard Labour." The mill works were never converted to steam, probably because in the mid-1800s the estate cultivated very little sugar cane, concentrating on livestock and ground provisions.

The Hawksbill resort includes five beaches, one of which is Antigua's only designated nude beach. The little beach at the entrance to the hotel property remains open for local use. In the bay itself there is a large rock formation which has the shape of a Hawksbill turtle emerging from the water. It is a natural feature, which provided this estate with its name.

In 1649, Antigua's first House of Assembly met at Hawksbill, presumably in a building long since gone.

Then in 1713, the will of James Hanson left his Five Island acreage *"half to Robert Hanson and half to (his) wife for son Robert till of age."* And in 1738, the will of Frances Hanson Hawksbill (Five Islands) and the 1759 will of Hugh Holmes "leaves *my 2 houses at St. John's, Antigua, and a legacy that was left to my wife on Hawksbill estate in Five Islands to my grandson Thomas Harrison, son to my brother-in-law Theodore Hanson in Antigua."* Somewhere in the mix there was a Samuel Hanson, an Antiguan planter, whose widow's will is dated 1763.

Pappy Smith, in the popular book *"To Shoot Hard Labour",* cites the following: *"The Hawksbill fun House was the top entertainment centre in the land for nearly forty years or so. There were three top houses at the Hawksbill Estate. The Great House, the Fun House and the Leap House. There was a passageway that lead from one to the other."*

"The Leap House was used every leap year at midnight on the 28ᵗʰ of February in the age old ritual of finding a mate. At Hawksbill there was the Irish 'hengman stone'. A big stone was the platform for the gallows on which the English use to hang slaves and Irish people. Don't mine who the enemy against the mother country, the Irish man was with them."

"For generations, a particular family use to mould the features of people (clay) painting or in wood. That was a big business at Hawksbill. This was a natural gift between the Hector, the Radison and the Goodall family. The planters used to get their features molded or painted. Massas George Goodwin and Affie Goodwin (Duers) dead left their image in their bluff that was done by those two people."

"Mandy Hector draw the plan for some of the great houses including Camacho great house at Millars Estate. And not a copper them get. Piece of bread or bun and some bebitch [drink] make them feel good."

"There was a Hawksbill comb produced by one Norris Billinghurst. He would cut a piece of wood six to eight inches long and use half the portion as a handle and drive nails in the other half. A simple comb for poor people."

"The Hawksbill area was popular too because Missy Mabel used to make soap and hot pepper sauce and pepper powder. Miss Mabel pepper vinegar tell for everybody else, tan-way. None could match hers.

"Hawksbill was known in the old days for healing the sick and they would come from near and far on the island. The women healers at the Sick Hark would try almost everything to revive the sick. Whatsoever the sickness, they would rub the bottom foot, rub and exercise the ankle properly, rub the back and place the palm of the hand at the back of the head for some time. The sick must get up in the mornings and walk on the dew grass when dew fall overnight. This Lady Jumbia tell the neighbors, make the body and limbs move freer. Besides knowing what

bush to apply, vinegar was a common medicine at the Sick Hark. As a matter of fact, no woman healer travel without vinegar, turpentine and allum.

"Any amount of meat was at Hawksbill. It was the chief cattle estate. Had the right for a long time to import livestock and supply some of the Estates with all the cattle they want. It had two jetties, one to land animals and the other to land goods."

"Before then was the people from Monserrat, St. Kitts and Nevis. For long years the planters, not poor people, go back and forth swapping their vegetables and meat, and fowl, rum and sometimes coal from the Hawksbill Market."

< >

In 1833, when the British Government abolished slavery, the Hawksbill estate was granted a Legacy award (Antigua 1041) of £10,851. 1s. 5p. for granting freedom to 59 enslaved.

< >

In the late 1800s, William Jeffrey O'Mard (born in Liberta) supposedly became the first black man to own an estate: Hawksbill. He also was one of the first black men to invest in Barclays Bank. It's believed that he lived part time in the buff house, which was constructed of stone and located on the right side of the road across from the Jeffrey family memorial at the entrance to the Hawksbill Hotel. The rest of the time he resided in his home in Greenbay with his family.

He rode a horse between the two locations and was often hailed by a Portuguese family on his way home asking him to stop, partake of refreshments and play a few hands of poker. He suspected them of atempting to get him drunk so he would gamble away his lands, a fairly common practice of planters in those days. His excuse, apparently, was that he would secure his horse and return, but instead he galloped out of there!

William had three daughters, two of whom married and had families, and it is the third generation who now own Hawksbill. The Hotel was built by a man called Sheppard, and an entail was put on the property and beaches allowing a 50-year lease (with option).   Kathleen (Jeffrey) Walter

In 2011, a reading of Mr. Jeffrey's will revealed that he stated the land could not be sold, but must remain owned by the Jeffrey family in perpetuity.

Top – the renovated sugar mill today functions as a gift shop for the Hawksbill Hotel.

Bottom – the mill set against the Caribbean sea in the grounds of the hotel. Agnes C. Meeker

The family has obviously grown over the years resulting in many heirs to the property, including Jeffreys, Richardsons, Francis, Browns, etc.

At the entrance to the Hawksbill Hotel is a memorial honouring the Jeffrey family "who bequeathed to his three daughters (Francis Richardson, Grace E. Francis and Sarah Brown) and to their heirs and assigns forever in equal shares." The Hotel has fallen into disrepair over the past fifty years. Apparently members of the extended family did not view the lease agreement as favourable, leaving the property's future uncertain. It is still being negotiated at this time (2016).

The plaque to the Jeffrey family outside the Hawksbill Hotel gates.

Agnes C. Meeker.

#33a - The Folly (Duncombe's) Plantation

The Ownership Chronology

1670:   James Vaughn.

1679:   Thomas Duncombe. A patent for 150 acres. In 1679, James Vaughn sells an additional 500 acres to Thomas Duncombe, who arrived from Surinam (c.1680) with 40 of his slaves.

1700:   James Weatherill. d. 1702.

1748:   James Weatherill. Baptized: 1722; d. 1770.

1750:   Colonel James Weatherill. d. 1765.

1760:   Mrs. Margaret Weatherill.

1777:   Alexander Willock, Esq.   1777/78 Luffman map.

1829:   John J. Walter. Acreage unknown, 255 slaves.

1851:   Heirs of John J. Walter.

1852:   Godschall Johnson.

1872:   Fryer's Concrete Company.

< >

Thomas Duncombe was, apparently, a rather irascible Scotsman who, according to General Codrington, *"Thomas Dunce (sic) of ye Council of Antigua being a grown Scot . . . in his drunken fits abuse govt. I have suspended him."*

1718: *"There being hardly any freight this season, several masters of ships petition against the payment of dues. A bridge was recently built at the end of Duncombes Folly for £100.*

1770: *Indenture -- lease for one year to Francis Farley of a plantation called Duncombe's Folly in St. John's Parish and Division of 456 acres bounded W with Oliver's (#201) and Bendall's (#37), N with Briggins (#22) S with Hon. S. Martin, E with Edward Williams, Esq. Schedule of negroes and stock: 78 men, 51 women, 10 boys, 11 girls."* "History of the Island of Antigua" by Vere Oliver, Volume III.

1748: *"The land owned by James Weatherill, border on the east by Edward Williams, south by Richard Oliver, west by Peter Thibou, and Samuel Martin, and north Robert Chester. Duncombe's Folly was indentured. It's 575 acres in St. John's Parish were bounded E(ast) by lands belonging to Peter Thibou, Esq. & Samuel Martin, Esq., W(est) by lands belonging to Peter Thibou, Esq., and N(orth) by lands formerly belonging to and in the possession of Robert Chester,*

Esq, but now or later held by Col. George Lucas and those 107 negroes and all cattle, horse, as such are or lately were in the possession or occupation of Michael Lambert.

Goldsmith Sir Charles Duncombe also had something to do with Thomas Bertram's Estate in Antigua."

Prior to 1767, the Folly Estate was owned by George Weatherill. On October 17, 1836, the estate had 199 slaves and received a Legacy award (Antigua 70) from the British Parliament of £2,980. 6s. 2p. for setting them free.
(Parliamentary Papers, p. 309. T71/877 Ann Bean Water, Jacob Daniel Walter and Peter Philip Walter were all executory of Jacob Walter, deceased. Further information on the Walter ownership of Bath Lodge -- Papers, Correspondence and Plans -- can be found in the National Archives, Kew, for the period 1869-1892,)

By 1872, The Folly contained 456 acres and was owned by the Fryer's Concrete Company. All of this sheds doubt on the 1851 claim of over 1,000 acres.

< >

In 1941, the Antigua Sugar Factory, Ltd. had estimated returns from The Folly of 1,628 tons from 641 tons of cane harvested on 125 acres of peasant land.

< >

In 2003, the Antigua Power & Utilities Association (APUA), with the help of Hydro Source, sunk an artesian well at The Folly. This was Antigua's first artesian well. Water was struck at 296 feet and the well produced 400 gallons/minute.

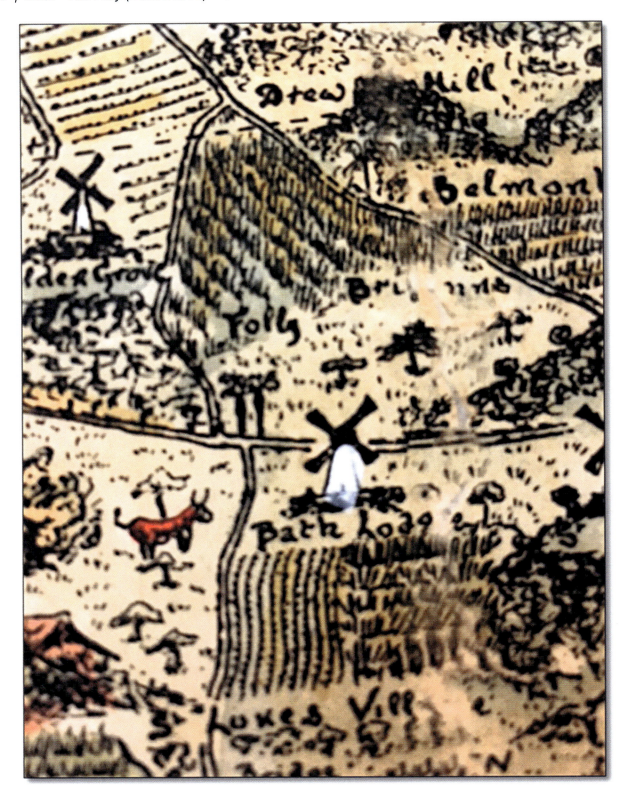

A combined map by Robert Baker 1773, Captain E. Barnett RN 1873 and Henry Martin Adams 1891 show both Folly and Bath Lodge. Today, there is no sign of Folly.

#33b - Bath Lodge Plantation

The Ownership Chronology

1869:   Jacob Walter.
1872:   Fryer's Concrete Company. 456 acres.
1891:   James Kirwin.
1928:   Heirs of Parson Emmanuel George.
1933:   E. L. Ward. 1933 Camacho map.
1946:   Returning World War II veterans given five acres of land each.
2004:   Alvin Christian, the buff house land.

< >

There is nothing left of the original buildings or sugar mill other than a large pile of stones and bricks. The land has been divided into separate holdings and house lots, and is known today as Bath Lodge.

In "Affairs of Antigua, 17th July 1841", Samuel Gore was a leasee of Bath Lodge and brought the following people to court:

* *John,* for ill usage of cattle entrusted to his care and by neglect occasioning the death of an ox. Sentence was one month's imprisonment in the House of Correction with hard labour.

* *Philemon,* for ill use of an ox. Sentence to forfeit to the estate 14 days labour.

* *Emanuel,* absent without leave. Reprimanded fourteen days imprisonment in the House of Correction with hard labour.

* *Simon,* absent for thirty-one days. Received fourteen day's imprisonment in the House of Correction with hard labour.

* *Edward B. Bryan,* withholding from wages of Samuel Barter. Defendant agreed to pay wages.

* *Francis,* quitting estate before his notice had expired. Ordered to return to work the 2 days required. W. Walker was the Justice of the Peace

< >

Following World War II, returning veterans were given three-to-five acres of farmland by the Colonial Government on various parts of the island, including

Brason Hill, Bath Lodge and Liberta. Roland Morris was in charge of land distribution, and a Mr. Page was responsible for surveying.

Those returning soldiers -- including Selvyn Spencer, Wilden Richards and Hudson Christian -- were billeted in the area prior to obtaining the land. Alvin Christian inherited his land from his father, which was the original site of the bluff house and works. He is farming the land and has a large collection of fruit trees.

< >

The property includes a red brick tomb, which Mr. Christian has been told originally featured glass doors on both the east and west sides. A Dr. Knight, of obeah (black magic) fame, from Ovals, apparently conducted some of his ceremonies at this tomb which included live chickens. The practice of obeah was declared illegal in the early 1900s, and there are several interesting cases in the Court records.

Also on the property is a large cistern, which had been used to collect water from the roof of the cattle pen. It no longer exists.

< >

Parliamentary Papers, p. 309. T71/877 Ann Bean Walter, Jacob Daniel Walter and Peter Philip Walter were all executory of Jacob Walter, deceased. Further information on the Walter ownership of Bath Lodge -- Papers, Correspondence and Plans -- can be found in the National Archives, Kew, for the period 1869-1892,)

Above – Remains of the crypt said to be used in the practice of Obeah.
Below – the remains of the cistern which was fed off the roof of the animal pen.
Agnes C. Meeker

#34 - Thibou/Jarvis Plantation (aka Mount Joshua)

The Ownership Chronology

1600s: Louis (Lewis) Thibou. d. 1716. Father of ten girls, Rachael was the oldest.

1716: Thomas Jarvis. d. 1747.

1749: Thomas Jarvis II. b. 1722; d. 1785. Married 1. Jane Whithead; 2. Rachael Thibou.

1790: Thomas Jarvis III. b. 1784; d. 1807.
1777/78 Luffman map.

1829: Bertie Entwhistle Jarvis. b. 1793, d. 1859/62.

1843: Bertie Entewhistle Jarvis. 830 acres.

1872: Thomas Jarvis. b.1835; d. 1877. 568 acres.

1891: John C. Jarvis.

1921: C. D. Ledeatt.

1933: Joseph Turner Dew. b.1867; d. 1941. 1933 Comacho map.

c1940: Anthony & Ferdinand Shoul.

2003: Heirs of the Shoul's.

< >

The surname Thibou was originally derived from the Old French personal name of Theobold, meaning "bold" or "Brave". Louis (Lewis) Thibou was born in the Province of Orleans, in France, and was the first member of the family to arrive in Antigua.

The Thibou Jarvis sugar mill remains in excellent condition, but except for the remnants of some stonewalls and stone "footprints" in the bush, there is little left of this estate. The works inside the mill are one of three remaining on the island. It was refurbished to working condition and donated to the Betty's Hope Trust (#77a/b) by the Shoul family. The original house was built on fairly flat land but the elevation was sufficient to provide both the house and the works with a view of the surrounding landscape all the way to the sea.

Thomas Jarvis inherited his father-in-law's Antigua estate in the Popeshead Division, in 1716, and the mansion on the plantation was known as Mount Joshua. It was considered to be one of the most commodious on the island.

Top, Mount Joshua with mounting block for horses and water dripper as flower pot.
Bottom – the interior filled with Victorian bric-a-brac – Maybert Dew nee Jarvis

The plantation grew and prospered, remaining in the Thibou/Jarvis family for 200 years. It eventually included 1,000 acres in both St. John's and St. George's parishes, as well as Long Island and Bird Island. When the elder Thomas died in 1749, the estate was inherited by his son Thomas Jarvis II, who served in the Government of Antigua. He eventually became Chief Justice of the Court of Common Pleas. He and his wife, Rachael, had numerous children, including Thomas Jarvis III, George Ralph Payne Jarvis, Bertie Entwhistle Jarvis, and James Nibbs Jarvis (1794 - 1842). James and his wife, Lorne (Campbell) Jarvis, had a son, Thomas Jarvis (1835 - 1877), who served in the General Legislative Council of Antigua.

Jarvis family papers, William Clements Library.

The Jarvis family owned Doddington Hall in Lincolnshire, England.

In 1750, Thomas Jarvis II inherited Long Island and Mount Joshua. He also inherited Blizards (#54) with his first wife, Jane Whitehead, who died in 1797. He left a will dated 1779 in which he gave *"to my wife, Rachael, my dwelling-house built on land called Mount Joshua of 18 acres for life, also furniture, plate, provisions, cattle, coach, post chaise, whiskey and carriage horses."*

"History of the Island of Antigua" by Vere Oliver, Volumes II and III.

Thomas Jarvis II had considerable influence with Antigua's governors because of his position as Chief Justice of the Court of Common Pleas. His family built the famous Massa Grave, which *"the planters at Thibou Jarvis estate use to say, was better than those at Big Church."*

Sammy Smith in *"To Shoot Hard Labour"*

< >

Patsy Harley (deceased), Maybert Dew's niece, who lived in New Zealand, found an architectural drawing of the cemetery among her aunt's papers. The drawing shows a stairway beneath a central stone, leading to a crypt below. Mrs. Dew often spoke of a skeleton of a one-legged man in the crypt, whose identity had long been lost. When her mother, Mrs. Jarvis, died, the Government would not permit burials except in the public cemetery or church yards, so neither were interned in the Thibou/Jarvis family plot which is difficult to find now that the bush has totally taken over. The unpaved road that went by the small cemetery to Mount Joshua from the Village of New Winthropes, no longer exists.

The burial site of the Jarvis Family - Patsy Harley.

The website www.tomstonesbb shows grave stones recorded in Antigua for Jameson/Mary, Jarvis/Thomas, Taylor/Annie, Jarvis/John Campbell, Jarvis/Thomas, Jarvis/Mabel Cecilia, Jarvis/Bertie Hill and Jarvis/Alice.

< >

In 1768, *"a demurer recites that Catherine Thibou, being possessed of a plantation in St. John's parish -- by indenture of demise dated 1768 made between her of the 1st part and Walter Thibou, Esq of the other -- assigned her estate to him for 99 years at the yearly rent of 700 UKL for the first year and 800 UKL a year after."* This presumably refers to another plantation not named.

Thomas Jarvis III noted in a 1790 letter that *"in the last two crops I made only 45 hogsheads of bad sugar"* and also noted his *"hogsheads sold for 54/-; my neighbour Mr. Byam sold his for 69/- in London."*

< >

The William Clements Library, in Michigan, has two old hand-drawn maps of the Hart's & Royal's Plantation (#3), Thibou's and Blizzard's (#54). The undated material in the Jarvis family papers, placed at the end of Box #2, includes two small manuscript maps of land in Antigua. The first, dated c1800 and entitled 'Plan of Harts' and Royals' Estate Buildings', shows the buildings of a sugar mill, including

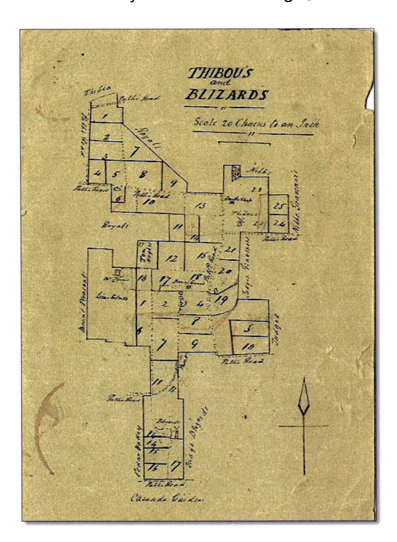

the 'Chaff machine room, Rum cella under Stillhouse, Curing house and the house and kitchen of the overseer. The other manuscript map of the "Thibou's and Blizard's Estates in Antigua' reveals public roads, shops and burial grounds.

In 1829, Thibou's was combined with Blizard's and contained 830 acres including both Long and Bird Islands. There were 319 registered slaves.

When the British Parliament abolished slavery in 1833, Thibou's Estate was given a Legacy award (Antigua 30) of £4,194. 12s. 7p. for freeing 276 enslaved. Successful claimants were Hardman Earle, Christiana Richardson Jarvis, Thomas Ridding, Thomas Ward, Rev. Alexander Scott and Hayward Turner. Unsuccessful were John Hopkins Forbes, Bertie Entwhistle Jarvis, Grace Jarvis, Mary Wilelmina Lindsey (nee Jarvis), William Chacon Lindsey and Joseph Maberly. Previous owners were listed as Mary Elizabeth Shepherd Freeman Jarvis (nee Blackwell) and Thomas Jarvis, Sr.

< >

James Howell managed the estate by 1837 when James A. Thome wrote the following report: *"The negro village on this estate contains one hundred houses each of which is occupied by a separate family. Mr. H. next conducted us to a neighboring field where the 'great gang' were at work. There were about fifty persons in the gang -- the majority females -- under two inspectors or superintendents, men who take the place of the quondam drivers, though their province is totally different. They merely direct the laborers at their work, employing with the loiterers the stimulus of persuasion, or at the furthest, no more than the violence of the tongue. (The people on most estates are divided into three gangs: first, the great gang composed of the principal effective men and women; second, the weeding gang consisting of younger and weekly persons; and third, the grass gang, which embraces all children able to work.*

"There had been much less pretended sickness among the negroes since freedom. They had now a strong aversion to going to the sick house, so much so that on many estates it had been put to some other use."

"Emancipation in the West Indies – 1837" by James A. Thome

One of the last members of the Jarvis family to reside in Antigua was Catherine Anne Maybert (Jarvis) (b. Dec. 22, 1911; d. June 9, 1999). She and her husband Dalmer Dew, of Dew's & Son, rebuilt the oldest house on the island -- the Hodges Estate house (#4) on Hodges Bay -- after they were married in the 1930s.

In 1933, Thibou's was owned by Joseph Turner Dew who had an engineering business in Antigua, Dew's & Son. He was born in 1865 and had four children. His third daughter was Lillian Betty Dew, who married Ronald Cadman, the Managing Director of Dew's & Co. Joseph's fourth child was Dalmer; he married Maybert Jarvis, and together they were instrumental in renovating the oldest house in Antigua. It is located at Hodges Bay (#4).

Dew's & Co. was the agent for Morris cars and imported various other makes when privately ordered. The author's grandmother told her that Major Dew was the first person to bring a car onto Antigua. When she got married in 1915, there were only two vehicles on the island, both of which were hired for her wedding.

Dew's & Co. also opened a supermarket and hardware and lumber business. Major Joseph Turner Dew, OBE, VD, was one of the best known engineers in Antigua, and almost his entire professional career he was engaged in the erection of sugar factories and the marketing of sugar processing machinery. He had been connected with the sugar industry in Antigua since 1887, when he first arrived on the island after completing a five-year apprenticeship in the Leeds Works of

Messrs. John Fowler & Sons. Subsequently, Major Dew broadened the scope of his business to include shipbuilding repairs. He also was a consultant to a large number of sugar factories and to the Government pumping plant at St. John's waterworks. He also held the position of Agent for a number of British engineering firms.

He was keenly interested in the welfare of Antigua and was a member of its Executive Council. He was also Chairman of the Board of Directors on the Antigua Light Company, Ltd., and of the Antigua Cotton Factory, Ltd. He died in Antigua on 7th October 1941 at age 75.   Grace's list.

< >

In the 1940s, when Anthony Shoul owned the estate, his wife Themene recalls when *"hog cholera broke out at Thibou's and 480 pigs had to be burnt with one gallon of kerosene, including Lady Fine who weighed 450 lbs. and had 18 piglets. Also, in 1939, the estate had the largest crop of cotton ever, and during the war years produced one million lbs of yams."*   Themene Shoul, memories of . . .

In 1941, the Antigua Sugar Factory, Ltd. had sugar cane returns of 1,794 tons from the Thibou estate, drawn from 1,375 tons of cane on 111 acres, equaling 12.39 tons per acre.

< >

This author states: *"My grandmother, Margaret (McSevney) Conacher, rented Thibou/Jarvis estate for a short time in the 1920s after her father had been 'let go' as manager of Parham New Works due to the accident that left him wheelchair bound. Both Annie Duncan (her sister) and my grandmother had returned home to Antigua with their children after losing their husbands at an early age, and a large property was needed to house them all. It was while they were at Thibou/Jarvis that my grandmother found and purchased Court Lodge in St. John's, where the City View Hotel is today, next to the Antigua Girl's High School (AGHS). She later sold Court Lodge in the 1950's to Dr. Wizenger (dentist).*

"Thibou/Jarvis was supposed to have its share of ghosts, and many a night the silver could be heard rattling in the drawers: rats?"   Agnes C. Meeker.

The Thibou/Jarvis mill when it still had the wooden 'sails' – Mrs. Themene Shoul

#35 - St. Clare/Williams Plantation
(Originally known as The Body)

The Ownership Chronology

1713:   Edward St. Clare. 320 acres.
1750:   Edward Williams.
1790:   Samuel Williams.
1829:   Roland Williams. 384 acres.
1872:   Dr. James B. Thibou.
1891:   Louisa Martin.
1921:   W. T. Malone.
1933:   Dr. Robert Andrew Raeburn. d. 1987.
1980:   Raymond Raeburn and his wife, Ursula.
2003:   Heirs of the Raeburn's.

< >

The sugar mill on this plantation is in fairly good condition and features an unusual squat barrel shape, much different from any other sugar mills on the island. The workmanship in the cut stone is quite rough. This mill was never converted to steam.

The original house was changed slightly by Dr. Raeburn and his wife in the 1930s, when they apparently used many of the old burial stones on the property as fill when they built the new stairs to the entrance. Rita Raeburn, the doctor's daughter, has said there was a slave burial ground marked by a copse of large old tamarind trees. One marker remained when she last looked. The estate has a beautiful view of Bendal's Estate (#37) and McNish mountain, together with the Allen's (#48) and Gillead/Providence (#189) plantations.

When known as the Body this plantation was rented for £900 annually, and occasionally "underlet" for £120 per year.

"History of the Island of Antigua" by Vere Oliver, Volume II.

< >

The estate house surrounded by beautiful gardens during Dr. Raeburn's time.   Raeburn family.

With the abolition of slavery in 1833, the British Parliament granted the St. Clare estate a Legacy award (Antigua 115) of £10,041. 6s. 9p. for granting freedom to 62 enslaved. Rowland Edward Williams was the sole awardee.

< >

Both Vere Oliver and the 1872 edition of the Horseford Almanac show St. Clare owned by "The Honorable James B. Thibou, a member of the Assembly for St. John's City". The estate had 354 acres, with an additional 10 acres owned by William Alsas.

Dr. Robert Raeburn was the chief Government veterinarian on the island during the 1940s, and along with Robert Hall at Smith's (#161), established a dairy farm. Their gardens were beautiful and very extensive, with a very large variety of trees and plants, including an ancient Sandbox tree which still stands just west of the original house. Peacocks continue to roam the grounds.

Above one of the out buildings is a plaque, which reads: *"St. Clare formerly known as The Body Plantation of Colonel Roland Williams and his heirs from 1680-1842. Surveyed by Edward St. Clare in 1772."*

The estate had an 18-inch bell forged by Mears & Staenbank Founders, London in 1860. Although now cracked, it still lies in the yard. Most of the plantations had large bells such as this which were used to summon the workers on the estates.

The St. Clair mill with
its barrel shape.
Agnes C. Meeker

The Raeburn family also possesses a lovely 1773 hand drawn map of the estate, drawn by Alexander Willock, Esq. It shows the complete layout with numbered fields, acreage, roads and the location of the sugar mill and buildings. John Killian was the surveyor.

< >

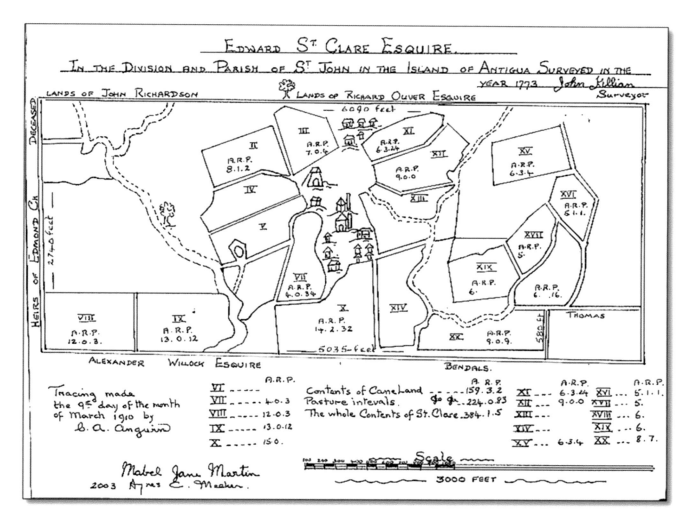

Hand drawn map dated 1773 by John Killian, Surveyor.   Re drawn by Mabel Jane Martin and in
2003 by Agnes Meeker. Shows the fields, acreage, roads and location of the mill & houses.
Raeburn Family

#36 - Belle Vue/Stoney Hill Plantation

The Ownership Chronology

1750:   Rowland Ash.

1790:   William & Joseph Warner.

1814:   Indenture between Thomas Warner and his wife, Dorothy, and the Honourable Samuel Warner conveying to Samuel "all that plantation in the Division of New North Sound and parish of St. George's called 'Stoney Hill' or 'Belle Vue', containing 149 acres of cane and 89 acres of pasture . . . and all slaves reputed to be amounting in number to120."

1829:   Honorable Samuel Warner.

1843:   Francis Shand & Company, Liverpool. 527 acres; 261 slaves.

1870:   Francis Shand.

1872:   Fryers Concrete Co., one of 24 steam works in St. Mary's Parish.

1878:   Aubrey J. Camacho.

1891:   James Maginley. On Sept. 7 of this year, Queen Victoria "has been pleased to give directions for the appointment of James Maginley, Esq., to be a Member of the Executive Council of the Island of Antigua."

London Gazette.

19xx: Heirs of W. Maginley.

1921:   Aubrey J. Camacho.

1933:   M. V. Camacho.   1933 Camacho map.

1930s: John I. Martin.

< >

The sugar mill on this plantation no longer exists, but in the mid-1800s it was most certainly converted to steam as evidenced in photographs of the old brick chimney, which regrettably was demolished by the earthquake of 1974.

Across the main road to the south of the estate, in the bush, are the remains of old walls and evidence of cut and rubble stone where the brick chimney of the estate house had stood. The chimney was hexagonal in shape, similar to those found on the island of Nevis. On Antigua chimneys tended to be square. Most of the bricks which formed this chimney have been removed most likely scavenged for rebuilding.

Left - Destroyed by an earthquake in 1974, this chimney indicates the sugar mill had been converted to steam power in the mid-1800.

Mrs. Daley.

Right – The Boa-bob Tree supposedly marks the grave of the owner of Belle Vue. These trees are known to have the largest trunk of any tress on the Island, 30 feet in diameter. There are approximately 9 mature trees on the island.

Agnes C. Meeker.

To the west of this estate stands a very large Baobob tree (*adansonia digitala*) on the property of Mr. Walter, which features the largest trunk of any tree on Antigua (30 feet). *"Historically, the tree marks the resting place of Robert Ashe, a former owner of Stoney Hill Estate, who vowed no stone would mark his grave. Pappy Smith's mother called it a 'Devil Tree' and it was known as a 'place of wickedness'."*

"Heritage Treasures" by Desmond Nicholson

On the main road nearby is considered the exact center of the island. At one time, an engraved stone marked the location, but it was covered up by a construction crew when the main road was widened.

"About five miles east of St. John's is the exact center of the island at a spot on the hill now known as Clarke's Hill. Back then it was called Centre Hill, for about half a mile east of the tee road at the hill is the exact centre of Antigua. The centre was marked by a big stone -- put in the middle of the road -- about three feet long by three feet wide and about eight inches thick. The surveyors carved out the crown and date on that spot."

"The Bear Bob Tree also use to mark the place where the slave market was. On Tuesday the slaves for sale or swap was taken there. Later on the market was move to another tree about 400 yards east of the Bear Bob Tree. A slave by the name of Grandy Two happen to die at that tree while she was up for sale and the pond take its name after her. That tree and that pond is still there. On the north side, a little way east of the tee road is a gulley about three-quarters of a mile long running from south to north called Stoney Hill Gulley. RSD (Goodwin) said that that was the place where the slaves meet and plan the revolt in 1736.

The Goodwins know plenty of what happen at the Stoney Hill Gulley.

He used to say that slave go there to worship them King and them African God. They would dance around fire, drink wine and inhale the smoke from the roasted cashew nuts."

"A little away from the gulley -- was the spot where almost all negas that was killed at North Sound, Blackman's and Jonas was buried. After I get to know the spot, I never like to pass that way because of the sad memories it a bring back. That place was very hard and stony, a spot the planters and them couldn't use to grow sugar cane. That place so hard that man could hardly dig a grave there, so the graves have to be shallow and the massa use to make sure they give us white lime to rotten the body way quickly. People use to have to pile stones on top of the graves, they were so shallow." Pappy Smith in "To Shoot Hard Labour".

< >

1840: Francis Shand's slave ownership in Antigua was accomplished through the family's merchant firm, C. W. & F. Shand, of Liverpool, England. Francis, John and Alexander Shand were sons of Charles Francis Shand, who was associated with the West Indian merchant firm, Rodie & Son, located at Rupert House near Liverpool. Francis Shand also operated in British Guiana in partnership with Alexander Simpson.

T71/877 Antigua claim nos. 3 (Willick's Spyes), 9 (Christian's Valley & Biffins), 22 (Harts & Royals), 36 (Cedar Valley), 52 (Collen's Estate), 303 & 321 (Crabb's Estate), 351 (Belle Vue), 354 (Fitch's Creek) and 835 Profile 7 Legacies Summary.

< >

When the British Parliament abolished slavery in 1833, the Belle Vue estate was granted a Legacy award (Antigua 352) of £36,741. 13s. 1p. for granting freedom to 246 enslaved. William Shand was the sole awardee; Dorothy Warner and Samuel Warner were unsuccessful applicants. Francis, John and Alexander Shand were sons of Charles Francis Shand.

< >

Antonio Joseph Camacho (died 1894) arrived in Antigua from Madeira around 1960 and by 1861 he owned A. J. Camacho Co., an export and merchant business and was the sole owner of Briggins (#22), Herbert's (#20), and Dunning's (#7) estates between 1871 and 1878, and Jonas (#85), Otto's (#16) and Langford's (#6) between 1878 and 1891. By 1887, he also owned Woods (#12), Lower Freeman's (#81b) and Oliver's (#46). His son Emanuel O. Camacho inherited the business. By the time Emanuel died he held over 1,600 acres of sugar land under cultivation, the single largest landowner besides the Maginley family. He was a staunch supporter of the Roman Catholic Church.

In 1941, the Antigua Sugar Factory, Ltd., estimated sugar returns of 1,739 tons from the 160-acre estate (120 acres of peasant land) based on 4,260 tons of cane delivered, averaging 18.58 tons/acre.

The 1970s, the brutal murder of Mrs. Thomson occurred in the Estate's bluff house. The crime was never solved, and was attributed to the practice of obeah because her eyes had been slit to prevent identification of the murderer. A concrete blockhouse has been built on the original buff house site and the pond has been filled in.

Helen Abbott noted that when she accompanied Desmond Nicholson on one of his historical exploration hikes and in the area of Belle Vue Plantation they came across an old headstone dedicated to a Captain "Somebody" with a skull and cross bones symbol. In an attempt to read the middle initial, they used their drinking water and some grass to scrub the headstone, but the engraving was too faded. She noted that none of the old grave stones found in the bush are preserved, and usually get ploughed under or used to tether cows.

Helen Abbott, Memories of....

#37- Bendal's Plantation

The Ownership Chronology

1728:   Hopefor Bendall. d. 1727. He was Collector of Customs, and presumably had some involvement with this plantation, hence the name.

1733:   Mr. Bendall was reported to be *"an eminent Quaker in the minorities, reputed to be worth £20,000."* *"History of the Island of Antigua"* by Vere Oliver, Volume I.

1750:   Richard Oliver. d. 1791. 1777/78 Luffman map.

1790:   Thomas Oliver.

1820:   Messrs. Robert & Thomas Hyndman. By 1829, the estate contained 503 acres, 249 slaves.

1843:   Hyndman.

1872:   Fryer's Concrete Company, which also owned Belvedere (#38), and George Byam's (#39) for total acreage of 1,690. All three sugar mills were converted to steam in the mid-1800s.

1891:   L. I. P. Company.

1904:   Bendals Sugar Factory built to handle area crops.

1933:   S. W. Estates Company.

1940:   The closing of the Bendal's Sugar Factory.

1943:   Antigua Syndicate Estates

1958:   Antigua Government

< >

The sugar factory on this estate no longer exists, but the manager's house still sits up on the hill overlooking the factory site below, along with several stone walls, the tennis court, and the foundation stones of several of the staff houses. The author was born in one of the staff houses in 1940, when her father, James McIndoe Watson, was dismantling the closed factory. One of the storerooms was purchased, at auction, by Robert Hall. He moved it to the Smith's estate (#161) by oxen, and later enlarged it to accommodate his growing family.

"A scene of peculiar interest is found near Bendal's Estate, whose Sugar Works and offices with a bridge in the foreground one might almost imagine to have been placed by the hand of an artist."

"Historical & Descriptive Account of Antigua, 1830."

Top – Plymouth engines in the yard
Middle – Factory from the hill above, staff houses.
Bottom – Bringing lunch in pails for the workers.
Gerrald Thomas

There were three cane sidings in the Bendals area — York, Rigby and Bendals — where cane was loaded onto carts (or "bagoons)" to be transferred by locomotive to the factory. From 1940 the cane from Blubber Valley and Cashew

Hill was not brought by rail to the Antigua Sugar Factory. It was a strenuous climb so two locomotives were used to pull the bagoons, #9 and #10. Mr. Roland Morris worked at Bendals and wrote out all of the tickets for each peasant farmer as cane was loaded into the bagoons (cane carts).

The loading began at six AM and was repeated later in the afternoon, so each engine made two trips daily. The tickets were checked against the cane as it was weighed so each peasant could be paid the correct amount. There was no room for error.

The Hewlett family now lives in the manager's house which overlooks the rest of the compound and the location of the Bendals Sugar Factory, which shut down in 1940.

< >

An 1805 article in *The Antigua Times* stated: *"Last Saturday evening the Court House was filled with a most influencing gathering of ladies and gentlemen who had been invited to listen to a lecture on Sacchorometry and Concrete, which Mr. A. Fryer had consented to deliver. This gentleman is head of the well-known sugar refining firm Fryer, Benson & Foster, of Manchester, and is the inventor and patentee of an apparatus which has condensed the syrup, which he calls the Concretor.*

"The firm has purchased a number of estates on the island of Antigua, and Mr. Fryer has been here for several weeks making arrangements for the manufacture of concrete on an extensive scale. He has at the same time been prosecuting various and important scientific researches bearing upon sugar cane and its constituents. Several gentlemen who had an opportunity of private intercourse with Mr. Fryer, conceiving that if he were willing he might impart in the form of a lecture information valuable to the planters generally. I addressed to him the request to do so, to which request he willingly acceded, and on the issue of the invitation the interest felt in Mr. Fryer's communication was shown by the presence of all the leading proprietors and planters from every part of the island."

< >

When the British Parliament abolished slavery in 1833 the Bendal's estate was granted a Legacy award of (Antigua 95) of £2,854. 16s. 6p. for granting freedom to 225 enslaved. Awardees were George Betts, Samuel Boddington, Thomas Boddington the younger, Richard Davis, and Nicholas Kirwan. Unsuccessful were

John Allan, Robert Hyndman, Thomas Hyndman Sir William Martin 2nd Bart, Josiah Martin, and James Shannon. Thomas Bartrum was listed as "other association".

(Papers. Correspondence and Plans: Hyndman, Bendal's, Antigua 37; available from the Colonial Office and Predecessions; West Indian Encumbered Estates Commission from the National Archives (UK) - 1866-1892 Ref. CO 441/7/1.)

< >

Originally the Belvedere factory was the site of the Fryers Concrete Co., and later became the location of the Bendals Sugar Factory when it was converted in 1904/5 to produce sugar crystals. The Bendals Sugar Factory never produced more than 1,800 tons of sugar annually and eventually closed in 1940.

On August 18, 1903 Arthur Morier Lee published an 11-page paper entitled "Contract as to Advances of Bendal's Sugar Factory in Antigua." And in 1904, Bendal's became one of the three central Sugar Factories built on the island. The last manager of the factory was Mr. Martin; the junior engineer was James McIndoe Watson (the author's father), who later became one of the last managers of the Gunthorpes Sugar Factory in the late 1950s. The Bendal's Sugar Factory ceased operation in 1940 when it was decided that cane was to be processed at the main factory, Gunthorpes.

Very few photographs of the Bendal's Sugar Factory exist, although Jean Thomas possesses several negatives which belonged to her husband Gerald Thomas who, with his brother Lionel, grew up at Bendal's. Gerald later worked at the Bendal's Sugar Factory, and moved over to Gunthorpes with Jimmy Watson. Gerald once told the author that her mother, Mae Watson, would have her maid deliver a tray at tea time (4 PM) every afternoon for the men to share.

In 1910, the government of Antigua issued two postal stamps with images of the Bendal's Sugar Factory.

Top – view of Bendals Factory from the North.
Bottom – view of Bendals Factory from the East – Anthony Gonsalves Collection

"People today mostly hear of Bendal. Very little is heard of the estates within close proximity of Bendal because almost everybody now name the whole place Bendal. In my young days, each plantation was known and identified separately. To refer to the whole area as Bendal is misleading. Breaknock [#40] is about one and one half miles from Bendal Estate works. At one time Antigua's largest sugar factory was located at Bendal. That may be the reason why the name Bendal keeps ringing above the names of other estates." Aunty Dood in *"Symbol of Courage"*

"Back in the old days members of the Lewis family monopolized the cooper trade at Hamilton, Bendal and Jennings (#187) plantations. The sugar industry was the main source of livelihood, and coopers played an important part of the operation. As result, the sugar estates could not function properly without the coopers." Aunty Dood in *"Symbol of Courage"*

< >

In the late 1990s, the author met Roy Edwards, a Bendal's Sugar Factory employee, who took her on a tour of the old factory site behind the Bendal's Clinic, where there are some old loco rail lines visible and was able to identify the loco yard, concrete walls and bits of machinery. Agnes C. Meeker.

Around 2000, several homes in the community of Bendal's were relocated due to the bombarding of stones from the government quarry nearby. In 1980, a young girl playing in the schoolyard was hit by rocks and her foot was later amputated.

The Green Castle Agricultural Government Station is located in Bendals across from the medical Clinic. Plants are propagated for sale, and during mango season the mangoes are harvested and sold to the public. Behind and to the west of the Station are several wells which continue to provide fresh water to the St. John's area.

< >

"Kooka bendal" referred to by Pappy Smith in *"To Shoot Hard Labour"* is supposedly derived from the African word "kooka" (cacca) meaning excrement, and "bendal" is an English word for an area used to dump; hence, the kooka bendals were where the villages dumped their excrement prior to the introduction of pit latrines by the Chinese. Nothing to do with the plantation Bendals.

< >

Hamilton's (aka Hamberly)

Hamilton's was a village in the hills above Bendals, known locally as Hamberly. Founded in 1679 by Captain John Hamilton, it originally consisted of 250 acres (granted) by the Honorable Jeremiah Watkins, as surveyed in July 1679. In February 1680, 233 acres were indentured to Sir William Stapleton. The village was destroyed by two back-to-back hurricanes in 1950 ("Dog" and "Cat"), and because of its remoteness many of the inhabitants opted to move down into the Bendals valley rather than rebuild. Ulrica Pierce, who was from Bendal's, recalled walking to visit people in Hamiltons when she was a girl, and at that time there were only three houses left standing.

Currently, plantings of flamboyant and lilies attest to the existence of the village, and a spring a little further up the hill still provides water for irrigation. Known as 'Salt Spring', the water tends to be a little brackish.

Mark Lewis was a well-known blacksmith in Hamilton's who could *"shoe horses and donkeys and he made bits for them, also cart wheels; he could bend iron into any shape. He also made cutlasses, knives, scrapers and then tempered them so they would remain sharp for long."* *"Symbol of Courage" by Keithlyn Smith.*

< >

St. Luke's Anglican Church

In 1715 *"The vestry think of building a new church on church hill belonging to me, for 5s. we give the land, S and N 80 feet E & W 50 feet on trust."* By 1752, the land was owned by Archibald Hamilton. On January 1ˢᵗ, 1758, Mr. Hart purchased the Hamilton estate. *"History of the Island of Antigua"* by Vere Oliver, Volume II.

St. Luke's Anglican Church is on a small outcrop just before entering Bendals. It has been a place of worship since slavery days. The building has been renovated several times after hurricane damage. There is an old cemetery behind the church; Mary Gleadall has recorded several of the memorial encryptions on her web site of graves in the early 1900s.

A magnificent wedding held at St. Luke's. – Museum of Antigua & Barbuda.

Aunty Dood (Mary Lewis), of "Symbol of Courage" fame, was from Breaknocks and recorded a number of her memories:

"The Lewis family was the corner stone of St. Luke's Anglican Church for over a century. At one time, the well loved and distinguished Anglican Bishop George Sumner Hand served at St. Luke's. It was there that he became close to the Lewis family, and showed by his words and deeds that he thought very highly of them. Priest after priest could call on them to do anything for the church. The family worked hard during the construction of the church and later maintained it with extreme care and devotion over the years."

Aunty Dood learned from Bishop Hand that the Lewis's were descendants of the Ashanti tribe from the Gold Coast in West Africa. He also said the *female slaves that disembarked from the boat at Point Wharf in St. John's"* were given the name Elizabeth, which became the most popular name in the Southern part of the island.

For further review, there is an 11-page paper written by Arthur Morier Lee on the "Contract as to Advances for Bendals Sugar Factory in Antigua" dated 18th August 1903.

#38 - Belvedere Plantation
(aka Horne's)

The Ownership Chronology

1682:   Edward Horne.

1760:   Valentine Morris Horne. b. 1739. Sold to,

1771:   Honorable Dr. Ashton Warner.

1789:   Mary Ann Massett. The heir of Dr. Warner, who left her *"all liquors in my house at St. John's and on my estate called Belvedere. I do not wish Belvedere to be sold. 1/2 of the plantation and slaves in the Old North Sound Division (Pares) and also a plantation I purchased of the late Valentine Morris Horne, Esq."*

1820:   Messrs. Robert & Thomas Hyndman. By 1829, the estate contained 361 acres worked by 125 slaves.

1843:   T. Sanderson.

1852:   Heirs of T. Sanderson. 361 acres.

1872:   Fryer's Sugar Concrete Company.

1891:   Lee Spooner & Company.

1921:   Lee Spooner & Company.

1930:   M. V. Camacho.

1933:   E. L. Ward.   1933 Camacho map.

1940s: John I. Martin.

< >

The estate house still exists on the hillside with views over the valley extending to Body Ponds (see St. Clair #35 and Body Ponds #41). The sugar mill no longer exists, but it is known that this mill, with Belvedere (#38), Bendals (#37), and George Byam's (#39), converted to steam in the mid-1800s.

Ms. Gay Byam visited this estate around 2009 in an attempt to trace the footsteps of her ancestor, Lydia Byam (c. 1800), who had kept a diary then in Gay's possession. The diary extolled the beautiful gardens on the estates, and Belvedere was described as one of the most beautiful, with walled tiers accessed by steps and planted with tropical plants. Lydia Byam used to enjoy horseback riding all over the plantation on her visits.

The Belvedere house nestled against the hills. Agnes C. Meeker

Gay Byam did find seveal of the steps leading to the different levels of the garden and old walls which were covered in coralita. She also entered the original foundation below the house, which is still standing. The foundation had walls three feet thick with narrow slits for shooting at marauding Caribs or French. It was obviously a place of refuge in time of attack. When approaching from the direction of the Bendals estate there are the remains of an old structure, which may have been the works for Belvedere.

< >

When the French captured the island of Montserrat in 1676, Lieutenant Colonel Sutton of that island escaped into the woods and found *"Henry Ashton, Esq., son of _____ Ashton, formerly Governor of Antigua and a current resident of Montserrat, lying desperately wounded."* He carried [him] into the house of Mr.

Angus, *"which the Indians then burnt down and they said Henry Ashton was burnt alive."*
"History of the Island of Antigua" by Vere Oliver, Volume III.

Some of the ruins on the approach to Belvedere – Agnes C. Meeker

In 1682, carpenter Edward Horne held a patent for 400 acres, and in 1702 he was granted another patent for 750 acres in the Body Division of Antigua. A letter dated c.1697 states that *"Sam Horne, Collector of ye Duty in Antegoa [sic], a man of very morose temper, who by his trading and concessions has got a great Estate [and] a few years ago was servant to one Mr. Cole in Nevis."*
"History of the Island of Antigua" by Vere Oliver, Volume II.
(A comprehensive history of the Morris and Horne family from Wales, may be found in the National Library of Wales Journal.)

In 1787, there is an indenture record which shows *"Horne's containing 247 acres, 3 roods and 30 perches. Schedule 1. Belvedere Plantation [with] men 44, women 73, children 30, mules 12 and 1 old, cattle, 9 oxen, 7 bulls, 11 cows, 5 calves. Also owned Pare's Plantation (#84)."*
"History of the Island of Antigua" by Vere Oliver, Volume III.

"There were hard times on the estates around 1846, but even then there was the occasional spark of new enterprise. One gentleman, Mr. Fryers acquired eight Antiguan properties: Bendel's (#37), Belvedere (#38), George Byam's (#39), Bath Lodge (#33), Halliday's Mountain (#49), Bodkins (#142), Green Castle (#163) and Rigby's (#162). [His] intention was to introduce a shortened manufacturing technique. The cane juice was to be brought in as rapidly as possible by evaporation to a solid state of 'sugar concentrate' which would be exported in 'blocks' to Britain for processing and refining. A patented 'concretor' costing about £1,000 had been designed and was to be manufactured by Messre. Manlove, Elliott & Company of Nottingham for Fryer's Concrete Company. The enterprise was not successful."

"First of the Leewards" by Robert Hall

"If we wish to know, after the composition of concrete sugar and good 4th, what would be the return in concrete sugar No. 4 and molasses, we arrive at the following result:

Extractible sugar calculated..................58%
Molasses...16%
Or in good sugar No. 4..........................74%
In Colonial Molasses............................26%

< >

In 1941 the Antigua Sugar Factory Ltd. estimated cane returns from Belvedere at 3,344 tons from 218 acres including 160 acres of peasant land, 4,348 tons of cane delivered averaging 12.52/acre.

#39 - George Byam's Plantation

The Ownership Chronology

1700s: George Byam. b. 1704; d. 1779).
1750:   Heirs of George Byam.
1790:   Dr. James Athill. b. 1759; d. 1822. 1777/78 Luffman map.
1820:   Heirs of James Athill. 336 acres; 132 slaves.
1843:   James Athill.
1851:   John Foreman. b. 1820. 300 acres.
1872:   Fryer's Sugar Concrete Company.
1933:   E. L. Ward. 1933 Camacho map.
2000:   Joseph Horseford.

< >

The sugar mill on this site no longer exists and there is nothing to remind one of this plantation except for some stones and remnants of old walls. The mill had been converted to steam power in the mid-1800s along with the mills at Bendals (#37) and Belvedere (#39).

There is nothing left to indicate there were estate buildings except for an old wall and a broken 'dripper' .
Agnes C. Meeker

In 1763, George Byam was painted by portrait artist Gainsborough in the artist's Bath studio, along with Byam's wife, Louise, and their daughter Selina. George was the son of a sugar plantation owner and colonial official from Antigua. By 1763, the Byam's sugar plantation was one of the largest on the island, and was worked by 132 slaves.

Dr. James Athill was one of three brothers who were the first of the Athill family to settle in Antigua. Dr. John Athill and his wife Jane (Dunbar) Athill, were the parents of Joseph Lyons Athill, born August 30, 1748, and baptized at St. Paul's on September 8, 1748.

In 1820, Brother Newby went to George Byam's Plantation, then the property of Dr. James Athill where, during the breakfast hour, the negro slaves assembled to hear the lessons of the day.   Moravian Archives, Bethlehern, PA, US.

< >

With the abolition of slavery by the British Parliament in 1833, the Byam's Plantation was granted a Legacy award (Antigua 92) of £2,238. 2s. 3p. for granting freedom to 133 enslaved. Henry Moreton Dyer was the sole awardee. Alexander Coates was listed as "other associate" and John Athill was unsuccessful. Additionally, the plantation also was granted a second Legacy award (Antigua 126) of £932. 4s. 2p. for freeing 63 enslaved. Samuel Athill Turner was the sole awardee.

(For further information on the Byam family, see #74a/b - Upper & Lower Cedar Hill.
For more information on Fryer's Sugar Concrete Company, see #38 - Belvedere.)

#40 - Brecknock's Plantation

The Ownership Chronology

1718:   Peter Gaynor. d. 1738.

1750:   Miss Mary Gaynor. b. 1754; d. 1818.

1777:   Sir. George Colebrook, to 1790. b. 1761; d. 1839. He inherited the estate from Mary Gaynor. He was Chairman of the East India Company and a banker in London.

1829:   Messrs. Turner. 220 acres, 234 slaves.

1833:   John Adams Wood. b. 1783; d. 1833, age 53.

1843:   John W. Bennet. Arrived in Antigua in 1830.

1872:   Heirs of John W. Bennet. 234 acres.

1891:   Heirs of John W. Bennet.

1933:   Thomas Symister. b. 1906; d. 1971. 65 years old. 1933 Camacho map.

< >

The landscape of hills and valleys looking north from Breaknocks - Agnes C. Meeker.

This estate has essentially disappeared with the ravages of time. The sugar mill still stands, but is deteriorating on the windblown hill. The land was quite fertile, and received a considerable amount of rainfall, which made it conducive to growing sugar cane, other crops, and for grazing cattle. The view north of the estate is spectacular, overlooking valleys and water reservoirs.

Between Brecknock's and Allen's (#48) there was an "estate" called "Hamilton's", which is shown on the 1777-78 map produced by cartographer John Luffman (see #37). It is shown where the small village of Hamilton -- or Hamberly, as it is usually called -- was obliterated in the hurricanes of the 1950s.

Peter Gaynor was the father-in-law of Sir George Colebrook. He was born in the village of Longwood, County Meath (Ireland), and was encouraged at an early age to migrate to the West Indies. His nickname was "Peter Big Brogues" because of the huge shoes he wore when he left home. He left an estate worth £200,000 to his daughter, Mary Gaynor, when he died in 1738. He made his fortune in sugar and rum.

The merchants and planters of Antigua were far more likely to pay for their provisions and supplies shipped from Ireland by shipping the merchants in Ireland rum rather than paying cash. Antigua was Dublin's largest source of rum in 1744, and, like Peter Gaynor, several Irishman on Antigua grew rich from their combined businesses as merchants and planters.

< >

"Not many people hear of Breaknock (sic) nowadays. In earlier times people referred to it as the Evergreen Village because it was not known to be ever really out of water. The frequent drought from which Antigua suffers never had the kind adverse effects on Breaknock as on other places. Its green surroundings and high trees protected the water from rapid evaporation. The water would get very low at times when the drought was extremely hard and long, but luckily the rain would come in time before the water dried up completely. The estates surrounding Breaknock were fruitful. The belief was the people of Breaknock and the surrounding estates were not that badly off because they did not have to bear the extreme hunger and starvation that was the main taker of life on the island. This does not mean that life was not bad with them. The circumstance was, the people living there could find a little thing to bite when people in some other places had nothing or very little to eat. Breaknock was in the rain belt of the island. There were gardens with all types of fruit trees, sapperdilla, marmiesupport, custard apple, breadnut, breadfruit, mango, sugar apple, guava, lime and oranges are

some that I can remember. I would say that Breaknock is close to the mid-south of the island.

"It is a little south of Warner and lies east of the Hamilton Estate. It is west of Body Pond Estate (#41) and close to Body Pond that became well known because it was the main source of water for the whole island for many, many years. Breaknock is also a stone throw from Sawcolts (#174) in the south."

Keithlyn B. Smith. Aunty Dood "A Symbol of Courage".

< >

In 1833, when the British Parliament abolished slavery, Brecknock's estate was granted a Legacy award (Antigua 93) of £989. 10s. 1p. for granting freedom to 63 enslaves. John Adams Wood was the sole awardee. Sir James Colebrook appeared under "other association."

< >

John Bennett, who arrived in Antigua in 1830, was an Agent for Lloyd's of London and resided on the island until 1863. He was acting for Joshua Kentish, according to a newspaper story dated July 26, 1830. There was a court case *John A. Wood vs. John P. Anderson*, and later John Horsford; the partnership between Wood and Bennett was taxed £2. 8s. on property owned on Newgate Street. Bennett acquired Brecknock's in 1843, a small provisional estate of 220 acres. He was appointed Coleboork's attorney in 1833. John A. Wood was the man connected to the slave Mary Prince, who contested her freedom (see The Wood estate, #12).

In 1864, *"the daily yield from the three principal springs, all situated about six miles from St. John's, was measured during a period of drought. The water from these springs was collected and carried by pipes to a large reservoir situated at Barnes Hill (#71) to the southwest of St. John's: Sawcolt's 12,960 gals.; Mill Hill (#176): 20,160 gals.; Breaknock's: 8,640 gallons."* *"History of the Island of Antigua"* by Vere Oliver, Volume I.

Breaknock's village is a small place where the Mullins, Lewis, Jarvis and Philip families come from. An Englishman call "One Man Band" lived up there and was murdered around 2000 walking home late at night. He was an entertainer, hence his nickname. Roland Morris, 2004.

View of mill from both sides
showing weathering on east side.
Agnes C. Meeker

#41 - Body Ponds Plantation
(aka: Carleton)

The Ownership Chronology

1679: Redmond Stapleton. d. 1688. 700 acres.

1750: William Young. b. 1726; d, 1788. He was a surgeon.

1777: Richard Adney. 1777/78 Luffman map.

1790: Thomas Oliver. b. 1733/34; d. 1815. Lt. Governor of Massachusetts.

1829: George Doyle. 210 acres; 102 slaves. d. 1830.

1843: John Hyde Doyle. b. 1805; d. 1894.

1877: Heirs of John Hyde Doyle. They owned 210 acres, which they leased to E. Melchertson; another 20 acres were owned by James Barrett.

1843: David Cranstoun. b. 1795; d. 1865.

1865: John Duer Cranstoun.

1891: Charles Shand.

1915: Langford Sully Cranstoun. d. 1920.

1921: J. A. Harney.

1960s: The actor Richard Burton, the Buff only. b. 1925; d. 1984.

1994: Rob Sherman, the Buff only.

< >

The sugar mill still exists, and a chimney gives evidence of having been converted to steam. The estate house was constructed of stone. Not only has it survived, but it has been completely refurbished by the current owner, Rob Sherman, and his wife Bernadette. It features an unusual hexagonal brick entryway similar in style to that used at Milly Byam (#145), now in ruins, and the Pare 's Estate (#84).

The valley below the house is very fertile thanks to abundant rain and its proximity to Body Pond. That catchment was used by the residents of St. John's as their primary source of fresh water. The original pumping equipment decorates the old Redcliff Tavern in St. John's, which is now a clothing shop.

Top - The beautifully remodelled home.   Rob & Bernadette Sherman.
Bottom – the original structure which overlooks the mill and chimney.

In 1912, when the Wallings reservoir was empty, a water supply from Body Ponds was considered for St. John's. That same year Body Ponds was dammed and water wells dug. In 1925, Governor Ffiennes had Body Ponds enlarged from four-to-five times its original size. In 1933, the first water treatment plant for Body Ponds was built at Grays Hill. *The Antigua Times*, in July 1863, referenced the existence of "rivers" at Body Ponds, Tom Moore's Old Mill Estate (#175) and the Jonas Estate (#85).

Body Pond is actually a series of three ponds -- Fisher's, Fiennes and Swetes -- northwest of the village of Swetes and quite close to Wallings. They cover an area of 2,000 acres with a water storage capacity of 96 acre/ft. The name, Body Pond, most likely is derived from the following quotation in an 1801 diary: *"We passed what are called the Body Ponds, that is a circle of spacious ponds in the body of the island. These are surrounded with trees under the shade of which we observed a table spread, and a company of gentlemen at dinner. It was a meeting of the Sprat Club...."*

At the time of his death in 1686 William Stapleton owned, or had an interest in sugar plantations on four islands, and had become a very wealthy man. His first acquisition was

Body Ponds

Agnes C. Meeker

on Montserrat, where he was granted the Waterwork plantation in St. Peter's Parish. He also owned a plantation on Nevis, where he resided. He granted this estate to Major Charles Pim on May 1, 1678, and then re-purchased it on the same day for 400,000 pounds of muscovado sugar! But, William wasn't done!

He also owned two plantations on Antigua, called Carleton, which he granted on behalf of the Crown to his brother, Redmond Stapleton, in 1679. Three years later, in 1682, William re-purchased these two estates from his brother for 100,000 pounds of muscovado sugar. (He must have loved muscovado sugar!) Then, in 1684, Philip de Nogle assigned his plantation in Cayon Quarter on St. Kitts as a gift to Stapleton.

William died in Paris on August 3, 1686. In his will he bequeathed half of his Nevis plantation and all of the storehouses in Charleston to his wife, Anne Rusell, for her life. The other half of the estate he bequeathed to his eldest son, James (1672 - 1690), his main heir, or in default to his second son, William, or his third son, Miles, and their respective male heirs.

He left his plantation on Monserrat to his son William and the two Antigua plantations to his son Miles. He also directed that Philip de Nogle's plantation on St. Kitts was to be sold after the present occupier's death, and that an estate in Ireland should be purchased for his son William.

Bangor University Stapleton-Cotton Manuscripts.

"Probably the oldest conservation law in the Caribbean was enacted in 1721, the Body Ponds Act, No. 14. It prohibited the felling of trees within 30 ft. of the edge of the ponds. It stated that the trees 'keep waters fresh and cool, (for if they are) exposed to heat and exhalations of the sun, the waters are in great danger of being dried up." "Heritage Treasures" by Desmond Nicholson

By 1831, the Moravian community represented two-thirds of the slave population on Antigua. The Rev. Maynard said Sister Salome Cuthbert, who was born at Body Pond, was one of the negro helpers when the Grace Hill Church was still at Bailey Hill. Sister Cuthbert had been a slave of Mrs. Cuthbert of Falmouth, and when her mistress died she willed that Salome should be set free and given £10 annually from her estate.

Howard A. Samuel, Sr.

When the British Parliament abolished slavery in 1833 the Body Ponds estate was granted a Legacy award (Antigua 91) of £1,704. 6s. 11p. for granting freedom to 102 slaves. The sole awardee was John Hyde Doyle; Charles M. Clarke was listed as "other association".

It appears that both George Doyle and his son John Hyde Doyle were absentee landowners, as both lived in England, yet John's marriage license from 1830 states that he resided in Antigua. The genealogy site states that he was married at St. James Church to Laura Sarah, second daughter of the late Vincent Kennet, Esq., of Portland Place.

John was awarded compensation for the Body Ponds estate on Antigua, although the estate had belonged in part to Mary Doyle, presumably John's mother. The will of John Hyde Doyle, proved in 1830, makes no reference to Antigua nor the Body Ponds estate, which was registered to George Doyle in 1821, 1826 and 1828. The will of George Doyle, late of Barton Street but then of the War Office, Horse Guards, was proved 19/07/1830, Pro. 11/1773/307.

It is said that David "Justice" Cranstoun owned Body Ponds estate and left it to his son, John Duer Cranstoun.

For further information on the Cranston family, see Cochrane's (#139).

< >

Jules Walters recalls white swans swimming in the dam. A photograph of the swans is located in the Antigua & Barbuda Museum.

There is a small grave marker made of green stone on the hill above the Body Ponds estate house, but weather has obliterated the words engraved on it.

The Harney family was at Body Ponds at some point in the 1930s. Mortuary records discernible at the Harney burial site on Montserrat include demographic, burial and artifact information derived from 17 skeletons, 19 unmatched bones, 10 graves, and 134 artifacts. The cemetery dates from the late 18th century and provides data on the mortuary practices of enslaved people at a time when sugar production dominated the economy of the West Indies.

(The National Archives at Kew hold some papers relating to J. A. Harney, Ref. CO 950/470 Memorandum of evidence 1938/39.)

In 1941, the Antigua Sugar Factory, Ltd. reported cane returns from Body Ponds from 82 acres of peasant land on the estate, and 582 tons of cane delivered.

< >

Richard Burton, CBE, (1925-1984) was a famous Welsh stage and cinema actor noted for his baritone voice and great acting talent. He established himself as a formidable Shakespearean actor in the 1950s; later married actress Elizabeth Taylor. It is purported that he purchased the Body Ponds bluff house, but it is doubtful that he actually ever lived in it prior to it being resold. Wikipedia

#42 - Cedar Valley Plantation

The Ownership Chronology

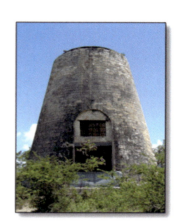

1748: Elizabeth French. Married: 1748; d. 1781.

1781: Heirs of Nathaniel French. d. 1818.

1790: William Blizard. b.1743; d. 1835.
       1777/78 Luffman map.

1829: George Doyle. d. 1830. 128 acres.

1872: Messrs. William (d. 1784; d. 1848) & Francis
       Shand. 128 acres. Francis d. 1868.

1872: Heirs of Francis Shand. 218 acres.

1933: DuBuisson & Alexander Moody-Stuart.

1940: Gunthorpes Estates Ltd.

1943: Antigua Syndicate Estates Ltd. 240 acres.

1958: Antigua Government

< >

The mill is in excellent condition, and portions of a stone wall and old building still exist, but the property is currently the site of the Cedar Valley Golf Course, built by Ralph Aldridge, a Canadian. It is Antigua's only 18-hole championship course. The first nine holes were completed in 1972 and house lots were sold to finance building the course. The second nine holes were not completed until 1980, when the Antiguan government provided land on the north side of the clubhouse. An old photograph of the Cedar Valley works, though not particularly clear, conveys an idea of what the estate looked like.

"The main house (of the estate) was wooden on a stone foundation. In those days because of the fear of fire, the kitchen was separated from the house by a walkway about the length of a cricket pitch. The walkway was covered by a grape vine. A row of casurinas grew on the south side of the approach from the east.

"Large square water tanks in the yard on the west side gravity fed the prolific kitchen garden, which grew on the slope below. The only other building on the estate was the overseer's house, and just outside the yard, beneath a large avocado tree, was a little grocery shop where everyone congregated on Saturdays when the workers on the estate were paid. It became very lively and was the place to be.

"Dr. Raeburn was the farrier (vet) and he came regularly to look after the animals. The horses were curried and clipped around race (horse) season and I would line up at the end and get a haircut at the same time! I remember walking up the hill to preschool at Blizard's (now New Winthrops, #56) to Teacher Dollo (Henrietta Knowles) and later, when I was older, I rode a donkey to school.

"We felt we were very privileged at Cedar Valley to have electric lights, though they were a bit dim -- difficult to read by. The batteries were charged during the day by a wind generator which provided enough electricity till bed time which was very early on the estate."   Lawrence Royer, 1944 Memories of ...

< >

In 1940, the Antigua Sugar Estates reissued 18,000 shares at £1 each to three DuBuissons (James Memoth DuBuisson, Mrs. Edith Manus Dubuisson, and William Herman DuBuisson) as well as Alexander Moody-Stuart and Judith Gwendolyn Moody-Stuart. This signaled the final shift to the next generation, as George Moody-Stuart was offered shares, but declined (ASE minutes, 4 January 1940; 1 May 1940). The estates to be controlled by the new company, in addition to Cedar Valley, were Gunthorpe's (#64), Cassada Garden ($13a), Paynter's (#61), Tomlinson's (#17), Fitches Creek (#67), Donovan's (#65) North Sound (#66), Galley Bay (#30) and Five Islands (#31).

Not a very good picture but it does depict the works in the front and the estate house in the upper right corner.
Foote Family Album.

That same year the Antigua government passed the Lands of Antigua & Barbuda Sugar Factory Limited and the Antigua & Barbuda Syndicate Estates Limited (Vesting) Act., which specified that "all piece or parcel of land forming part of Cedar Valley, approximately 240.225 acres as contained in Certificate of Title No. 1111940 dated 26th April, 1940 and registered in Register Book P Folio 11." (Cedar Valley lands totaled 240.2 acres as noted in a Certificate of Title No. 1111940 dated 26th April; 1940. Register Book P, Folio 11.)

On August 1, 1943 Gunthorpes Estates, Ltd., was restructured (see Gunthorpes #64) into a new company renamed Antigua Syndicate Estates, Ltd. The original company's estates -- Cassada Garden, Cedar Valley, Fitches Creek and North Sound -- were bought for £30,700, while Delaps (#137) was bought for £7,734.

Cedar Valley mill – Agnes C. Meeker

#43 - Hill House/Dry Hill

The Ownership Chronology

1750: Tobias Lilse. Baptized at St. John's 1723.

1790: Ladwell & Scott. 1777/78 Luffman map.

1829: James Baker.

1843: James H. Baker. 167 acres.

1860: Samuel Williams.

1872: Heirs of Samuel Williams. 100 acres, plus 10 acres belonging to Paul Horsford.

1878: Samuel L. Athill.

1933: Mary S. Athill. 1933 Camacho map.

1940s: Asot Michael.

2000: Heirs of Asot Michael.

< >

The sugar mill still stands on this site, situated on a bluff above the sea with a terrific view of ships approaching St. John's harbour and Fort James to the south, with Goat Hill in the background and Corbison's Point to the north. Cattle and provisions were raised on this estate.

The beach area, now known as Runaway Beach after the hotel of that name, was formerly known as Dry Hill.

The Cove estate owned by John Taylor Esq. (1777/78 Luffman map) was situated just south of the Dry Hill estate house and was probably incorporated at a later date.

< >

Elizabeth Lisle, the daughter of Henry Pearne, of Antigua, was granted 100 acres in 1681 by William Stapleton. In 1711/12, Captain Toby Lisle of the *HMS Diamond* wrote about a sloop he had captured. Samuel L. Athill, a native Antiguan, married an American woman and built the house now situated on Dry Hill. *"Mother used to visit and Mr. Athill would offer everyone something to drink, then turning to Mrs. White would ask 'if she would care for a glass of water' knowing she was diabetic."*

Margaret White, Memories of ….

Samuel and a Thomas N. Kerby jointly owned an extensive cargo of corn meal, flour, staves and fish, which had been loaded aboard the S/V *Hannah,* a 143-ton brig built in 1796. The vessel was owned by Walt and Isaac of Weathersfield, Connecticut: mastered by James Barclay. The vessel departed New York on March 8, 1800 bound for Antigua. However, it was seized on April 5 by Captain Chaufort, a French privateer aboard in *L'Unise* and taken to Guadalupe, where the vessel and cargo were condemned.

The mill with Dry Hill house behind. – Agnes C. Meeker

Top left – a good example of the 'fire hole' used to provide light within the mill when grinding at night.
Agnes C. Meeker

The view from within the mill looking across St. John's harbour to Fort Barrington
Agnes C. Meeker

#44 - Rose Hill & Hammersfield

The Ownership Chronology

1750:   Nathaniel Humphrey. b. 1722; d. 1758.
1843:   James Thibou. 63 acres in 1851.
1872:   Heirs of Sarah Adamson.
1878:   F. J. Edwards.
1933:   Amanda Crogman.   1933 Camacho map.

< >

Very little is known about this estate, which is situated halfway between Renfrew's (#21) and Buckley's (#45), very near Oliver's (#46). The letter below is from a John Rose in 1785, and the Museum of Antigua & Barbuda has a photograph of Rose's Valley under cane cultivation. It was taken from Jolly Hill, not near the location of the Rose Hill/Hammersfield estate. Also noted on the 1933 Camacho map is a "Rose Cottage." When googling Rose's estate, an area is shown on the internet in the hills overlooking English Harbour in St. Phillip's Parish.

Roses' Valley from Jolly Hill, Antigua, B.W.I. (Photo: Jose Anjo)

In Vere Oliver's History of the Island of Antigua, Volume III, there appears the pedigree of Rose showing a John Rose (d. 1711) of New North Sound, Antigua. He was a merchant. There is also an indenture *"30 December 1710 between Robert Weir of Antigua, planter, and Mary his wife, of the 1 part and John Rose of Antigua, merchant, of the other, the latter agrees to let his plantation in New North Sound to the former, late in the occupation of William Glanville of Antigua, merchant, for lease of twelve years at £300 a year."*

1785, from John Rose:

"Dear Sir! I have the pleasure to inform you of the safe Arrival of the Ship Joshua. The late arrivals from all parts of America has sunk Lumber near 50-150p Cent. Our Men of War are stationed at all the English Islands to prevent the Americans from trading." M30s The Beineke Collection.

The above picture taken from Jolly Hill facing east, shows a lovely scene of cultivated fields of sugar cane going right up the valley. With little information on the Rose/Hammerfield plantation, it is noteworthy to see that the Rose name persisted in several locations on the island. This is not the location of the estate mentioned above

#45 - Buckley's Plantation

The Ownership Chronology

1672: Elias Buckley. Named in the 1672 will of John Bridges of Antigua.

1750: Colonel Daniel Mathew.

1759: Richard Buckley. His 1759 will stated the estate was to be sold.

1790: Daniel Hill. d. 1808. 1777/78 Luffman map.

1828: David Cranstoun. b. 1795; d. 1865.

1843: Plots sold to establish the free village of Buckleys.

1872: W. B. Nibbs. 98 acres. Several smaller holdings of 10 acres each were owned and farmed by Samuel Edwards and the heirs of Isaac Kilsick.

1878: Reverend Thomas Nibbs.

1933: Reverend W. M. Williams. 1933 Camacho map.

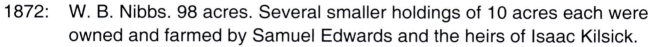

< >

The village of Buckley's was founded after 1843 and the abolition of slavery, a decade earlier. The Buckley's area is noted for being especially fertile, receiving more than the average rainfall than in the rest of Antigua. The sugar mill stands as testimony to the days when sugar was king and the giant rollers used to crush the cane were powered by wind in the mill's blades. There is no record that the mill was converted to steam.

In *"1665/66 Colonel Buckley played an active part in the conflicts with Holland, Denmark and France. During the signing of the capitulation with the French, Lt. Colonel Bastien Baijer, Colonel Buckley, Joseph Halliday, Capt. Samuel Winthrop, Capt. Phillip Warner and James Halliday, all arms, ammunition, forts, buttresses, &c., were to be given up to the French, but the English were to be allowed to retain their property, have free exercise of their religion and Colonel Carden, a prisoner of war, was to be restored to liberty."* "Antigua and the Antiguans" by Mrs. Lanaghan

Elias Buckley, an Antiguan planter, was named in the 1672 will of John Bridges, also of Antigua.

There were two men named Daniel Hill, the Elder and the Younger. The elder is purported to have died in 1808, and there is record that William Lee and

George Wickham Washington Ledeatt were their executors, but no will has been located for Daniel Hill the Elder.

< >

"The Cranstouns are the one family for which there is a direct heritage line from the free coloured family into the 20th century. The living Cranstouns descendants had no idea of their heritage until advised by a relative that their great-grandfather had been a prominent free coloured gentleman.

"As with the Shervington's the earliest family identification begins with the petition signers. There is no Cranstoun genealogy in Vere Oliver's historical volumes. By the 1830s, the free coloured family was prominent: two brothers, David and George, signed the free coloured petition, while a sister, Ann, was President of the Female Orphan's Aslyum. She never married, but a second sister, Jane, married into another prominent free coloured family named Weston."

Dr. Susan Lowes

In 2011 David Cranstoun began extensively researching his family's genealogy, and noted that David Cranstoun — his great, great grandfather — a man of colour, purchased Buckley's from Daniel Hill (1790) and was compensated for 23 slaves by the British government, most likely a Legacy payment from Parliament for granting freedom to the slaves.

The estate was not cultivated after 1820, and was leased in 1836 to U.S. Ambassador Ralph Higgenbottom, a manager of the Athill estate, and Buckley's was later sold when, like his neighbors in nearby Swetes, David Cranstoun sold some of his estate to the laborers, encouraging Buckley's as a free village. David managed Seaforths (#160) for Justin Casamajor, plus Robert Sutton's mother on the Willis Freeman estate (#143), and several other plantations during his lifetime. He was attorney for William Manning, and in 1830, when Manning and Anderdon of the New York Bank Building in the City of London purchased the Carlisle's estate (#60), he was appointed their "true and lawful attorney." Cranstoun was known as "Mr. Justice."

Joseph Gravenor Buckley married Elizabeth Doig, a spinster, in 1801. However, we do not know of his connection to Buckley's estate, if any.

The decaying mill at Buckley's – Agnes C. Meeker

#46 - Oliver's (Stock Estate)

The Owners Chronology

1670:   Richard Oliver. d. 1681. One of the original settlers.
1708:   Richard Oliver. Will: 1714. 520 acres in St. John's Division.
1716:   Richard Oliver inherited half of his father's 520 acres.
1750:   Richard Oliver. Baptized 1734/5 d. 1784.
1770:   Rowland Oliver. b. 1779.
1780:   Thomas Oliver. b. 1733/34; d. 1815.
1785:   William Smith. Cousin to Thomas Oliver.
1790:   Thomas Oliver. d. 1784.   1777/78 Luffman map.
1791:   Peter Langford Brooke. b.1739; d. 1840.
1860:   Thomas W. Langford Brooke.
1878:   Heirs of Thomas W. Langford Brooke. 279 acres.
1891:   Antonio Joseph Camacho. d. 1894.
1933:   M. V. Camacho.   1933 Camacho map.
2003:   Antigua & Barbuda Government.

< >

There are no old buildings left on this site, which was known to have raised cattle. The Government Veterinary Clinic established by Dr. Lionel Thomas was located on this land until destroyed in a major hurricane. Nearby is the new site of the Island Academy School. To the west is the St. Clare estate (#35) and to the south is the Buckley Plantation (#45).

Richard Oliver was returning to England from Nevis in 1784 for the recovery of his health. He died while traveling on board the Sandwich packet. He was formerly an alderman and MP for London. He was married to his cousin, had two children, but his property on Antigua would have descended to his nephew Richard Oliver, Esq. He was the son of the elder Richard's brother, Thomas. That Richard had formed an agreement with a William Smith, his cousin, that whomever survived the longest would inherit all of the other's property. William sold the Oliver's estate in 1791 to the Langford Brooke's.

< >

A plan of this estate, drawn in 1821 and very difficult to read, is titled *"A Plan of STOCK ESTATE called Olivers in the Parish of St. John's, Antigua, the property of PETER LANGFORD BROOKE, ESQ."* The estate is shown bounded on the north by the property of Chalmers & Daniell, to the east by Heirs of Elizabeth Colebrooke-- and heirs of Williams, to the south by John Boyd and Robert Hyndman and to the west by Samuel Williams, Esq. It appears the estate covered 279 acres. 'A' through 'P' on the plan list the position of various buildings: 'A' the old windmill; 'B' the boiling house; 'C' the cattle pen; 'D' ponds; 'E' the negro houses; 'F' water courses; 'G' negro ground; 'H' ???; 'I' formerly the garden; 'J' ??? now disused; 'K' private road through Williams (#50); 'L' ???; 'M' rocky or barren ground; 'N' stone ???; 'O' copse or bushwood; 'P' ???. Due to the illegibility a copy of the map is not included here. A copy can be seen in *"History of the Island of Antigua"* by Vere Oliver.

< >

By 2012, some of the land was being used as part of the stock and animal husbandry farms connected to the Government. Most interesting is that pieces of petrified wood litter the area, indicating the one-time presence of an age-old forest. Several large tree trunks, some 18 inches across have been found, a sample of which can be seen at the Museum of Antigua & Barbuda.

< >

"Richard Oliver of Bristol, (was a) linen draper and merchant trading to Virginia, and owner of plantations beyond the seas." Will dated 15 Sep. 1676: proved 1 Dec. 1681. *"History of the Island of Antigua"* by Vere Oliver, Volume II.

In the book *"Sugar and Slavery"*, there is mention that much of the sugar arriving in London from about 1745-1780 was consigned to the two Richard Olivers (father and son), who were descended from a prominent merchant/planter family in Antigua. (There were actually five men named Richard Oliver at that time.) Richard III, born in Bristol in 1664, was most likely the merchant and planter in Antigua. When the Council list was published in February 1745, Richard Oliver was reported absent in England and was presumably engaged in his sugar processing factory at that time.

In 1714 *"the Hon. Colonel Richard Oliver of Antigua and his wife Sarah for 10s. convey to the Hon. Colonel Thomas Williams and Captain Thomas Oesterman of Antigua, 5 negroes for his dau. Frances, his son Thomas, Mary, his dau. Anna, and his son Samuel, children of the said Richard Oliver by his said wife Sarah."*

In 1725 *"an indenture informs us that Richard Oliver has sold a plantation in Virginia and houses in St. John's Town on account of the very great debts of his father Richard Oliver, deceased, and has paid one thousand pounds on the marriage to Frances Otto-Baijer. A division of their father's estate has now taken place between Richard Oliver and Rowland Oliver, consisting of 520 acres in St. John's Division bounded E(ast) with John Sawcolts and Ashton Warner Esq., S(outh) with John Hughes, W(est) with Elizabeth Symes and Thomas Warner Esq., N(orth) with Baijer Otto-Baijer Esq."*

Extensive information of the Oliver family may be found in Volume II of Vere Oliver's "History of the Island of Antigua."

< >

In 1941, the Antigua Sugar Factory, Ltd., had cane returns of estimated 500 tons from an unknown number of acres. 158 tons of cane per acre were delivered for processing.

#47 - Potter's Plantation

The Ownership Chronology

1750: Nathaniel Gilbert. d. 1774.
1800: Honorable William Gunthorpe. b. c1785; d. 1826) 77 acres.
   1777/78 Luffman map.
1826: Alicia and James Gunthorpe, wife and son of William.
1843: John Joseph Ronan. He purchased 40 acres at auction for £3,065 and sold it the following year to George Richard White for £4,500.
1844: George Richard White. Married Tryphena Ronan, 1834.
1851: McDonald & Co.
1891: John R. McDonald. b. 1865.
1930: Captain Geoffrey George David Downing. d. 1941.
1941: Philip Downing.
1945: Joseph Lake. b. 1890; d. 1958.
1960: Mona Lake. d. c.1960.
1964: Mrs. Ena Phyllis Judkins
19--: F. O. Benjamin.
2012: Mrs. Gwen Edwards. Bluff house.

< >

The sugar mill no longer exists at this site, but the estate house, which is quite small compared to most estate homes, still exists on the rise west of Potters main road. The estate raised provisions and had a herd of milk cows. The village of Potters lies north and took its name from the estate. The Herbert's estate (#20) is south of Potter's.

"There was a lovely view from the veranda over No. 2 dam towards the factory. During crop time the lights sparkled and the twin stacks (chimneys) were silhouetted against the night sky. Nearby there was a pond where the calabash tree grew. Mother kept chickens and the old man had some milch cows and sent milk daily up to the factory houses in the cart." Evelyn (Lake) Joslyn, Memories of . . .

< >

The 1777/78 map drawn by John Luffman shows Potter's owned by the Honorable William Gunthorpe, who also owned the Gunthorpe's estate (#64). He died in 1826, specifying that the proceeds of the sale of this estate should go to his wife, Alica (Jackson) Gunthorpe, and to James Gunthorpe, presumably their son.

A headstone at Potter's reads:
To the Memory of
Lucy Gunthorpe
who departed this life
December 9th, 1832
aged 103 years.

It is said Lucy was probably a negro slave...

"*History of the Island of Antigua*" by Vere Oliver, Volume II.

McDonald & Company was a reputable and respected firm in St. John's. It began to incur problems around 1874 when the partnership of John S. McDonald, James R. McDonald and W. W. Maclachlan expired. John and James continued to work together until 1884. John married his first cousin, Katherine Dora Maclachlan, in Glasgow, Scotland. They lived at Gray's hill and had eleven children there. The McDonald family home is now owned by the Henry family (related), and still enjoys a marvelous view overlooking St. John's harbor.

The Honorable J. P. McDonald was a senior partner of McDonald & Co, West Indian merchants. He was born in 1865 and educated in private school either in Scotland or London.

"Sons of An Islander".

Kitty (Lake) Yarnold recalls that Philip Downing, her brother-in-law, inherited Potter's from his father, Captain Downing. In 1945 Phillip Downing sold the estate to her father, Joseph Lake, shortly after he lost Marble Hill estate (#9). Phillip then immigrated to the United States.

< >

Mr. Maharaj, who worked at the Sugar Factory, recalled that in 1954, a locomotive pulling a sugar train, ran off the tracks in the vicinity of Gilbert's estate (#80). Members of the "Weigh gang" and the "Porter gang" were sent to assist in the emergency. Joseph Lake was the foreman of the Porter Gang at that time.

< >

Steve Cranstoun, who had been researching his family's genealogy, mentioned that his grandfather, Langford Sally Cranstoun, sold Potters at public auction for £570. However, the dates of ownership are missing, and he is not listed in the Ownership Chronology.

The Potter's bluff 2001 – Agnes C. Meeker

The London Gazette, in 1976, listed Mrs. Ena Phyllis Judkins as receiving honours for welfare services in Antigua.

#48 - Allen's Plantation
(aka: Mount View)

The Ownership Chronology

1668: William Allen. Granted 297 acres.
1720: Robert Allen. d. 1730.
1730: William Allen. b. 1709; d. 1804. 232 acres,
      71 slaves.
1780: William Allen. 182 acres, 85 slaves.
1785: Thomas Allen. 1777/78 Luffman map.
1790: Robert McNish. b. 1755; d. 1828. 239 acres,
      81 slaves.
1852: Heirs of Richard McNish. 239 acres.
1933: John Davis.
1965: John Rowan Henry.
2003: Winston Derrick, owner of *The Antigua Observer.* d. 2013.

< >

    The sugar mill still stands, although trees and roots are causing considerable deterioration of the stonework. The mill is situated on McNish Hill, one of the highest in Antigua. The mill was often called by that name instead of Allen's. Reaching the mill is a difficult climb, prompting one to wonder how slaves ever cultivated, harvested and ground sugar cane at that altitude.

    The elevation does provide an amazing view of the surrounding countryside from atop McNish Hill, and one can understand why the estate was named Mount View. Partway down the hill are the remains of a building, which may have been part of the works. There is also a brackish Salt Spring, which never seems to run dry, plus the old site of Hamilton (Hambleton) Village nearby, which was destroyed by hurricanes in the 1950s. Three families were living in the Village at the time, and were forced to relocate to Bendal's (#37). Huge royal palms, flamboyants, lilies and mother-in-law tongue continue to grow on the slopes.

< >

Allen's mill nestled in a vale before the final climb to the top of McNish – Agnes C. Meeker

William Allen's only son was murdered in 1768, his 20th year, by soldiers in St. George's Field. The inscription on his tombstone asserts that he was "inhumanely murdered on the 10th May by Scottish detachments of the army."

"History of the Island of Antigua" by Vere Oliver, Volume I.

An un-sourced 1734 family tree notes that Robert McNish was born in Antigua and married Mary Brodie on November 2, 1796. One of their sons, the Rev. Alexander William McNish, was Robert's trustee. Their other two sons were Brodie George McNish, Alexander's executor, and John McNish. All three sons were jointly awarded compensation for Antigua claim No. 1009.

William McNish is recorded in Antigua as having died in 1798, but it is not known if he owned this estate prior to Robert McNish, a planter, who died in 1828. The Rev. Alexander William McNish died in 1829, all of the same family.

With the abolition of slavery by the British Government in 1833, the Allen's estate was granted a Legacy award (Antigua 137) of £1,369. 19s. 3p. for granting freedom to 99 enslaved. The awardees were James H. Barker, Robert McDonald, Brodie George McNish and Mary Elizabeth (Johnson) McNish. Robert McNish and Rev. Alexander William McNish, both deceased, were beneficiaries.

Unsuccessful were William Croll, R. Louisa Eldridge and Benjamin Nicholson.

There also was a secondary Legacy compensation (Antigua 1009) where all three sons -- Brodie George McNish, the Rev. Alexander William McNish (born 1708, died 1837) and John McNish, were granted £143. 10s.9p. The Reverend McNish was Rector of St. Peter's Church.

The 1777/78 map produced by John Luffman shows a "Biffan's" (Bevan's) estate near the McNish property (Allen's). "Biffan's" is shown as owned by Ledwell & Scott, but the name is no longer used, and the estate seems to have disappeared over the years; may have been annexed to Allen's.

The Allen mill showing signs of deterioration. Roots from invading trees destroy and break up the stone work.
Agnes C. Meeker

< >

Rowan Henry purchased the Allen's plantation in 1965 for $16,000. He was one of the few Antiguans who went to England during World War II, where he joined the RAF. Upon his return to Antigua, he became a leading attorney and aspired to challenge V. C. Bird for the office of Premier. Rowan and his wife were murdered by a crazed gardener; the details are in a 2003 book on diplomatic wanderings written by Bill Cordiner.
"Cyclone & Cucumbers"

"I was with John Henry on 37 Squadron; we lived in the same tent when we were based at Misurata and Kairouan. At the end of our tours, was also a Wireless operator, air gunner. We both were posted back to Egypt. I last saw John at the training camp in Tunis. I would love to hear from him or his family. All the best, from Tommy."   Observer Newspaper

< >

John Pierce, Bill Cunningham and the farmer who helped us that day, resting within the mill's interior. The top of McNish can be seen in the background. Agnes C. Meeker.

In 2005, a year after the Allen's property was acquired by Winston Derrick, a road was cut following a 100-year-old path through Jennings (#187) and by the dam at Dunnings (#190), to provide easier access to NcNish. Observer Radio installed a communications tower on top of the hill. Derrick was co-founder of Observer Publications with his brother, Samuel "Fergie" Derrick, who predeceased him. Winston was described as "fearless", "fair-minded", "humble", "confident" and a "man of indelible character." Observer Radio 91.9 FM, the *Daily Observer,* and Observer Printery, were all part of the Derrick media empire, founded in 1993.

#49 - Halliday's Mountain
(aka: Gillead's, Gilliat's or Providence)

The Ownership Chronology

1668:   Anthony Gilliat, a planter. 38 acres, in
        Popeshead estate.
1719:   Thomas Gilliat. Will: 1714.
1740:   Joshua Gilliat. d. 1791, in Jamaica.
1750:   John Halliday. b. c1717; d. 1779.
        300 acres, 137 slaves.
1777:   John Delap Halliday. 1777/78 Luffman map.
1872:   Fryer's Concrete Co.
1933:   James John.   1933 Camacho map.
1940s: Antigua Syndicate Estates Ltd.
1990s: Nigel Lee, leased the land around the mill (cane field #7) from the
        Government.

< >

A stone above the sugar mill's doorway bears the inscription "CFS 1732". The initials remain a mystery, but could be attributed to the builder. The mill is crumbling at its top, but was converted to two levels in the 1990s to house Nigel Lee's Family. It has a wonderful view of the Bendals Valley, and the current owner, Nigel Lee, has tilled the surrounding soil to provide a prolific garden.

In 2009, this mill was hidden by bush and basically forgotten until Nigel Lee leased the land from the Government in the 1990s. He was told the designation for the cane field was No. 7, but never knew the actual name of the plantation nor mill. His goal is to entirely repair the sugar mill one day.

< >

There were Gilliat families in both Antigua and Jamaica. Three hundred years of history on the web provided the author with the following: Chris Codrington, who has researched his own prominent family (see Clare Hall #13b), had some family connections with the Gilliats of Jamaica. Indeed, Mr. Codrington says his research showed that there were family connections with the Gilliats of Jamaica.

Samuel Gilliat, born in 1717 at Crowie in Lincolnshire, may have been the first, although Anthony Gillyat (sic), born March 9, 1644 at South Ferriby, is also thought to have relocated to Jamaica. (The two spellings of the last name reflect the birth registrations.) A daughter, Lucy Gilliat, was born in 1647 to an Anthony Gilliat of South Ferriby. The two villages, Crowie and South Ferriby, are close geographically and border the Humber River.

Mr. Codrington could find no further record of the Gilliat family in the UK, so it is possible they had left the country. Assuming the Anthony Gilliat born in 1644 is the same individual who owned Halliday's Mountain in1688, he would have been 24 years old. It may have been his father

300 years of Gilliat history, Public Records, Kew, London.

< >

The name Halliday does not appear on a 1933 map of Antigua, but it is the name best known by residents of the Bendals/Greencastle area. The family figured prominently in the history of Scotland, County Galloway, since the sixteenth century. John Halliday, a collector, was born in Antigua, and was a nephew of William Dunbar (see Boone's #1) and son-in-law of Francis Delap.

"James Halliday of Antigua, signed the Capitulation to the French in 1666, his 1,400 acres reduced to 800 in 1668. In 1780 John Delap Halliday was rated on 300 acres, 137 slaves (St. Mary's Vestry Book). In 1788 John Delap Halliday owned the following plantations: Blizard's (#54) in St. Paul's Parish, Delaps (#137) and Rockhill and one un-named in St. Mary's Parish; and in St. John's Parish: Boone's (#1), Gamble's (#14) and Blizard's (#54); in St. Philip's Parish, Laviscount's.

"Halliday Hill, which was another popular hill to climb, was best known for its history of slave masters, who would put slaves in barrels and roll them to their deaths. In that area also was Warner plantation, which held a significant interest in the land because some slaves started a rebellion there during the last years of slavery."

Aunty Dood in *"Symbol of Courage"*

"We found Mr. Martin at the Church door with our carriages, into which we mounted and were soon at Mr. Halliday's Plantation, where he this day dined; for he has no less than five, all of which have houses on them. We had a family dinner, which in England might figure away in a newspaper, had it been given by a Lord Mayor, for the first Duke in the kingdom. Why should we blame these people for their luxury? Since nature holds out her lap, filled with everything that bestow, it were sinful to them not to be luxurious.

"They never make but two, the soup and the shell. The first is commonly made of old Turtle, which is cut up and sold at Market, as we do butcher meat. It is remarkably well dressed today. The shell indeed is a noble dish as it contains all the fine parts of the Turtle baked within its own body, here is the green fat, not the slabbery thing my stomach used to stand at, but firm and more delicate than is possible to describe." "Journal of A Lady of Quality" by Janet Shaw

Documents relating to John Halliday's Antigua estates 1777-1857 are held by Cheshire Archives and Local Studies. Ref. #DTW/2343/D/11.

Top - Haliday's mill with a view down into the valley and the village of Bendals to the right.
Bottom left – Two Princesses. Bottom Right – the north side of the mill , plaque on west entrance.
Agnes C. Meeker

#50 - Williams Plantation

The Ownership Chronology

1700s: Rowland Williams.
1730:   Roger Williams. Indentured, 470-500 acres.
1775:   Joseph Williams. b. 1760; d. 1814.
1777:   Samuel Williams. 1777/78 Luffman map.
1851:   William Williams. 41 acres.
1933:   Olive & Lauchland Charity. 1933 Camacho map
2000:   Denely Nibbs.

< >

It is difficult, if not impossible, to locate this estate. It is not shown on any maps, but nearby Buckley's (#45) was owned by a Reverend Williams and also close by were two Williams farms. The mill is reportedly made of flint stone, which made for a fairly rough exterior finish and is known as the Williams mill.

The remains of a buff house may be found on a small rise to the northwest, along with clumps of spider lilies, which usually denote the grave of a slave, since slaves did not have the financial resources to erect a stone monument. The pond has never been dry, and Mr. Nibbs intends to look into the possibility of researching the spring that supposedly feeds it.

The reason this mill does not appear on both Baker's or Luffman's maps may be the following:

"As regards the Williams of Williams Farm, the 'WW' on the old mill was William Williams, son of Joseph Williams. This family sprung from the Old Road Williams family, but was coloured and illegitimate. William Williams' brother was a manager here and his daughter married a black man, who is well known here today in business circles - Mrs. S. I. Athill. The last of them left the island years ago and the above lady is dead. The flintstone windmill was built from money obtained under the 'Earthquake Loan' of the forties, but apparently did not remain long in operation."

Archibald Spooner Bendals, Antigua 1900

The Williams mill showing plaque
in the stones above the arch.

In 1743, Edmund Williams owned Tom Moore's Plantation (#1 of 120 + 50 acres) and the Cistern Plantation of 954 1/2 acres, both in St. Mary's Parish, as surveyed in that year. Roland Williams owned The Road, Tom Moore's and the Cistern in 1784. By 1867, Rowland Edward Williams owned Claremont (#177) and Mountain (#178), both in St. Mary's Parish, with total acreage of 938.

The Williams Plantation was bounded on the north by the property of James Vaughn, south by the property of William Horne, west by the property of Samuel Martin, and east by property originally owned by John Lucas, later by Edward Byam, Jr.

An Internet search disclosed the will of a Joseph Williams, Antigua planter, proved in 1817. According to Vere Oliver's historical volumes, a memorial to Joseph Williams, located on the Williams estate in Antigua, says he died in 1814, at age 54.

< >

The Earthquake Act of 1853 was enacted to assist with the sale of estates when owners were unable to pay their debt, often by auction. At the time, three estates fell under this Act: Mannings (#124), Lower Walrond (#117) and *"Williams Farm (#50), which contained 41 acres in St. John's Parish. The property of William Williams [is] charged with the sum of £94. 10s. amount of installment and interest up to the first day of May, last past £395. 10s, payable as in the said here-in before mentioned Act is set forth and the respective plantations or estate have been twice put up for auction by the Provost Marshall."*

< >

There was another Williams estate, also known as Brodies/Windy Hill in St. Paul's Parish [see Volume II]. That estate may be the one now known as Windy Hill/Howard's (#148).

The Plantation Index

Registry of Plantation Owners

Plantation Owner	As of:	Plantation
Abbott, W. J.	1921	# 2 Crosbie's
Abbott, Fred	1950	#10 McKinnon's
Abbott, Mrs. M.	1921	#31 Five Islands
Abbott, heirs of:	2000	#10 McKinnons
	1985	#12 The Wood
Adam, Alex M. & L.L.P. Co. Ltd.	1891	#18 Drew's Hill
	1891	#19 Belmont/Murray's
Adamson, Sarah heirs of	1872	#44 Rose Hill/Hammersfield
Adney, Richard	1777	#41 Body Ponds
Allen, George	1869	#20 Herbert's
Allen, Robert	1730	#48 Allen's (McNish)
Allen, Thomas	1785	#48 Allen's (McNish)
Allen, William	1750	#48 Allen's (McNish)
Allway, John	1852	#32 Hawksbill
Anthonyson, John C.	1878	#26 Cook's
Antigua & Barbuda Govt.	2003	#46 Oliver's
Ash, Rowland	1750	#36 Belle Vue/Stoney Hill
Athill, Dr. James	1790	#39 George Byam's
heirs of:	1829	#39 George Byam's
Athill, Samuel L.	1878	#43 Hill House/Dry Hill
Athill, Mary S.	1933	#43 Hill House/Dry Hill
Baijer, Colonel Sebastian	1600s	#19 Belmonht/Murray's
		#16 Otto's
Baijer, J. Edward	1722	#26 Cook's
Baijer, Honorable Edward Otto	1750	#26 Cook's
	1750	#29 Yepton's
Baijer, Colonel John Otto	1722	#16 Otto's
	1777	#25 Denfield's
	1722	#26 Cook's
Baijer, Edward Otto	1750	#26 Cook's
	1700	#31a/b Five Islands
	1790	#29 Yepton's
	1790	#19 Belmont/Murray's

Baijer, John Otto		1829	#16 Otto's
		1790	#29 Yepton's
		1790	#26 Cook's
Baker, James		1829	#43 Hill House/Dry Hill
Barreto, John		1944	#21 Renfrew's
Baxter, Ralph W.		1851	#29 Yepton's
Beckett, Edward		1878	#10 McKinnon's
Benjamin, F. O.		19??	#47 Potter's
Bendal, Hopefor		1728	#37 Bendal's
Bennett, Harry Ogilvie		1891	#11 Friars Hill
		1921	#12 The Wood
Bennett, John W.		1843	#40 Brecknock's
	heirs of:	1891	#40 Brecknock's
Bennett, John W. et al		1878	#40 Brecknock's
Bennett, George W.		1878	#40 Brecknock's
Billinghurst, J.		1829	#32 Hawksbill
Bird, Vere Cornwall		1970	#11 Friars Hill
		1981	#17 Tomlinson's
Burke, Walter	prior to	1678	# 1 Boone's
Burton, Richard		1960s	#41 Body Pond's
Blackburn, Thomas		1829	#15 The Villa (Daniel's)
		1829	#18 Drew's Hill
Blizard, William		1790	#42 Cedar Valley
Boone, Joseph		1733	# 1 Boone's
Boone, Samuel		1715	# 1 Boone's
Boone, William		1678	# 1 Boone's
Bott, Mrs. A.		1829	#18 Drew's Hill
Bradshaw & Richard, F. Shand & Co.		1843	#18 Drew's Hill
		1843	#19 Belmont/Murray's
Brooke, Jonas Langford		1790	# 6 Langford's
Brooke, Thomas Langford		1872	# 7 Mount Pleasant
Brooke, Peter Langford		1829	# 6 Langford's
		1791	#46 Oliver's
Brooke, Thomas Langford		1878	# 6 Langford's
		1878	# 7 Mount Pleasant
		1878	# 9 Dunbar's
		1878	#12 The Wood

Brooke, Thomas W. Langford	1860	# 46 Oliver's
Bryson's	1950	#15 The Villa
Buckley, Elias	1672	#45 Buckley's
Buckley, William	1750	#23 Golden Grove
Bunrthorne, William	1829	#20 Herbert's
Burke, Walter	1698	# 1 Boone's
Burton, Richard	1960s	#41 Body Pond's
Byam, George	1700s	#39 George Byam's
Camacho, Antonio Joseph	1893	#11 Friar's Hill
	1891	#7 Mount Pleasant
	1891	#16 Otto's
	1891	#12 The Wood
	1891	#19 Belmont/Murray's
	1891	#22 Briggin's
	1891	#46 Oliver's
	1894	#24 Gray's Turnbull
Camacho, Aubrey J.	1891-1833	# 6 Langford's
	1891	#16 Otto's
	1891	#22 Briggin's
	1933	# 7 Mount Pleasant
	1933	# 8 Dunbar's
	1921	#11 Friars Hill
	1921	#12 The Wood
	1921	#19 Belmont/Murray's
	1921	#36 Belle Vue/Stoney
Camacho, Emmanuel O.	1921	#20 Herbert's
with Mrs. M. T.	1921	#22 Briggins
	1933	#11 Friars Hill
	1933	#25 Denfield's
	1933	#27 The Union
Camacho, M. V.	1933	#36 Belle Vue/Stoney
	1933	#38 Belvedere
	1933	#46 Oliver's
Camacho, Mrs. J. J.	1933	#12 The Wood
Camacho, John J.	1900s	# 1 Boone's
	1894	# 7 Mount Pleasant
	1894	#24 Gray's Turnbull

	1894	#19 Belmont/Murray's
	1921	#16 Otto's
Carden, Robert	1678	#31a/b Five Islands
Carlisle, Captain Francis	1679	#11 Friars Hill
Chambers, M.	1872	#21 Renfrew's
Chester, Edward	1720	#14 Gamble's
	1708	#22 Briggins
	1710	#13b Clare Hall
Christian, Alvin	2004	#33 The Folly/Bath L.
Clarke, Dorothy prior to	1679	#11 Friars Hill
Codrington, Sir C. Bethel	1800s	#13b Clare Hall
Colebrook, Sir George	1790	#40 Brecknock's
Coltart, Alex	1878	#29 Yepton's
Combermere, Lord	1871	5 Weatherills
	1878	#14 Gamble's
	1878	#15 The Villa/Daniel's
	1878	#18 Drew's Hill
Lord & C. J. Thomas	1891	#14 Gamble's
Conyers, John	1790	#18 Drew's Hill
Cook, John & Lady Elizabeth	1600s	#26 Cook's
Cotton, Colonel R. S.	1921	#14 Gamble's
	1921	#15 The Villa
	1921	#13b Clare Hall
	1921	#18 Drew's Hill
Crogman, Amanda	1933	#44 Rose Hill
Cranstoun, John Duer	1865	#41 Body Pond's
Cranstoun, David	1843	#45 Buckley's
	18—	#41 Body Pond's
Cranstoun, Langford Selly	1915	#41 Body Pond's
Crosbie, Charles	1872	# 1 Boone's
Crosbie, John	1790	# 2 Crosbie's
Crosbie, General John	1770	# 2 Crosbie's
Crosbie, G. John	1878	# 1 Boone's
	1878	# 2 Crosbie's
Crosbie, General William John	1797	# 2 Crosbie's
Crosbie, Colonel heirs of:	1891	# 2 Crosbie's
Daniel, Earl Lindsey	1829	#19 Belmont/Murray's

	1813	#15 The Villa
Daniel, Thomas	1790	#15 The Villa
	1811	#18 Drew's Hill
Davey, James	1891	#28 Creekside
Davis, John	1933	#48 Allen's (McNish)
December, F.	1921	#27 The Union
Derrick, Winston	2003	#48 Allen's (McNish)
Dew, Joseph Turner et al:	1921	#18 Drew's Hil
	1922	#24 Gray's/Turnbull
	1933	#34 Thibou/Jarvis
Dew, Ernest J.	1910	#28 Creekside
Dew. Mrs. Ernest J.	1921	#28 Creekside
Dew, Joseph D. & Sons	1933	#18 Drew's Hill
	1933	#19 Belmont/Murray's
	1933	#34 Thibou's
Dew, Dalmer	1930s	# 4 Hodge's
Dobee & Sons	1878	#16 Otto's
	1878	#19 Belmont/Murray's
Dobson, Robert	1878	#27 The Union
Dowe, Ellis	c.1960	#13b Clare Hall
Downing, Philip	1941	#47 Potter's
Doyle, George	1820	#41 Body Ponds
	1829	#42 Cedar Valley
Doyle, John Hyde	1843	#41 Body Ponds
heirs of:	1878	#41 Body Ponds
Drew, J. et al	1923	#24 Gray's/Turnbull
Dubuisson & Moody Stuart	1933	#13a Cassada Gdns.
	1921	#17 Tomlinson's
	1921	#30 Galley Bay
	1934	#42 Cedar Valley
Dunbar, John	1780	# 8 Dunbar's
Dunbar, Colonel William	1750	# 1 Boone's
	1829	# 8 Dunbar's
Dunbar, Charles Warner	1790	#13b Clare Hall
	1790	#14 Gamble's
	1821	# 8 Dunbar's
Dunbar, Robert Skerritt Nugent	1794	#14 Gamble's

	1821	# 8 Dunbar's
Duncombe, Thomas	1679	#33a The Folly
Dyett, Colonel I. E.	1933	#10 McKinnon's
	1933	#18 Drew's Hill
	1933	#15 The Villa
Dyett, Colonel I. E. & W. J. Abbott	1933	#14 Gamble's
heirs of :	1933	#15 The Villa
	1933	#13b Clare Hall
	1933	#18 Drew's Hill
Edwards, F. J.	1878	#44 Rose Hill
Edwards, Edna	1920	#24 Grays/Turnbull
Edwards, Mrs. Gwen	2016	#47 Potter's
Edwards, Keith	1970s	#31 Five Islands
Edwards, Malcolm	1985	# 3 Harts & Royals
Emerson, Edward	1831	#21 Renfrew's
Entwhistle, Bertie	1790	#23 Golden Grove
	1840	# 9 Marble Hill
heirs of:	1843	#23 Golden Grove
Erskine, Joseph	1933	# 2 Crosbie's
Este, Millie	1940s	#15 The Villa
Fanning, Charles J.	1878	#18 Drew's Hill
	1878	#19 Belmont/Murray's
Farr, Sara E.	1871	#32 Hawksbill
Francis. Ralph	2000	#29 Yepton's
Ferris, Elias	1790	#32 Hawksbill
Foreman, John	1851	#39 George Byam's
Freeman, Thomas	1878	#30 Galley Bay
French, Elizabeth	1748	#42 Cedar Valley
French, Nathaniel, heirs of:	1750	#42 Cedar Valley
Fryer's Sugar Concrete Co.	1878	#37 Bendal's
	1878	#38 Belvedere
	1878	#39 George Byam's
	1879	#38 Belvedere
	1872	#33a The Folly
	1872	#49 Halliday's
	1872	#36 Belle Vue
Furlong, John	1829	# 3 Harts & Royals

Gabriel, Dennis	1940	#21 Renfrew's
Galley Bay Hotel	1960s	#30 Galley Bay
Gamble, George	1668	#14 Gamble's
Garling, Samuel Henry	1860	#16 Otto's
	1860	#19 Belmont/Murray's
Garling, Daniel Burr	1857	#16 Otto's
	1857	#19 Belmont/Murray's
Garroway, F.	1872	#16 Otto's
Gaynor, Peter	1718	#40 Brecknock's
Gaynor, Miss Mary	1750	#40 Brecknock's
George Parson Emmanuel, heirs:	1922	#33a/bThe Folly/Bath
Gilbert, Nathaniel	1750	#47 Potter's
Gilliat, Anthony	1668	#49 Halliday's
Gilliat, Thomas	1719	#49 Halliday's
Gilliat, Joshua	1740	#49 Halliday's
Gonzales, Amelia	1921	# 3 Harts & Royals
	1921	# 9 Marble Hill
Goodwin, Robert	1891	#20 Herbert's
Gray, Honorable John	1790	#24 Gray's/Turnbull
Gregory, William	1829	#22 Briggin's
Guffay, Victor	1891	# 3 Harts & Royals
Gunthorpe, Honorable William	1788	#47 Potter's
Gunthorpe, Alicia & James	1826	#47 Potter's
Gunthorpe, Estates Limited	1940	#42 Cedar Valley
Hapsburg, Dominic	1976	# 9 Marble Hill
Haddon, Captain John	1678	#27 The Union
Haddon, Richard	1700	#27 The Union
Halliday, John Delap	1760	# 1 Boone's
	1788	# 5 Weatherill's
Halliday, F. D.	1790	# 5 Weatherills
Halliday, John Delap	1777	#49 Halliday's
Halliday Tollemach, Rear Adm. J.	1788	# 1 Boone's
	1829	# 5 Weatherill's
	1788	#14 Gamble's
Hanson, Will Frances	1730	#32 Hawksbill
Hanson, James	1710	#32 Hawksbill
Hanson, Richard & Robert	1713	#32 Hawksbill

Harper, Bessie & family	1900s	#21 Renfrew's
Harney, J. A.	1921	#41 Body Ponds
Harrison, Thomas	1738	#32 Hawksbill
Hart, Barry C.	1788	# 3 Harts & Royals
Hawksbill Hotel	1964	#32 Hawksbill Hotel
Haynes, Captain R. N.	1829	#11 Friars Hill
Haynes, H. E.	1921	# 4 Hodge's
Heath, Dr. Ivor	2000	#14 Gamble's
Henckell Du Buisson & Co.	1950s	#31 Five Islands
Henry, George Alexander	1933	#21 Renfrew's
Henry, O. E.	1974	#
Henry, Rowan	1965	#48 Allen's (McNish)
Henzell, Leonard I.	1933	# 3 Harts & Royals
Herbert, Sir Richardson	1773	#20 Herbert's
Herbert, John F.	1790	#20 Herbert's
Hill, Jacob	1669	#23 Golden Grove
Hill, Daniel	1790	#45 Buckley's
Hill, Sir Stephen J.	1878	#31 Five Islands
Hodge, Commander 1660	1960	# 4 Hodge's
Hodge, Henry	1790	# 4 Hodge's
Hodge, Isabella	1820	# 4 Hodge's
Hodge, James Lovell	1817	#27 The Union
Hodge, Langford Lovell,	1829	#26 Cook's
	1829	#27 The Union
	1852	#16 Otto's
	1841	# 4 Hodge's
Hodge, Reverend H. O. B.	1878	# 4 Hodge's
Hodgson, Granada	1780	#22 Briggin's
Horne, Edward	1682	#38 Belvedere
Horne, Valentine Morris	1760	#38 Belvedere
Horseford, Joseph	2000	#39 George Byam's
Humphreys, John	1666	# 7 Mount Pleasant
Humphreys, Nathaniel	1700s	# 7 Mount Pleasant
	1750	#42 Rose Hill
Humphreys, Mrs. Nathaniel	1822	# 9 Marble Hill
Hyndman, Messrs.	1829	#29 Yepton's
	1820	#37 Bendal's

	1820	#38 Belvedere
Ireland, Benjamin	1790	#22 Briggin's
James, John	1933	#49 Halliday's Mtn.
Jarvis, Thomas	1872	# 3 Harts & Royals
	1749	#34 Thibou's
Jarvis, Bertie Entwhistle	1840	# 9 Marble Hill
	1829	#24 Thibou's
Jarvis, Mrs. M. E.	1878	# 9 Marble Hill
Jarvis, Thomas, heirs of:	1878	#34 Thibou's
Jarvis, John C.	1891	#34 Thibou's
Jeffrey, William	1800s	#32 Hawksbill
Jocquin, John	1891	#26 Cook's
Jocqiuin, F. A.	1921	#26 Cook's
Jenkins, John	1688	# 7 Mount Pleasant
Johnson, Clarence	1950s	# 4 Hodge's
Johnson, Godschall	1850	#33a/bThe Folly/Bath
Jones, Samuel	1671	#31a Cassada Gdns.
Joseph, Molwyn c.	1980	# 9 Marble Hill
Judkins, Ena	1964	#47 Potter's
Keynell, Harvey prior to:	1661	#22 Briggin's
Kirwan, John	1774	#13b Clare Hall
Kirwin, James B.	1891 - 1921	#33a/b The Folly/Bath
Laforey, Sir John	1790	#19 Belmont/Murray's
	1777	#21 Renfrew's
Ladwell, Scott	1790	#43 Hill house
Lake, Joseph	1945	#47 Potter's
Lake, Mona	1960	#47 Potter's
Lane, Edgar Henry	1882	# 5 Weatherill's
Lane, Edgar Casper	1945	# 5 Weatherill's
Langford, Jonas	1660	# 6 Langford's.
Langford, Jonas	1679	#13a Cassada Gdns.
Langford, Jonas	1790	# 6 Langford's
Langford, James	1750	#12 The Wood
Langford-Brooke, Jonas	1790	#12 The Wood
	1790	# 6 Langford's
Langford-Brooke, Thomas	1851	#12 The Wood
	1851	# 6 Langford's

Langford-Brooke, Peter	1829	#12 The Wood
	1829	# 6 Langford's
Lapp, et al.	1969	13a Cassada Gardens
Ledeatt, Mr.	18—	#13a Cassada Gdns.
Ledeatt, C. D.	1921	#34 Thibou's
Lee, Nigel	1990s	#49 Halliday's
Lee Spooner & Co.	1891	#38 Belvedere
Lenaghan, Ann Hodgson &	1828	#22 Briggin's
Rev. James Lenaghan		
Lewis, James C.	1891	#10 McKinnon's
Luvin, James C.	1891	#10 McKinnon's
Liggins, Joseph	1800	#13b Clare Hall
Lindsey, John	1767	#15 The Villa
Lindsey, William	1742	#15 The Villa
	1742	#18 Drew's Hill
Lisle, Tobias	1750	#43 Hill House/Dry Hill
L. I. P. Company	1891	#37 Bendall's
Locker, Dr.	1962	#21 Renfrew's
Lovell, Langford	1843	#16 Otto's
	1843	#19 Belmont
Lynch, John	1820	#13b Clare Hall
Macandrew, George & Kathryn	1900	#20 Herbert's
MacLean, Marina	2000	#20 Herbert's
Maginley, James	1891	#36 Belle Vue
Maginley, Mrs.	1945	# 5 Weatherill's
Maginley, W. heirs of:	19—	#36 Belle Vue
Malone, Reverend P.	1878	#32 Hawksbill
Malone, W. T.	1921	#35 St. Clare/Williams
	1922	#16 Otto's
	1933	#19 Belmont/Murray's
Manning, Charles J.	1878	# 3 Harts & Royals
	1878	#20 Herbert's
Margetson, Dr. Noel	1878	#20 Herbert's
Margetson, D. Noel	1960s	#15 The Villa
Martin, George Savage	1843	# 7 Mount Pleasant
Martin, Louisa	1891	#35 St. Clare/Williams
Martin, John J.	1940	#19 Belmont/Murray's

Martin, John I.	1933	#20 Herbert's
	1940s	#22 Briggin's
	1940s	#25 Denfield's
	1940s	#27 The Union
late	1930s	#36 Belle Vue
late	1930s	#38 Belevedere
Heirs of late	1930s	#22 Briggin's
Martin, George	2000	#25 Denfield's
	2000	#27 The Union
Martin, Mrs. George Savage	1852	# 7 Mount Pleasant
Martin, Samuel	1777	# 2 Crosbie's
Massett, Mary Ann	1789	#38 Belevedere
Mathew Fathew, Colonel David	1750	#45 Buckley's
Mathew, Captain William	1750	#18 Drew's Hill
McCarthy, Owen	1717	#23 Golden Grove
McDonald & Company	1851	#47 Potter'McDonald, John R.
	1891	#47 Potter's
	1891	#20 Herbert's
McDowell, Alex	1843	#29 Yepton's
McKinnon, Daniel	1700s	#10 McKinnon
McKinnon, William	1790	#10 McKinnon's
	1710	#23 Golden Grove
Messrs.	1829	#10 McKinnon's
McKinnon, Wm. Alexander	1843	#10 McKinnon's
McLean, Marina	2000	#20 Herbert's
McNish, Robert	1790-1829	#48 Allen's (McNish)
Michael, Asot	1940s	#43 Hill House/Dry Hill
Heirs of:	2000	#43 Hill House/Dry Hill
Michael, Victor	2013	# 5 Weatherill's
Milder, William	1660	#23 Golden Grove
Montgomerie, Elizabeth	1830	#17 Tomlinson's
Moody, Stuart & Dubuisson	1943	#31a Cassada Gnds.
	1921	#17 Tomlinson's
	1921	#30 Galley Bay
	1934	#42 Cedar Valley
Moore, John H.	1878	#28 Creekside
Moore, H. D. C.	1933	# 2 Crosbie's

Morgan, Jacob		1743	#15 The Villa
Morgan, Rice		1667	#15 The Villa
Morgan, Samuel	prior to	1742	#15 The Villa
		1700s	#18 Drew's Hill
Murray, Honorable John		1750	#19 Belmont/Murray's
Musgrave, Dr. Anthony		1843	#20 Herbert's
		1852	#18 Drew's Hill
Musgrave, Burnthorn		1852	#18 Drew's Hill
Nesbitt, James		1716	#26 Cook's
Nibbs, Thomas Franklyn		1829	#28 Creekside
Nibbs, James		1738	#27 The Union
		1738	# 9 Marble Hill
Nibbs, James Langford		1790	# 9 Marble Hill
		1790	#27 The Union
Nibbs, Jonas Ian		1751	#27 The Union
Nibbs, Samuel		1750	# 9 Marble Hill
Nibbs, Rev. Thomas F.		1829	#28 Creekside
		1878	#45 Buckley's
Nibbs, Denely		2000	#50 William's
Nibbs, W. B.		1872	#45 Buckley's
Nugent, Walter		1690	#13b Clare Hall
Nugent, Oliver		1757	#13b Clare Hall
Nugent, Robert Skeritt		1765	#13b Clare Hall
Nugent, Nicholas		1806	#13b Clare Hall
Nugent, Oliver		1757	#13b Clare Hall
Nugent, Sir Oliver		1891	# 4 Hodge's
Nugent, Robert Skerritt		1765	#13b ClareHall
Odlum, William	Heirs of:	1891	#24 Gray's Turnbull
Okey, C. H.		1872	# 8 Dunbar's
Oliver, Richard		1750	#37 Bendal's
		1700	#46 Clare Hall
		1716	#46 Oliver's
Oliver, Rowland		1770	#46 Oliver's
		1716	#13b Clare Hall
Oliver, Thomas		1790	#11 Friars Hill
		1790	#37 Bendal's
		1790	#41 Body Ponds

	1790	#46 Oliver's
+ Lauchland Charity	1933	#50 William's
Osborne, John	1829	#17 Tomlinson's
Parke, Governor	1710	#14 Gamble's
Parker, Peter	1777	#13b Clare Hall
Paul, Elinor	1650	#23 Golden Grove
Peters, Rev. Thomas Heirs of:	1891	#23 Golden Grove
Peters, T. E.	1921	#23 Golden Grove
Phillip, Cosmos	19??	#47 Potter's
Phillips, Walter	1708	#17 Tomlinson's
Poyntz, Gen. Major	1651	#13a Cassada Gdns.
Powell, Edward	1684	#23 Golden Grove
	1678	#22 Briggin's
Powell, D. Daniel	1702	#23 Golden Grove
Powell, Colonel Henry	1716	#22 Briggin's
Purvis, Mrs. Emma	1872	#18 Drew's Hill
	1872	#19 Belmont/Murray's
	1872	#20 Herbert's
Raeburn, Dr. Robert Andrew	1933	#35 St. Clare/William's
Raeburn, Ursula & Raymond	1933	#35 St. Clare/William's
Redwood, William	1709	#13a Cassada Gdns.
Redwood, Honorable Abraham	1750	#13a Cassada Gdns.
Redwood, J & L.L.	1829	#13a Cassada Gdns.
Redwood, Heirs of	1851	#13a Cassada Gdns.
Robinson, Marmaduke	1833	#31 Five Islands
Ronan, John Joseph	1843	#47 Potter's
Royal, Isaac	1750	# 3 Harts & Royals
Ross, Charlesworth	1960s	#47 Potter's
St. Clare, Edward	1713	#35 St. Clare/William's
Sampson, John prior to:	1679	#13a Cassada Gdns.
Sanderson, T.	1843	#38 Belevedere
C. F. S.	1732	#49 Halliday's
Seager, Mare	1782	#22 Briggin's
Shaffler, Martin & Lee	1940s	# 5 Weatherill's
Shand, C. William & Francis	1843	# 3 Harts & Royals
	1872	#42 Body Ponds
Shand, A. Francis	1870	#36 Belle Vue

Heirs of:	1878	#13a Cassada Gdns.
Heirs of:	1891	#17 Tomlinson's
Shand, Charles	1891	#41 Body Ponds
Shand, Francis & Company	1843	#36 Belle Vue
	1843	#42 Cedar Valley
Sherman, Rob	1994	#41 Body Ponds
Shoul, Anthony & Ferdinand	1940s	#34 Thibou's
Smith, Bob	1933	#13b Clare Hall
	1945	#14 Gamble's
Smith, William	1785	#46 Oliver's
Stamers, A. H.	1933	# 9 Marble Hill
Stapleton, Redmond	1679	#41 Body Ponds
Sun Sail Club Colonna Hotel	1970s	# 4 Hodge's
Sutherland, Dr. Bill & Millicent	1940s	#31 Five Islands
Millicent	1938	#12 The Wood
Sutherland, George Scott	1978	#12 The Wood
	1950s	# 3 Harts & Royals
Sutherland, Dr. J. W.	1940s	#30 Galley Bay
S. W. Estates & Co.	1933	#37 Bendal's
Symister, Thomas	1933	#40 Brecknock's
Syndicate Estates, Antigua	1940s	# 6 Langford's
	1940s	# 8 Dunbar's
	1950s	# 3 Harts & Royals
	1957	# 9 Marble Hill
	19—	#11 Friars Hill
	1969	#17 Tomlinson's
	1940	#31a/b Five Isands
	1943	#42 Cedar Valley
	1940s	#49 Halliday's
Sydserfe, Walter	1750	#31 Five Islands
Thompson, Philip Lyne	1833	#15 The Villa
Thibou, Isaac	1730	#28 Creekside
Thibou, Walter	1790	#28 Creekside
Thibou, James	1848	#44 Rose Hill
Thibou, Dr. Jesse W.	1878	#35 St. Clare/William's
	1891	#21 Briggin's
Thibou, Minister Jacob	1750	#34 Thibou's

Thibou, C. J.		1891	#30 Galley Bay
Thibou, C. J. & Lord Combermere		1891	#15 The Villa
Thibou, Louis (Lewis)		1600s	#34 Thibou's
Thomas, C. I.		1891	#30 Galley Bay
Thomas, Mary		1852	#11 Friars Hill
Thomas, Sir & George T.,		1750	#30 Galley Bay
		1790	#30 Galley Bay
		1800	#29 Yepton's
Heirs of:		1829	#31 Five Islands
Thomas, Inigo Freeman		1843	#30 Galley Bay
Thomas, Freeman		1872	#30 Galley Bay
Thomas, George White		1821	#29 Yepton's
Tollemach, Rear Admiral John H.		1788	#14 Gambles
Tollemach, John		1852	# 5 Weatherill's
		1843	#14 Gamble's
		1852	# 1 Boone's
Tomlinson, John		1750	#17 Tomlinson's
Heirs of:		1790	#17 Tomlinson's
Turnbull, Merrick		1750	#24 Grays/Turnbull
Turner, Messrs.		1829	#40 Brecknock's
Turock, Sid & Norma		1945	#20 Herbert's
Vaughn, James		1670	#33a The Folly
Walker, Thomas	early	1700s	# 8 Dunbar's
Heirs of:		1750	# 8 Dunbars
Heirs of:		1750	#11 Friars Hill
Walker, John J.		1820	#33a The Folly
Heirs of		1843	#33a The Folly
Walkin, Thomas		1745	#11 Friar's Hill
Ward, E. L.		1933	#38 Belevedere
		1933	#39 George Byam's
Warneford, "Frankie" Henry S.		1940	#29 Yepton's
Warneford, Robert		1891	#29 Yepton's
Warneford, R. A. L.		1921	#29 Yepton's
Warner, Honorable Ashton		1798	#38 Belvedere
Warner, William & Joseph		1790	#36 Belle Vue
Warner, Samuel		1829	#36 Belle Vue
Weatherill, Charles P.		1766	# 5 Weatherill's

Weatherill, James	1679	# 5 Weatherill's
	1670	#33a The Folly
Weatherill, Mrs. J.	1750	# 5 Weatherill's
Weatherill, Margaret	1740	# 5 Weatherill's
	1750	#33a The Folly
Weatherill, Michael Lambert	1766	# 5 Weatherill's
Weeks, John	1738	#27 The Union
Weir, J. Robert	1679	#22 Briggin's
Westcott, Lee	1940s	# 1 Boone's
Westcott, Lee H.	1930s	# 2 Crosbie's
Heirs of:	2000	# 2 Crosbie's
White, George Richard	1844	#47 Potter's
White, Montague	1878	#11 Friars Hill
White, William	1812	#17 Tomlinson's
William, Edward	1750	#35 St. Clare
	1742	#20 Herbert's
Williams, Joseph	1775	#50 Williams
Williams, Roger	1730	#50 Williams
Williams, Thomas	1750	#20 Herbert's
Williams, Samuel	1777	#50 Williams
	1790	#35 St. Clare
	1860	#43 Hill House
Williams, Colonel Thomas	1733	#20 Herbert's
Williams, Roland E.	1700s	#50 Williams
	1829	#35 St. Clare
Williams, Rev. W. M.	1933	#45 Buckley's
Williams, William	1851	#50 Williams
Williams, Edward	1742	#20 Herbert's
Williams, John E.	1790	#20 Herbert's
Williams, Col. Edward	1760	#35 St. Clare
Willock, Alexander	1777	#33a The Folly
	1790	# 7 Mount Pleasant
Willock, Frank Gore	1830	# 7 Mount Pleasant
Winter Clinic	2012	#15 The Villa
Wood, John	1671	#12 The Wood
Wood, John Adams	1833	#40 Brecknock's
Young, William	1750	#41 Body Ponds

Acknowledgements

This historical research project has been a labour of love for more than twenty years. It could not have been accomplished without the devoted assistance of so many others who gave of their time and expertise.

Prints, old maps, plans and photographs were either copied from files at the Museum of Antigua & Barbuda, given to me by members of families (the Goodwins, the MacDonalds, the Moody-Stuarts, the Raeburns, the Ledeatts, the Abbotts, the Barretos, the Robert Halls, the Nunes, the Footes, the Dews, the Cranstouns and Jake Underhill) who formerly resided on the estates, or from various archival collections in the U.S. and U. K. Many of the photographs I took personally as I searched out each and every mill site. Many records and photographs, like the mills themselves, have been lost to hurricane damage.

To those individuals who have contributed their knowledge of anecdotes past and present, I thank you. Any story always denoted the teller, and if I have omitted anyone I apologize for I feel those personal stories help tell a stronger tale.

To Desmond Nicholson, who plotted the original plantation sites for the Mill Survey of 1995/97, and began an ownership list of the estates from old maps. This was an invaluable contribution to build upon.

To the "bush beaters" who spent countless hours hacking through prickly cassie (acasia), up mountains and down vales, in hot tropical sun, broken by a rain storm or two, to help me personally locate every single estate site and sugar mill on this island of Antigua: to them, I owe an enormous debt of gratitude: Vonnie and Anne Delisle, Rosemary Magoris, Anne Thompson, John and Ulrica Pierce, Bill Cunningham, Maudlin Evans, Louise Barreto and Agnes Lurz, Jane Seagull and David Sutherland, the Hash House Harriers. To the friendly farmers who downed their garden tools to lead us through the bush to hidden sites. Last but not least, to my dear husband Robert Meeker, who allowed his white Isuzu "Amigo" jeep to traverse every marked and unmarked trail, getting scratched and gouged in the process, and not to mention innumerable flat tyres.

A big thank you to Rosemary Magoris and Hamish Watson who helped with the dreary work of proofreading.

And to Don Dery, a friend and former journalist, who volunteered to study my hundreds of pages of notes and reference materials and convert it all into editorial format in three massive volumes entitled *Plantations of Antigua: The*

Sweet Success of Sugar. He has been instrumental in guiding me through the entire editorial and publishing maze.

To all, my heartfelt thanks.

Agnes C. Meeker, MBE
Antigua, W. I.

Bibliography

Books:

Abbot, Elizabeth; *Sugar.*

Austin, Jane; *Mansfield Park.*

Coleridge, Henry Nelson; *Six Months in the West Indies in 1825.*

Drake, Samuel Adam; *Our Colonial Homes.*

Dyde, Brian; *A History of Antigua: The Unsuspected Isle.*

Evan-Wong, Susan and Cooper, Brian; *Sir Robert: His Life and Work in Agriculture.*

Farquer, David U.; *Caribbean Adventures: Extracts from Missionary Journals.*

French, George; *Answer to A Libel.* 1718.

Hall, Douglas; *Five of the Leewards: 1834 - 1870.*

Hyde, Thomas K.; *Journal of Caribbean Adventures* edited by David H. Farquar.

Johnson, J.; *Historical & Descriptive Account of Antigua, 1830.*

Lai, Walton Look; *The Chinese in the West Indies, 1806 - 1995.*

Mrs. Lanaghan; *Antigua and the Antiguans, Volume I.*

--------------------; *Antigua and the Antiguans, Volume II.*

Lane, Edgar Kasper; *Memoirs of ... (1986).*

Lowes, Susan; *The U.S. Bases in Antigua and The New Winthropes Story.*

-------------------; *Sugar & Empire.*

Lawrence, Joy; *Bethesda and Christian Hill: Our History & Culture.*

Mackinnon, John Daniel; *A Tour Through the West Indies in 1802 & 1803.*

Manegold, C. S.; *Red Hills Farm.*

Massei, Anton and Bartey-King, Hugh; *Rum, Yesterday and Today.*

Nicholson, Desmond; *Heritage Landmarks.*

Oliver, Vere; *History of the Island of Antigua, Volume I.*

---------------; *History of the Island of Antigua, Volume II*

---------------; *History of the Island of Antigua, Volume III*

Read, Mary Emma; *Diary, 1887.*

Shaw, Janet; *Journal by A Lady of Quality: Narrative of a Journey from Scotland to the West Indies, North Carolina & Portugal, 1774 – 1776*

Sheridan, Richard B.; *Letters From A Sugar Plantation in Antigua, 1739 – 1758.*

---------------; *The West Indian Antecedents of Joseph Martin, Last Royal Governor of North Carolina.*

Skepple, Ineta F. J.; *Our Caribbean Heritage in Context.*

Smith, Keithlyn B. and Fernando C.; *To Shoot Hard Labour: The Life and Times of Samuel Smith, An Antiguan Workingman, 1877 - 1982.*

---------; *To Shoot Hard Labour, Vol. II.*

-------- ; *Symbol of Courage: Aunty (Aunt) Dood.*

Thomas, James A. & Kimball, Horace; *Six Months Tour of Antigua & Jamaica.*

---------; *Emancipation in the West Indies, 1837.*

Walter, Selvyn; *Not A Drum Was Heard*

Wentworth, Trelawny; *The West Indian Sketchbook, Vol. II, London 1834.*

Williams, Ian; *Rum.*

Winthrop, Samuel; *From Puritan to Quaker.*

Other "sources" of the Bendals Factory

Abbott, Helen; *Memories of....*

Abbott, Philip; *Memories of....*

Antigua Almanacs: 1851, 1872 and 1878.

Baker's 1746-48 Map.

(The) Bienecke Lesser Antilles Collection, Hamilton College.

Chemical Notices from Foreign Sources, 1878.

Christian, Alvin; *Memories of . . . .*

Clements, William M.; Library at the University of Michigan.

(The) Codrington Papers, National Archives.

Contract on the Advances of the Bendels Factory in Antigua, 1903.

The Lands of Antigua & Barbuda Sugar Factory Limited and the Antigua & Barbuda Syndicate Estates Limited (Vesting) Act.

Garling, Daniel Burr; *Will of . . . .*

Groom, Margaret (Moody-Stuart); *Memories of . . . .*

(The) Hart Family Genealogy.

Hewlester, Samuel; *Birth of the Village of Liberta.*

Historical & Descriptive Accounts of Antigua, 1830.

Hochschild, Adam; *Bury The Chains: Prophets and Rebels in the Fight to Free an Empire's Slaves.*

Horseford Almanac: 1851,1872.

Jarvis Family Papers, William Clements Library.

Evelyn, Joslyn (Lake); *Memories of . . . .*

Meeker, Agnes C.; *Recollections by . . . .*

Profile & Legacies Summary.

Royer, Lawrence; *Memories of . . . 1944 & 1948.*

Murphy, Dr. Reginald; Letters by the President of the Antigua Historical and Anthropological Society.

Samuel, Jr., Hewlester, A., *Memories of . . . .*

Scotland, the Caribbean.

Shoul, Themene; *Memories of . . . .*

Stapleton-Cotton Manuscripts, Bangor University

Thomas, Jean Willock; *Memories of....*

Toulon, Simon; *Memories of . . . .*

(The) Tudway Papers; Museum of Antigua & Barbuda.

Scalpy, Nick; Maps and Postcards.

Walter, Selvyn; *Memories of....*

White, Margaret; *Memories of....*

Addendum

The Horsford Almanac gives a complete listing in 1871 and shows that some of the estates had multiple owners though often small acreage. The estates highlighted in blue have not been included in this previous write up and may have been incorporated at a later date.

HORSFORD ALMANAC ANTIGUA 1871

List of other Sugar Estates, Grazing and other Farms in Antigua, 1871.

St. John's Parish

In this Parish there are 31 sugar estates in cultivation, representing 11,971 acres. The proprietors of 12 are resident and 19 non-resident.

The resident proprietors represent 3,179 acres and the non-resident 8,792 acres. Total 16,510 acres of cultivated and uncultivated land. On 8 estates there are steam works, and on the others there are windmills.

Name of Place	Acre.	Names of Owner	Remarks
Adelaide Cottage	10	J.D. Cranstoun	Provisions
Brecknocks	222	Heirs John Bennett	Lessee M. Dickenson
Body Pond	20	James Barrett	
Blizard's	50	J.D. Cranstoun	
Body Pond	210	Heirs J.H. Doyle	Lessee F. Melchertson
Buckley's	10	Samuel Edwards	
Bendal's)		Steam Works	
Belvedere)	1690	Fryer's Concrete Co.	24 acres in St. Mary's
Geo. Byam's)			
Buckley's	10	Heirs Isaac Kilsick	
Belle Vue	527	Francis Shand	10 acres in St.George's
Briggins	440	Dr. J.W. Thibou	
Buckley's	98	W.B. Nibbs	
Bath Lodge	456	Fryer's Concrete Co.	
Blizard's Hill	16	Heirs Dr. Mara	
Crosbie & Boone	300	Charles Crosbie	
Clare Hall	613	Henry Liggins	Lessee Dr. Edwards Graze Farm
Cook's	500	J.E. Anthonyson	
Cook's	10	R.S. Heagan	

Cottage	24	Heirs John Haining	
Cedar Grove	10	George Hart	
Cove	6	Rebecca Isles	
Creekside	396	John H. Moore	180 acres in St. Mary's
Cassada Gardens	600	Francis Shand	60 acres in St. George's
Cedar Valley	218	Do	90 acres Do.
Dickeys Hill	26	M. Chambers & others	rented to Renfrew's.
Dunbar's	106	C.H. Okey & another	
Drew's Hill)			
Herbert's)	788	Mrs. Emma Purvis	Steam Works
Belmont)			
Ferris Farm	13	Edward W. Alleyne	
Ferris Farm	8	R.S. Heagan	
Five Islands	703	Col. S.J. Hill C.B.	Lessee S.B. Johnson
Friars Hill	327	Lady Thomas	
Gambles	290	Viscount Combermere	Steam Works
Gambles	157	J.E. Anthonyson	
(Five Islands)			
Golden Grove	254	Thomas Peters	Grazing Farm
Galley Bay	447	F. Thomas	
Huntley Lodge	24	W.H. Gordon	
Hawk's Bill	180	F. Peter Malone	
Halliday's Mt.	250	Fryers Concrete Co.	
Hodges Bay	192		Lessee W. Goodwin Jr.
Harts & Royals	209	Thomas Jarvis	
Hamiltons	40	Hugh Mc Kay	
Hill House	100	Heirs of Samuel Williams	
Hill House	10	Paul Horsford	
Langfords &)	621	T.W.L. Brooke	Steam Works
Mt. Pleasant)			
Law's Land	50	Heirs of James Law	Provisions
Law's Land	10	Geo. W. Bennett	
Marble Hill	172	Mrs. M.E. Jarvis	
Mt. Rural	20	Heirs of Wlm. Grant	
McKinnon's	633	Edward Beckett	Steam Works
Oliver's	313	W.L. Brooke	
Otto's	676	F. Garraway	Steam Works

Potter's	60	McDonald & Co.	
Rose Hill	63	Heirs of Sarah Adamson	
Renfrew	17	J.W.W. Watkins	
Saint Clare	254	Jas. B. Thibou	
Saint Clare	10	William Alsas	
Turnbull's	71	Heirs of John Gray	Rented to Otto's Est.
Turnbull's	10	John Gray Jun.	
Tomlinson's	600	Francis Shand	Steam Works
Thibou's	368	Thomas Jarvis	
Union	433	Robert Dobson	
Villa	280	S. Dobson & Sons	Steam Works
Weatherill's	300	Viscount Combermere	
William's Farm & Mut. Rural Wood	63	Edward McGuire	
Wood	280	T. W. L. Brookes	
Williams Farm	40	Heirs of Samuel Williams	Grazing Farm
Yapton's	343	Mrs. Sheil	

The following St. John's Parish estates are names which have appeared through history, but they are not well known estate names today. The estates may have been incorporated into larger holdings, or the name changed with new ownership. Some still lend their name to the area, such as Clarke's Hill.

Clarke's Hill (aka Staughton's, Burgess, Mathew's)

Ownership Chronology

1670: Nathaniel Clarke.

1680: Reverend John Clarke. 277 acres. Heir to his brother, Nathaniel.

1681: Colonel Bastian Baijer.

1730: Edward Warner. d. 1732.

1732: Ashton Warner. d. February 11, 1752. He was Attorney General of the Leeward Islands. He married Elizabeth Anne Clarke, the daughter of George Clarke. 110 acres in 1750.

1771:   Dr. Stephen Livingston.
1790:   Joseph Warner. d. 1801.
1801:   William Warner.
1933:   Mrs. D. Ford.   1933 Camacho map.

< >

This area is still known as Clarke's Hill and is known to have been where Government House was once situated. Now a residential area. A painting by Thomas Hearne depicts Government House in the hurricane of 1727 and is shown in the Preface.

Edward Warner's 1732 will states, *"To my son Wm. my gold watch, chain and gift seal. My plantation called Clarke's and 3 negros I drew from there & put with Staughtons (but none of the slaves bought with Staughtons nor any of the plantations lately bought called Nantons or Dimsdales . . . To my cousin Mary Burgess 100 pounds in discharge of a deed of purchase made by me to Admiral Thos. Matthew & M. A. Mathews of a plantation called Stoughtons or Burgess or Mathews or Clarke.*   "History of the Island of Antigua" by Vere Oliver, Volume III.

Ashton Warner's 1750 will states,*... and I hereby declare by Clarkes, I mean not only 110 acres which was my late wife's inheritance, but the residence and 100 acres I bought from Sam Byam, Esq., and the lands called 'Hunts' now in dispute between Otto Baijer and myself ...."* On November 18, 1786, records show that 28 slaves, 29 cows, 13 oxen, 17 heifers, 7 young bulls, 6 bull calves, 7 cow calves, 5 steers and 2 pasture bulls belonging to Clarkes Hill Plantation but removed and now on Hatton Garden Plantation in Dominica.
"History of the Island of Antigua" by Vere Oliver, Volume III.

In 1835, Thomas Shirley Warner (b. 1797; died in Trinidad). He was the Editor of the 'Antigua Herald'.

Ghosts: Evonne Delisle lived on the ridge at Clarke's Hill and can attest to the following ghost stories: Both Mr. Delisle, Sr. and Isabel, his granddaughter, have seen the ghost of a white lady holding her two hands up in the air as if balancing something on top of her head.

When the Maginley family lived there previously, they witnessed *"someone coming into their bedroom and sitting on the bed."* Many have also heard the sounds of a horse and carriage charging down the hill on a quiet night, at breakneck speed.

< >

De Witts (near Otto's #16)

Ownership Chronology

1778:   John Otto-Baijer.
1933:   Jacob Martin.   1933 Camacho map.

      This estate appears on the 1777/78 map produced by the cartographer John Luffman in the middle of Gray's Farm (#24) and Golden Grove (#23), south of Turnbull's. De Witts also is shown south of Otto's (#16).

Evansons's

Ownership Chronology

1755:   Edward Evanson. Will: 1759. He was from Guano Island.
1759:   Edward Byam, Thomas Warner & Joseph Farley.

< >

      It appears to have been two separate properties: one in St. John's Parish near Boone's (#1), and the other called Guiana Island (#92), which was owned by Edward Evanson. His kinsman, Nathaniel Evanson apparently came to Antigua from Bantry, County Cork, Ireland, because his son Charles, of Antigua, was married in St. John's on May 24 1759 and had two children.

      The Reverend Nathaniel Evanson (baptized 1752) was heir to Edward Evanson, and a Martha Evanson also was baptized in 1752 in Antigua. A will states: *"Ann Evanson and Mary Charity Knight grant to Thomas Warner and Joseph Farley all that their plantation in the Division of Dickenson's bay and Parish of St. John's, Antigua, containing 60 acres bounded northward by the lands of James Weatherill, Esq., deceased, eastward upon the lands of Nathaniel Knight, southward upon the lands of William Mackinaw, and westward with the sea… and all negro slaves (names given), etc., etc., in trust to the following uses… as touching one undivided third to the 1751 May 7 Mary Evanson wife of Edward*

Evanson, use of Ann Evanson for life, and at her death to Mary 1753 Jan. 14 Charles Evanson."   History of the Island of Antigua by Vere Oliver, Volume I

The December 19, 1759 will of Edward Evanson of Guiana states: *"To be bur. near my uncle Baptiste Looby in Parham Churchyard. To my cousin Eliz. Looby, dau. of Baptiste Looby, 30c. yearly. To my cousin Marg. Looby of Cork 20c yearly. To my kinsman Nathl. Evanston, senr. of Foremill Bantry, co. Cork, late of Antigua, but now of Great Britain, Esq., co. Cork, £200 a year, and if he came to the West Indies after my death, all my wine, old rum in the room south of the kitchen chimney where I now live, all of my wether sheep, hogs, poultry, 2 horses, chaise and liberty to live in either of my 2 houses at Guana Island & if Martha his wife should outlive him then IU give her £40 st. yearly. I give him also my furniture & plate ..... My Ex'ors are to hold my estate till legacies are paid, then I give it to Francis Farley, Saml. Martin, Rowl. Otto Baijer, Nathl. Evanson Senr., & Alexr. Hillock in trust for Nathl. Evanston Juhjr. Grandson on Narthl. Evanston Senr., & son of the late Chas. Evanston on Antigua & Ann his wife, & to his heirs, power, etc."*   History of the Island of Antigua by Vere Oliver, Volume I.

< >

Huyghues (aka Hughes)

Ownership Chronology

1750:   Mathew Christian. d. 1758.
1758:   Mathew Christian. d. 1779.
1778:   Gabriel Scott.   See 1777/78 map by cartographer John Luffman.

The younger Mathew was heir to his uncle, who apparently owned Red Hill (#207) with 200 acres, The Valley (#209) with 350, Elmes (#109) with 149 and Huyghues with 200. This estate apparently was east of Tom Moore's 170-acre plantation (#175).

A Hughes Plantation is shown on an early Herman Moll map as well as a 1933 Camacho map, and we also have the village of John Richard Hughes in St. Mary's Parish. According to Vere Oliver there was a John Hughes (will 1693) in Antigua in the late 1600s and a Richard Hughes planter, whose will is dated 1714/1715, *"to my son Isaac, my plantation in Popeshead with the houses, etc.,*

& 1/3 of all my negros, to be divided when my son David is 21. To my sons David and Benj. my plantation in Nonsuch with 2/3 of all my negros, to be divided at 21."

< >

French's Estate

128 acres, and 139 slaves, owned by Richard Musgrave. A Richard Musgrave (b. about 1832) appears in the Slave Register of former Colonial Territories.

Vere Oliver shows a Robert French of Elliots (#106) in the mid-1700s and a Nathaniel French of Cedar Valley (#42 - d. 1747/48) plus a Nathaniel Bogle French still owning Cedar Vallery in 1816. They were one of the original families whose estate was either renamed or annexed by another.

< >

Pimm's (aka Old North Sound)

Ownership Chronology

1671:   Robert Oliver. 10 acres

The 1777/78 map by cartographer John Luffman shows a Pimm's Pond to the west of Parry's (#88). Yeamans (#91 and Duers (#89) to the south.

There was very little reference to this estate.

Printed in the United States
By Bookmasters